Integrating Spirituality in Clinical Social Work Practice

Walking the Labyrinth

Maddy Cunningham

Fordham University Graduate School of Social Service

Boston   Columbus   Indianapolis   New York   San Francisco   Upper Saddle River
Amsterdam   Cape Town   Dubai   London   Madrid   Milan   Munich   Paris   Montréal   Toronto
Delhi   Mexico City   São Paulo   Sydney   Hong Kong   Seoul   Singapore   Taipei   Tokyo

Editorial Director: Craig Campanella
Editor in Chief: Dickson Musslewhite
Executive Editor: Ashley Dodge
Editorial Product Manager: Carly Czech
Director of Marketing: Brandy Dawson
Executive Marketing Manager: Jeanette Koskinas
Senior Marketing Manager: Wendy Albert
Marketing Assistant: Jessica Warren

Production Manager: Meghan DeMaio
Creative Director: Jayne Conte
Cover Designer: Suzanne Duda
Cover Image: © shock/Fotolia
Interior Design: Joyce Weston Design
Editorial Production and Composition Service:
  Nithya Kuppuraj/PreMediaGlobal
Printer/Binder/Cover Printer: R. R. Donnelley & Sons

Library of Congress Cataloging-in-Publication Data
Cunningham, Maddy.
  Integrating spirituality in clinical social work practice : walking the labyrinth /
Maddy Cunningham.—1st ed.
    p. cm.
  Includes bibliographical references and index.
  ISBN 978-0-205-59201-2 (0-205-59201-5) 1. Psychiatric social work. 2. Spiritual life.
3. Labyrinths—Religious aspects. I. Title.
  HV689.C86 2011
  361.3'2—dc23
                                                              2011033535

10 9 8 7 6 5 4 3 2 1 [DOH] 15 14 13 12 11

ISBN-10: 0-205-59201-5
ISBN-13: 978-0-205-59201-2

CSWE's Core Competencies Practice Behavior Coverage in this Text

Competency	Chapter
Professional Identity	
Practice Behavior Examples...	
Advocate for client access to the services of social work	
Practice personal reflection and self-correction to assure continual professional development	1, 2, 3, 4, 5, 6, 7, 8, 11, 12
Attend to professional roles and boundaries	1, 2, 3
Demonstrate professional demeanor in behavior, appearance, and communication	1, 2, 3
Engage in career-long learning	
Use supervision and consultation	1, 12
Ethical Practice	
Practice Behavior Examples...	
Recognize and manage personal values in a way that allows professional values to guide practice	1, 2, 3, 4, 5, 6, 7, 8, 9, 12
Make ethical decisions by applying standards of the National Association of Social Workers Code of Ethics and, as applicable, of the International Federation of Social Workers/International Association of Schools of Social Work Ethics in Social Work, Statement of Principles	2, 5, 7
Tolerate ambiguity in resolving ethical conflicts	2, 3, 4
Apply strategies of ethical reasoning to arrive at principled decisions	2, 5
Critical Thinking	
Practice Behavior Examples...	
Distinguish, appraise, and integrate multiple sources of knowledge, including research-based knowledge and practice wisdom	2, 3, 4, 5, 7, 8, 9
Analyze models of assessment, prevention, intervention, and evaluation	4, 5, 7, 8, 11
Demonstrate effective oral and written communication in working with individuals, families, groups, organizations, communities, and colleagues	
Diversity in Practice	
Practice Behavior Examples...	
Recognize the extent to which a culture's structures and values may oppress, marginalize, alienate, or create or enhance privilege and power	2, 4, 9, 10, 11
Gain sufficient self-awareness to eliminate the influence of personal biases and values in working with diverse groups	1, 2, 4, 9, 10, 11, 12
Recognize and communicate their understanding of the importance of difference in shaping life experiences	2, 4, 9, 10, 11
View themselves as learners and engage those with whom they work as informants	3, 5, 12
Human Rights & Justice	
Practice Behavior Examples...	
Understand the forms and mechanisms of oppression and discrimination	2, 9, 10, 11
Advocate for human rights and social and economic justice	11
Engage in practices that advance social and economic justice	11

CSWE's Core Competencies Practice Behavior Coverage in this Text

Competency	Chapter
Research-Based Practice	
Practice Behavior Examples...	
Use practice experience to inform scientific inquiry	
Use research evidence to inform practice	2, 5, 7, 8, 9
Human Behavior	
Practice Behavior Examples...	
Utilize conceptual frameworks to guide the processes of assessment, intervention, and evaluation	4, 5, 6, 7, 8, 10, 11
Critique and apply knowledge to understand person and environment	4, 5, 6, 7, 8, 10, 11
Policy Practice	
Practice Behavior Examples...	
Analyze, formulate, and advocate for policies that advance social well-being	
Collaborate with colleagues and clients for effective policy action	
Practice Contexts	
Practice Behavior Examples...	
Continuously discover, appraise, and attend to changing locales, populations, scientific and technological developments, and emerging societal trends to provide relevant services	1, 2, 9, 10, 11
Provide leadership in promoting sustainable changes in service delivery and practice to improve the quality of social services	
Engage, Assess Intervene, Evaluate	
Practice Behavior Examples...	
A) Engagement	
Substantively and effectively prepare for action with individuals, families, groups, organizations, and communities	1, 3
Use empathy and other interpersonal skills	3, 6, 7, 8, 10, 11, 12
Develop a mutually agreed-on focus of work and desired outcomes	5
B) Assessment	
Collect, organize, and interpret client data	4, 6, 7, 8, 9, 10, 11
Assess client strengths and limitations	2, 3, 4, 7
Develop mutually agreed-on intervention goals and objectives	5, 6, 7, 8, 10
Select appropriate intervention strategies	5, 6, 7, 8, 10, 11
C) Intervention	
Initiate actions to achieve organizational goals	11
Implement prevention interventions that enhance client capacities	5, 7, 8
Help clients resolve problems	5, 6, 7, 8, 10, 11
Negotiate, mediate, and advocate for clients	11
Facilitate transitions and endings	11
D) Evaluation	
Critically analyze, monitor, and evaluate interventions	5, 11

Contents

5. Intervention   54

11. Leaving the Labyrinth: Gifting the World   152

Preface

When we engage in clinical work we seek to understand the essence of our clients, find creative ways to support their strengths, and ease their suffering. In the past few decades there has been a growing interest in including spirituality in our assessments and treatment interventions. Many therapists, regardless of their own personal spiritual beliefs, recognize that for some clients spirituality is an essential part of what helps them cope with the everyday difficulties they encounter. For those who face life's tragedies spirituality may be what helps them endure. For others suffering brings about a sense of despair, a floundering when the beliefs they once relied on shatter in the wake of unspeakable loss.

Historically, social workers have overlooked or dismissed spiritual issues. In fact, until recently, most professional social work educational programs have not included course content on this issue. Many years ago, when I was studying psychology as an undergraduate, I had a persistent feeling that something was missing in the theories I was learning. I did not feel psychology alone could answer the "big" questions: "Why are we here?" "Why do we suffer?" "Why do we die and what happens after we do?" I remember thinking that we needed to somehow combine psychology and spirituality, not a usual trend at the time.

In spite of my insight, when I entered graduate school to begin my training for social work, I took the "road more traveled." My earlier understanding about the need to combine psychological and spiritual approaches was forgotten as I studied psychodynamic, cognitive, and behavioral theories. I rarely thought about the spiritual domain and its importance to therapeutic work. As I began my clinical work, I recognized that some clients were "religious"; others were not. If a client raised a spiritual issue, we discussed it, but I did not initiate the topic. When spirituality was a positive coping resource, I encouraged it; when it was a source of distress, we explored it, but from a psychological perspective. In retrospect, I wonder about the possible opportunities I may have missed with my clients by limiting exploration to only those times when they raised spiritual concerns.

From my work with trauma survivors, I began to realize the importance of the search for meaning in the wake of suffering. Survivors sought to understand why the trauma occurred, why it happened to them, and how they could "go on with their lives" now that it had happened. Perhaps due to the synergistic convergence of several factors in my life, I began to explore issues around the inclusion of spirituality in clinical practice and social work education. On a personal level, I approached middle age. Many of my contemporaries began to talk more frequently about their spiritual lives. Some of those philosophical questions from our college years began to have a different quality, a deeper dimension. My professional curiosity about how one sought and found meaning in the midst of suffering began to include that dimension as well. How, I wondered, could we truly understand clients if we fail to understand how spirituality shapes the lens through which they interpret the events in their lives?

When I accepted a faculty appointment at a Jesuit university, I had the opportunity to explore these issues further. For the past several years I have taught an elective course in Spirituality and Clinical Social Work Practice. The idea for this book emerged from my teaching experiences. Although there are excellent books on spirituality and psychotherapy, I wanted a textbook that was based on a strong clinical foundation and was written from a social work perspective. I teach my class by integrating spiritual issues into the clinical stages of engagement, assessment, intervention, and endings. Therefore, I wanted a text that reflected that approach and was scholarly but engaging for the reader.

Theoretical Basis

Throughout this book I use the metaphor of a labyrinth walk to suggest ways to integrate spiritual issues into the clinical process. The labyrinth is a single, purposeful path made up of twists and turns that leads to a center. Its cyclical nature resembles the therapeutic process and reminds us that our work with clients often includes moving toward and moving away before we achieve the goal. We will discuss the labyrinth and its parallel to clinical practice in several chapters throughout this book.

The content is based on a relational approach to therapeutic work. Thus, I emphasize the importance of the sacred (therapeutic) relationship between therapist and client. In our clinical encounters we not only influence our clients, but they influence us as well. Therefore, it is important for us to attend to our own inner processes. In several chapters, I stress the importance of understanding our countertransference reactions, exploring our own beliefs and biases, and reflecting on how they may affect our work. Inclusion of spiritual issues in therapy poses some unique challenges for us. When clients encounter a dark night of the soul (crisis in their belief system) or express spiritual beliefs that are very divergent from our own, we may have particularly strong reactions. The final chapter of this book explores in depth the experience of therapists when spiritual issues are included in treatment.

Approach and Language

To present the material in this book in a reader-friendly fashion, I have chosen to "speak" informally to you. With a few exceptions, I avoid the awkward "she/he" and alternate between the two pronouns. The content in this book is based on a variety of scholarly works, but my goal is to create a conversational tone. I hope that perhaps you feel as if you and I are in a classroom together having a discussion about spirituality and clinical practice. To achieve this, I primarily use the first person plural. I do not intend this as the "royal we," but rather to imply that you, as the reader, and I, as the author, are embarking together on a learning journey. I want you to know you are included in the exploration of these issues, and perhaps more important, that I am not exempt from the challenges or struggles of clinical work.

I pose questions for reflection in several chapters, some of which my students and I have used for our classroom discussions. You and your instructors may decide to use them in a similar fashion, you may decide to use them for journal reflection, or you may choose to ignore them. Many of the questions posed have no right or wrong answers. I cannot answer most of them for you. Perhaps you can answer them for yourself, perhaps not. However, I believe that by raising them, by reflecting on them, by discussing them, we deepen our work. The poet Rilke in *Letters to a Young Poet* (Letter 4) says, we must "try to love the questions themselves" (p. 27). Even if we cannot answer them, perhaps we can become more comfortable with "not knowing" the answers. Not knowing, a theme in several chapters throughout this text, is a difficult experience for most of us. Yet, it is the most respectful stance in our work with clients. When we do not know we acknowledge that our clients are the experts, and we are merely witnesses. We provide the sacred space for their own exploration, reflection, and discovery.

Ambivalence About Spirituality

Although there is increasing interest regarding the inclusion of spirituality in social work practice, it is not without controversy. Although some therapists welcome its inclusion, others are opposed and some are ambivalent. Reflective practice emphasizes the importance of recognizing that who we are as individuals affects our clinical work. We look at what we bring to the encounter and how what we think, feel, and believe plays out in our work with clients. Throughout this text, I encourage you to reflect on your own beliefs and attitudes and to think about how they shape your work. Therefore, I think it is important for you as the reader to have some sense of my thoughts about the ambivalence among professionals in our field regarding the inclusion of spirituality in clinical social work practice. Knowing my stance can inform your critical analysis of what you read.

I believe that spirituality has a pivotal role in shaping how we approach our lives. In fact, I question if we can truly understand our clients, their difficulties, or their strengths if we do not understand their spiritual worldview, including the possibility that they do not embrace spirituality in any form. I see many advantages to including it in our practice with clients. However, I also recognize the valid arguments that those who oppose inclusion raise. I am particularly concerned about the potential to proselytize or impose one's beliefs on clients. Spiritual beliefs are extremely personal and often core to how one makes meaning out of the events he encounters. When one is suffering, confused, or in psychological distress she may be particularly vulnerable to her therapist's suggestions or intimations of what one should believe. I think this can be potentially dangerous. In my opinion, some therapists walk a fine line between raising spiritual issues for exploration and imposing their own beliefs. For example, a therapist whose faith brought meaning and solace in his life stated, "I know I cannot impose my faith on others, but I wish I could." His intention was motivated by his desire to share what for him was a wonderful resource. And although he may refrain from actually stating what he thinks clients should believe, he may unconsciously attempt to influence them in subtle ways. So when I have encountered therapists like this one, I struggle. I question if course content on spirituality somehow gives them permission to blur that line. Do we "sanction" them in their subtle imposition on others?

On the other hand, I have been impressed with students and experienced therapists who have a strong personal faith, sometimes in what one might categorize as an ultraconservative tradition. Yet, unlike the therapist described above, these therapists strive to find ways to be respectful of others' beliefs, including those clients who identify themselves as atheists. They are curious to learn ways to bring spiritual issues into their work, while carefully attending to their own process to assure they do not influence clients' beliefs. They do not have a personal need to bring spirituality into treatment. They are aware that this is the client's choice, not theirs. They are open to exploring their countertransference and evaluating their practice. Their faith provides spiritual nourishment and comfort to them, but they recognize that it may not fit their clients' needs. They are truly professional in their approach to including spiritual issues in their work.

I have also encountered students who have little or no personal interest in the topic of spirituality. They may state that they "are not spiritual in any way." Yet, they take electives or workshops to learn how to integrate it into their work because they recognize its importance to their clients. Often these students are working in hospitals, nursing homes, or hospices. I have been touched by how selflessly they put aside their own interests and comfort level to take coursework they believe will enhance their clinical work with their clients.

So I have resolved my ambivalence about including spirituality in our social work curriculum. If we do not address and wrestle with these ideas openly in the classroom, we remain silent about the potential misuse of spirituality. When we offer coursework we can discuss and struggle with our own values and beliefs and the need for diligence so we do not subtly impose our spiritual worldview on others. Through dialogue there may be a better chance that those who might blur that line will "hear" the voices of those who are open and respectful of all spiritual expressions.

Distinguishing Spirituality and Religion

As we will discuss in chapter 2, distinguishing between the concepts of spirituality and religion is challenging. Like the authors of other texts, I have diligently tried to clarify these concepts. If this had been an easy task, others would have accomplished clarity long before I even attempted it. I do make every effort to let you know when I am referring to religion and the broader concept of spirituality. Despite my efforts, I know there are times I most likely muddle the two and "slip over the line" of clarity. So I ask you to read critically.

Critical Thinking

This text offers suggested content areas for assessment and treatment interventions to implement spirituality into clinical social work practice. It includes important information on when it is inappropriate to include these issues. As you read, it is important for you to think critically about the content. Despite the fact that the information is drawn from the scholarly literature and clinical practice experience, you need to reflect on whether it fits your professional values and, more important, your client's therapeutic needs. You are the one charged with the responsibility of assessing and selecting interventions for your clients. You are the one who molds these suggestions to fit your own therapeutic style and you are the one who will evaluate whether they are helpful and effective with your clients or not. I urge you to use your best clinical judgment. Supervision and consultation are important adjuncts to clinical work and may provide a sacred space for you to explore when and if you wish to use any of the material presented in this text.

So as you turn the page and begin this book, I hope you will find the material thought provoking, challenging, and valuable. I hope it is as enjoyable for you to read this book as it was for me to write it. Be respectful of yourself as you read. Some sections may intrigue you, others may challenge or even disturb you. As you note your reactions, you may wish to keep a journal or explore your feelings with a trusted mentor, spiritual advisor, or therapist. So let us together cross over the threshold of the labyrinth and begin our walk together.

Acknowledgments

A French proverb defines gratitude as the memory of the heart and it is with sincere gratitude that I acknowledge some of the many people who supported me in completing this book.

I received a Faculty Fellowship from Fordham University that provided me with the time and space to focus on my work. This was truly a gift and I believe both the process and product of my efforts were greatly enhanced by the University's generosity.

I have been most fortunate to work under the leadership of Dean Peter Vaughan. I am grateful for his consistent support of my work over the years, and especially for his support in my completion of this book. Dean Vaughan truly models both strong leadership and compassion.

I would like to thank Candace McCalla and Kathleen Ensor for their assistance.

With gratitude I would like to thank the fabulous staff at Pearson Publishing, especially Pat Quinlan, with whom I initially worked, Carly Czech, and Nicole Zuckerman. They were always cheerful and willing to help this first-time author. I thank my colleague Dr. Marlene Cooper for suggesting Pearson as my publisher when I was first thinking about writing this book.

I am grateful for the many friends, colleagues, and family who supported me during this time. There are too many to name specifically, but I appreciate all of you who asked, "How's that book of yours coming along?" In particular I wish to acknowledge my mother Madeline, while her memory is fading, her love is unwavering, my sister Maureen for her love and friendship, my Aunt Pat, who has been a consistent source of support throughout my life. I am grateful to Dr. Zulema Suárez, not only for her friendship but also for our many conversations about spirituality and the writing process. It is she, who after listening to how I wanted to approach the topic of diversity, suggested I use the concept of mystery. She also provided the case material for Esperanza used in chapters 4 and 5. I thank Angela Belsole for her support in my completing this project; I also thank all the students who have taken both my elective in spirituality and my clinical practice courses. Their questions and comments have taught me a great deal and helped shape my ideas for this book.

The greatest blessing in my life has been my family. It is with love and gratitude that I thank my husband Hugh, who has always been the strong, gentle encouragement behind all my life's endeavors. I wish to dedicate this book to him. I am grateful for my children Gregory and Karen, my daughter-in-law Jennifer, my son-in-law Jamie, and my four precious grandsons, Gregory, Declan, Caleb, and Brayden. It is with pleasure that I anticipate the arrival of my newest bundle of joy due at the beginning of next year.

1

Walking the Labyrinth

Advancing Core Competencies in This Chapter				
☐ Professional Identity	☐ Ethical Practice	✖ Critical Thinking	☐ Diversity in Practice	☐ Human Rights & Justice
☐ Research-Based Practice	✖ Human Behavior	☐ Policy Practice	☐ Practice Contexts	✖ Engage, Assess, Intervene, Evaluate

We are blest by everything and everything we look upon is blest.

–W. B. YEATS

Most of us, at some point in our lives, inevitably ponder existential or spiritual questions. Why am I here? What is the meaning and purpose of my life? Is there some Higher Power, Divine Being, or a God? Why do bad things happen? These questions may be part of a dark night of the soul, when we find ourselves in the midst of some unbearable personal tragedy. We may question the very foundation of our previously held assumptions about our lives, our world, or ourselves. However, natural life transitions such as adolescence, mid-life, the birth of a child, or the death of a loved one may prompt these questions as well. Similarly, moments of great beauty and awe may inspire us to ask profound questions, which ordinarily go unasked. These questions may unsettle us and ignite a quest for meaning, significance, and a connection to something greater than ourselves.

Although some prefer to conceptualize this search for meaning and purpose as an existential or a humanistic one, others see these questions as spiritual. The very deepest core of our being seeks answers to these profound questions, even as we recognize that they are not easily answered. Philosophy has pondered these issues for centuries; social work and psychological theories alone fail to answer them adequately. Although we are not theologians or philosophers, clients sometimes come to therapy because of these very questions. They may not present directly asking for answers, but as we scratch the surface of their presenting problems, if we listen carefully, we hear these unspoken questions. Why did this happen to me? What did I do to deserve this? How could God let this happen?

Many everyday problems in living are complicated by underlying spiritual concerns. It is easy to become hopeless when one has no guiding frame, no spiritual resources to call on in the struggle against poverty, job loss, marital difficulties, health concerns, trauma, grief, oppression, depression, and a host of other problems. In pondering whether these are existential or spiritual concerns, Maslow (1962) states that existentialism focuses on human aloneness. Spirituality embraces the human desire for connection. Would either of these foci influence your approach to the clients below?

A middle-aged couple with marital problems may question if they are entitled to happiness. Should they stay together because of some shared value, whether it is children or marriage vows? They may be members of a particular religious denomination that discourages or even forbids divorce. If we respond from social work or psychological theory alone, we may miss the critical meaning of their struggle. If we include a spiritual perspective, how might we respond to this couple? How do we as social workers walk the line between psychological needs and spiritual concerns?

Spiritual questions may be less specific. A young man, who faces job loss, may for the first time wonder about what he really wants to do with his life. Traditional social work theories provide an excellent framework and guide us in exploring his feelings and thoughts, but perhaps for this young man it would be more beneficial to address an underlying question: What is the purpose of my life? Am I here for some special reason? How would our response differ if we approach these issues from a spiritual perspective rather than a purely existential one?

Professional Identity

Practice Behavior Example: *Attend to professional roles and boundaries.*

Critical Thinking Question: In this chapter the search for meaning is viewed as a spiritual search. What issues may arise for therapists who conceptualize this search as spiritual rather than existential?

SOCIAL WORK AND SPIRITUALITY

In social work and other helping professions, there has been a growing trend to include the spiritual dimension in client treatment. Although this inclusion has not been without controversy, there appears to be more acceptance than opposition. There has been an increasing number of journal articles and professional books on the topic. Several professional organizations focused on the role of spirituality in health and mental health has developed, and the Council on Social Work Education has created standards requiring spiritual content in social work curricula. Some practitioners welcome the trend, others are adamantly opposed to it, and some remain ambivalent or undecided. In chapter 2 we will discuss this debate, including the important issues raised by opponents.

In this chapter we focus on the parallel between the spiritual journey and the clinical process, using the image of a *labyrinth* as a metaphor for both. For those therapists who are ambivalent or opposed to including spiritual issues in treatment, the similarities between the two processes may provide a space that allows them to comfortably meet an important client need without compromising their own value system.

THE HELPING PROCESS

Spiritually focused treatment must be based on a foundation of good clinical practice. It does not replace careful assessment, treatment planning, skilled clinical intervention, and the ability to develop and maintain a therapeutic relationship with each client. When we include spiritual issues in treatment we add a dimension, not replace what we ordinarily do. For some, the only difference between the two processes may be how they conceptualize or think about their clients or their work. For example, in chapter 3, we will discuss reframing the holding environment as the sacred space for therapy. Therapists with a spiritual perspective see their clients as sacred beings, which goes beyond the traditional view of positive regard. Although the therapist does not approach clients differently, the spiritual perspective changes how the therapist views clients. Acknowledging the sacredness of clients may provide spiritually focused therapists a more viable concept to sustain a positive therapeutic relationships with clients and may provide a vehicle for implementing spirituality in a nonintrusive manner.

Ethical Practice

Practice Behavior Example: *Recognize and manage personal values in a way that allows professional values to guide practice.*

Critical Thinking Question: Conceptualizing clinical work as sacred allows for the implicit use of spirituality. What precautions are necessary to ensure that therapists do not impose a hidden agenda on clients and thereby violate clients' rights?

TREATMENT APPROACHES

Many therapists work in agencies that mandate short-term treatment models. Constraints imposed by insurance companies have made long-term models almost obsolete. Applegate and Bonovitz (1995) state that these short-term approaches often prove more costly in the long run, because clients are not given the opportunity to address underlying issues that keep them stuck in old destructive patterns. Spiritually sensitive practice that recognizes the wholeness of individuals may provide an antidote to treatment approaches that reduce clients to symptoms, diagnoses, and outcomes. More lasting change can occur when clients are given the time and space to allow issues to unfold and when therapists and clients are able to identify, explore, understand, and ultimately change behavior patterns that create difficulties for clients. Practice approaches such as Woods and Hollis's (2000) psychosocial model provide a holistic view of clients and allow the space and time to explore issues in depth. Clients are often able to understand that their behaviors or feelings often cluster around specific patterns, which can bring about more lasting changes. Although many of the ideas in this book are based on the psychosocial model, they can be easily used as specified or adapted for other models.

George, a 33-year-old accountant, is an example of a client who benefited from a long-term, dynamic approach. He requested help with job-related stress and was able to identify his inability to stand up to his boss at work. With further exploration he connected this pattern to the fear he felt as the child of a raging, alcoholic father. In our work with George, it may have appeared that we were moving away from his presenting issue, focusing on his childhood rather than on his boss. However, the insights learned led to a fuller resolution of his issue than simply focusing on coping strategie. George was not only able to work more effectively with his boss, but was positioned to respond in a healthier manner in other situations in which he felt intimidated by authority figures.

THE LABYRINTH WALK

The subtitle of this text, "Walking the Labyrinth," was chosen because it seems a fitting metaphor for both the clinical process and the spiritual journey of the client. Each process begins with a yearning for something different, a stepping into the process, negotiating the challenges, a time of deep reflection and insight, and ultimately bringing the discoveries, changes, and benefits from the encounter back into everyday life. In this section we describe the labyrinth and draw parallels between walking the labyrinth, the spiritual journey, and the clinical process.

The Labyrinth

A labyrinth is a single path that leads to a center (Artress, 1996; McCullough, 2004) (see Figure 1.1). The twists and turns of the typical labyrinth make a "meandering, but pur-

---

Figure 1.1 • Diagram of a labyrinth

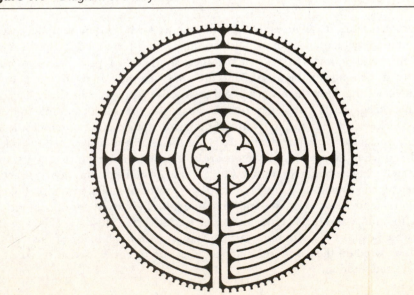

poseful path…" (Artress, 1996, xii). Circular labyrinths are most common, usually composed of a number of circuits, either 7 or 11, depending on the particular form (Artress, 1996; West, 2000). From afar, the design appears complex and confusing, but by placing one foot in front of the other, the individual comes to the center of the design, and by retracing one's steps, one comes back to the threshold (McCullough, 2004).

The labyrinth image has appeared throughout history, dating back to when our ancestors lived in caves. It is perhaps the "oldest artistic creation" (McCullough, 2004, p. 4). It is unique in that it does not copy anything from nature, but most likely was conjured up in the human imagination (McCullough, 2004). Found in the myths and legends of diverse cultures, the original purpose of the labyrinth is unknown. Like Stonehenge, however, there has been much speculation about its meaning, which varies by culture and has changed over time (McCullough, 2004).

Spirituality and the Labyrinth

We are naturally drawn to the labyrinth. It beckons us. It invites us to come and walk the concentric circles to the middle, wondering how that seemingly unruly mass of curves and turns leads us to the center, and ultimately back out again. The importance of the labyrinth image lies not its beauty but in its potential as a spiritual tool (Artress, 1996; McCullough, 2004), a tool for looking inward, a place to encounter the Divine (Artress, 1996; McCullough, 2004), or "an archetypal map of the healing journey" (West, 2000, p. 6). It is a "powerful spiritual symbol that speaks to our souls in a way that transcends all creeds and all beliefs. All spiritual traditions speak of life as a path, a spiritual purpose, with its own twists and unexpected turns, to the heart of the Spirit" (West, 2000, p. 9). "In surrendering to the winding path, the soul finds healing and wholeness" (Artress, 1996, p. xii).

The labyrinth has been used in spiritual practice, with images designed for use in cathedrals and other sacred places. It has been an adjunct to meditation and prayer. And more recently, recognizing the healing potential from walking the labyrinth, some hospitals and health spas have installed these sacred paths. Free from any specific dogma or creed, it is an image that appeals to both traditionalists and those who practice alternative spiritual rituals (McCullough, 2004).

The Maze

The labyrinth is often confused with the maze. McCullough (2004) states that "a labyrinth is a single circuitous path that leads uninterrupted to a center, while a maze is a puzzle with many forks in the road that demand choices" (p. 4). The maze is "tricky" (McCullough, 2004, p. 4). When one walks through a maze, one finds many possible wrong paths, many planned obstacles to avoid before one achieves the goal (McCullough, 2004). Mazes may "taunt, tease, and challenge" (West, 2000, p. 5) and can even lead to entrapment (McCullough, 2004) (see Figure 1.2). The labyrinth, however, has only one path to the center and the same path out (Artress, 1996; West, 2000).

Critical Thinking

Practice Behavior Example: *Distinguish, appraise, and integrate multiple sources of knowledge, including research-based knowledge and practice wisdom.*

Critical Thinking Question: Did you connect more with the image of the labyrinth or with that of the maze? Describe your experience and discuss how each helps you conceptualize your work with clients.

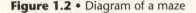

Figure 1.2 • Diagram of a maze

CLINICAL PRACTICE

Why is the labyrinth an apt metaphor for clinical practice? It is easy to get caught up in the "presenting problems" clients bring to treatment, in making assessments, in formulating diagnoses and treatment plans, in concerns about compliance with insurance companies, and in the need to adhere to agency policies and procedures. When we look at our clients from a spiritual perspective (and not coincidentally from a sound clinical perspective), we focus on the client's attempt to seek health, growth, and wholeness. We recognize that clients are more than individuals seeking relief from symptoms. Symptoms may have been the motivation for treatment, but we look beyond them to the deeper quest for growth, meaning, purpose, and a desire to flourish, a sense of fulfillment, or wholeness (holiness).

Maslow and Rogers emphasize our innate striving to reach mastery competence, to strive to be better, to achieve more than survival or material security, and to thrive or flourish (Keyes & Lopez, 2005). Artress (1996), in her introduction to *Walking a Sacred Path*, states that there is "a longing within the human heart to love and nurture, to create, and to discover the mystery we live [with] and that lives within us" (p. x). The labyrinth is an ancient tool that allows one to address both psychological and spiritual needs (Artress, 1996; West, 2000). "It connects us to our souls so we can remember who we are" (Artress, 1996, p. xi). The clinical process and the spiritual journey are endeavors to tap into our inner wisdom and connect to something beyond our intellect to grow, resolve, find strength, and move forward. Both involve a yearning to connect with our authentic self. The labyrinth, therefore, serves as a visual image of both processes.

The Labyrinth and the Clinical Process

The therapeutic process "is full of mystery, surprise, and unpredictable turns" (Welwood, 2000, p. 142). The image of the labyrinth helps us to remember the complexities of clinical work. In clinical work, as in the labyrinth, there are twists and turns. It involves "detours, uncertainty, failure, and reassignment of priorities" (Bien, 2008, p. 60). Clients' lives are complex, and the path to solutions can appear confusing at times. Yet, by stepping into the unknown process of therapy, clients hope that there will be resolution. Although they may wish for a quick resolution, progress in treatment, like human development, is not quick.

> We open (or expand) and we close (contract). We approach and then we retreat. We feel closer and then farther apart. We make progress and then we plateau or regress. Because we are made up of systems nested within systems, we are very complex expressions of interacting cycles. (Bien, 2008, p. 50)

Although the complexities of clinical work are natural and to be expected, our clients, and at times even us as therapists, wonder if we will get to the "center" in the treatment process. Will we get to the heart of the matter and a solution to the concern, or find a way for our clients to cope more effectively with an unchanging situation? We may feel we are close to a breakthrough, only to find circumstances that take us away from achieving a solution. Similarly, we may feel lost in the complexities of our clients' difficulties, fearing there is no solution to be found, when the client reaches a breakthrough, bringing about amazing progress. An understanding of the cyclical nature of change and growth may help clients and us to "understand the nonlinear and tacit aspects" of treatment (Bien, 2008, p. 50). The labyrinth is a visual map of this cyclical process. It allows us to see the client's movement toward and away from the work as a natural progression toward wholeness, rather than resistance to the work.

After the time spent at the center of the labyrinth, one begins the walk out, retracing the winding path outward. Just as the labyrinth walk comes to an end, after a time of reflection and insight, clients need to take what they learned from treatment and return to their lives, where they will use their new skills. The path back out from the labyrinth reminds us that after "resting" in the center for a period of time, clients need to return to their lives. So they take the gifts from therapy—the spiritual retreat, the time in the center of the labyrinth—back into their lives, as accountants, homemakers, physicians, lawyers, and so forth. Few are able to choose or want to choose the life of a hermit. In our times, we need to be spiritual beings in a secular world of relationships and work. Likewise, the lessons learned in therapy are intended to help clients live more fulfilling lives and not stay focused only on their own self-development and reflections. Therefore, we can see that the labyrinth gives clients and therapists an image of what the spiritual encounter or the therapeutic encounter is like: the decision to enter the process, a stepping into that process, time spent leading to the center—often by what appears to be moving away from that center only to come back to it—a time of discovery at the center of the process and feeling renewed and whole, and a return to one's life.

Trusting the Process

With clinical experience comes the realization that often opportunities or openings arise within the treatment session to raise important issues. This process occurs frequently, yet is not easily described. These moments allow us to realize that clients are ready to explore a topic or hear what we need to share with them. When we are attuned to these moments and wait to ask our questions or make reflective comments, our work has an apparently seamless flow. It is often difficult to anticipate when these moments will come. When we "trust the process," we "learn to rely on our practice wisdom, insight, and intuition built on practice experience," rather than theory and empirical evidence alone (Cunningham, 2004, p. 338).

Walking the labyrinth, as with therapy and the spiritual journey, requires courage and trust in the clinical process. If we cross the threshold into the unknown and persevere by placing one foot in front of the other, we will come to the center. In therapy, our clients enter the unknown, not sure if the twists and turns of the helping process will lead them to relief, a solution, or growth. They may wonder what they will face in treatment, what changes they will need to make. We all naturally resist change, while desiring the relief that only those changes can bring. If our clients embark on this journey, they can come to the center of who they truly are. The image of the labyrinth reminds us that the clinical process, like the labyrinth, has a center, where, after "walking" a sometimes circuitous path, the discovery is made, the healing takes place, the gift, whether it is peace, self-knowledge, understanding, compassion, guidance, advice, or encouragement, is realized.

Courage

Along with their problems and difficulties, clients bring their strengths and abilities to therapy. Perhaps one of their greatest assets is courage. It takes courage for a client to make the first phone call to request help. It takes courage for her to show up for her appointment and enter the unknown territory of therapy, trusting that it will help. Each session requires courage, as she explores her thoughts and feelings, making changes in how she approaches what had been familiar and now no longer is. Clients need courage to return to their everyday lives and use the insights gained and practice new skills learned to face the ordinary challenges of life. And it takes courage and trust for us to enter each session, each relationship with our clients. We need courage to open our hearts and witness our clients' suffering and struggles regardless of what we will hear and how it might change us.

Uncertainty

When our clients enter therapy they do not know how things will turn out. They face uncertainty; the path is unknown. We must recognize that regardless of how much we have learned, how well versed we are in theory, how capable of helping we might be, we too are uncertain. When we bear witness to our clients' struggles, we embrace our "not knowing" (Bien, 2008, p. 25). When we acknowledge that we are uncertain, we acknowledge that we do not know everything. We may have extensive information about our clients and their problems, yet we do not know everything about them, the whole of them. We may be quite skilled, yet we are not the experts; they are the experts on their life situations. We do not have control over what happens to them. Not knowing, although uncomfortable, is not problematic. Thinking we know everything is. When we believe we know, we cut off the client's experience. We do not hear what does not fit what we believe to be the truth. Uncertainty means that we give up attachments to specific outcomes (Bien, 2008). We approach our clients with interest and professional curiosity. We allow the process to unfold, as the client needs it to. Johanson and Kurtz (1991) point out that we can still be persons of wisdom in spite of uncertainty.

The Labyrinth and the Healing Process

The image of the labyrinth not only helps us to remember the complexities of clinical practice but also may assist us in assessing the phases of the treatment process. Clients rarely go straight to the center of their struggles. They often need time to reveal their story, often taking a circuitous path. The client follows his or her own rhythm in relating to us. The labyrinth reminds us that the story unfolds in a natural way, and we can trust that the client will lead us to the issues that need to be addressed. This is the antithesis of "manualized" treatment approaches favored by advocates of evidence-based practice. When we approach clients with respect and professional curiosity we recognize that the purpose of our questions is to learn about the client and form a relationship with them. "Embedded in our curiosity is our deep sense that learning about this individual is not about mechanically asking questions from an intake form nor is it related to solidifying or validating our quickly formed hypotheses about the client's struggle" (Bien, 2008, p. 72).

At times it is natural for us to feel anxious and unsure that our client's presentation will lead to the needed work. How do we know if we can trust the process? Are we off target and need to help the client get to the real issues? Is this a positive digression, which, as in the case of George (see example earlier), would lead to a better outcome? The challenge is to understand when something "should be trusted, and when something has become disconnected from the thread and needs attention" (Johanson & Kurtz, 1991, p. 56). When one walks a labyrinth, one can step outside the walls of the path, one can misstep and lose direction. The metaphor of the labyrinth can be used to reflect on the progress of the individual session or the overall treatment process. For a therapist in doubt, supervision is an excellent place to help distinguish the natural twists and turns of therapy and when one is off the mark.

The Labyrinth and Client Progress

The image of the labyrinth can be used with clients to help them understand the need for patience with themselves and help them understand the process of healing. It may remind therapists that true healing is often circuitous. Sometimes, clients expect that therapy means social workers will give them good advice. Although it is appropriate to occasionally give advice, we help clients understand the problem-solving process more deeply when we assist them in coming to solutions that are both effective and discovered by them or in collaboration with us. This takes more time, and, like walking the labyrinth, may appear to not be getting them anywhere.

After I had introduced diagrams of the labyrinth and maze in class, one creative advanced year student implemented the concept in her work with an adolescent girl who was struggling with her school attendance and grades. After the student asked her client about her career goals, she wrote the identified goals in the center of the labyrinth diagram. Then they discussed what the client would have to do to achieve her goals. They identified these actions to be staying in school, doing her schoolwork, and several other tasks. The client, who had seen school as interfering with what she wanted to do, now had a visual image that what had appeared to take her away from her goals actually led to them. She would need to continue with the social worker's support, but it was the first time she seemed to understand the connection between her current behavior and what she wanted for her future.

Phases of Treatment and the Labyrinth

As clinicians we are familiar with the phases of treatment: engagement, assessment, intervention, and ending. The tasks of each stage overlap and there are no clear distinctions.

As we move from one phase to the next we frequently need to revisit the tasks of previous stages. When clients become anxious or resistant, we need to engage them in facing a particular issue or concern that causes them to be fearful. If there is a misunderstanding between us, we need to focus our efforts on repairing our relationship, which requires more attention to engagement skills than intervention skills. At times new information necessitates major changes in our earlier assessments. The winding path of the labyrinth parallels the twists and turns of the therapeutic process and reflects its cyclical nature.

CONCLUSION

In this chapter we discussed the labyrinth as a metaphor to conceptualize clinical practice and the inclusion of spiritual matters in our work. Walking a labyrinth has phases similar to the therapeutic encounter as well as the spiritual journey. In each, the individual yearns for authenticity and wholeness. Each process, used in response to a call for healing, involves a commitment to begin, a stepping into the unknown, a meeting of challenges, and healed and renewed, one brings the benefits of each process into one's everyday life.

In subsequent chapters we will parallel walking the labyrinth with the phases of treatment. The tasks of engagement and assessment will be compared to the decision to cross the threshold of the labyrinth and walk the twisting path to the center. Time spent in the center will be used to discuss the intervention phase of our work and the walk out, the ending process of treatment.

Some of the issues discussed in this book are focused on the explicit use of spirituality in clinical practice. Included are guidelines for spiritual assessments and intervention techniques. Some of the suggestions, however, can be used implicitly. Please note that this does not amount to advocating a hidden agenda. With some clients, explicit use of spirituality is not appropriate but can be used to shape our professional worldview. For example, we can implicitly use spirituality by viewing clients as sacred beings and providing a sacred space for treatment (see chapter 3). We will include guidelines that are based on spiritual principles to prepare therapists for clinical practice.

This book is based on the belief that spiritually focused treatment must be based on sound clinical practice. Without such a foundation, treatment can be potentially harmful to our clients. Our goal is to develop an approach to therapeutic work that respects clients' values, implement effective helping, and find techniques that sustain us in our work and provide us with meaning.

PRACTICE TEST The following questions will test your knowledge of the content found within this chapter and help you prepare for the licensing exam by applying chapter content to practice. For more questions styled like the licensing exam, visit **MySocialWorkLab.com**

1. A social worker who is a devout Christian is working with a client who reveals that she is an agnostic. The social worker tells the client that she should believe in God. The social worker's behavior

   a. is inappropriate and she should apologize to the client.

   b. is inappropriate and she should not see clients until she can resolve her issues.

   c. is inappropriate and she should treat only clients who share her beliefs.

   d. is appropriate because it is consistent with her beliefs.

2. Social workers ethically integrate spirituality into their practice when they

   a. take special training in religious diversity.

   b. use it for a holistic approach.

   c. recognize that spirituality is appropriate for all clients.

   d. integrate spirituality and clinical practice theory.

3. A social worker who embraces a New Age philosophy is working with a client who tells him she is infertile. He should explore

   a. her spiritual beliefs about having children.

   b. if negative thinking created her situation.

   c. how spirituality would help her cope.

   d. spirituality only if the client raises it.

4. When social workers embrace a not-knowing stance in clinical practice it means they recognize they are not experts

   a. with a specific client population.

   b. on their clients' experiences.

   c. with a particular treatment modality.

   d. in a particular content area.

1. Anabella seeks clinical services. She is feeling confused and wonders if her life has meaning or purpose. What are some reasons for including the spiritual dimension with Anabella? How should the social worker determine if this would be appropriate?

2. Although social workers may have practice knowledge and expertise they are not the experts on the client's life. Discuss how social workers can use the concept of uncertainty or "unknowing" to balance their expertise with the clients' experiences.

SUCCEED WITH

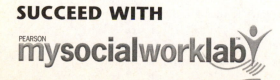
PEARSON
mysocialworklab™

Visit **MySocialWorkLab** for more licensing exam test questions, and to access case studies, videos, and much more.

2

Spirituality and Religion

Advancing Core Competencies in This Chapter				
✘ Professional Identity	✘ Ethical Practice	✘ Critical Thinking	◾ Diversity in Practice	◾ Human Rights & Justice
✘ Research-Based Practice	◾ Human Behavior	◾ Policy Practice	◾ Practice Contexts	Engage, Assess, Intervene, Evaluate

We are not human beings having a spiritual experience; we are spiritual beings having a human experience.

–P.T. de Chadin

Over the past several decades there has been an increasing interest in the topic of spirituality and its inclusion in clinical social work practice. Some therapists argue strongly for this inclusion, others are adamantly opposed, some remain ambivalent. Part, but certainly not all, of the difficulty for opponents and those who are ambivalent is the lack of clarity between the concepts of spirituality and religion. Research issues complicate matters further. How does one define *spirituality* in a manner that lends itself to measurement? Spirituality usually focuses on the inner life of the person, rather than behavioral observations. Spirituality is difficult to articulate, and, therefore, measure. And, finally, the current political context may increase opposition or ambivalence toward the domain of spirituality. For the past few decades the topic of religion has received much attention in the media. For example, it played an important role in the 2000 and 2004 Presidential races. Candidates were asked about their personal spiritual beliefs and practices, and for some voters the answers to these questions influenced their vote more than the candidate's stance on other issues. Several social and medical issues, including sexual orientation, right to life, the right to die, and stem cell research, have been addressed in the context of moral and religious values. Meanwhile, religious conflict and strife are rampant in several places in the world. Among some groups there is little room for those who do not share their beliefs and values. In chapter 9 we will discuss destructive forms of spirituality, but for now our point of concern is the potential for these issues to exacerbate the opposition or ambivalence toward including spirituality in clinical practice.

We begin this chapter with a brief historical context of the relationship between the social work profession and the issue of spirituality. We will discuss the concepts of spirituality and religion, along with the differences, similarities, and overlap, and finally we will explore the concerns and benefits regarding the inclusion of spirituality in clinical practice.

HISTORICAL CONTEXT

Although the debate about including spirituality in clinical practice is fairly recent, there is a long history regarding the role of religion and spirituality in our profession. Social work roots are grounded in the early Christian social movements and Charity Organizations of the 19th century. Early social workers, "friendly visitors," aimed to improve the lives of those living in poverty. Their approach, however, was "moralistic and ethnocentric," distinguishing the "deserving" from the "undeserving" poor (Krieglstein, 2006, p. 22). In the 1940s, in an attempt to develop a scientific basis for the profession, there was increased emphasis on empiricism and the medical model. At the same time Freudian influence became evident (Krieglstein, 2006; Woods & Hollis, 2000). Freud, along with Skinner and Ellis, had a very negative view of religion. Freud (1913, as cited in Palmer, 1997), in *Totem and Taboo*, states that religion is a form of neurosis. In *The Future of an Illusion* (1927), he states that religion is an illusion people use rather than face the realities of life (as cited in Palmer, 1997). Ellis equated religious or spiritual belief with irrational thoughts (as cited in Swinton, 2001), and Skinner (as cited in Pargament, 2007) believed that religious institutions used aversive methods to achieve social control. Thus, spirituality and religion were viewed as indicators of an unhealthy personality (Solari, 1995) and omitted as an important area for therapeutic exploration.

RELIGION AND SPIRITUALITY

Pargament (2007) asks how we can integrate spirituality into clinical practice if we do not know what spirituality is. It is a "slippery" (Swinton, 2001, p. 12), "fuzzy" concept (Spika, 1993, as cited in Pargament, 2007, p. 32), difficult to define and at times almost impossible to distinguish from religion. Until recently *spirituality* and *religion* were used interchangeably (Pargament, 2007; Swinton, 2001), but currently the terms are more polarized (Pargament, 2007). In most spirituality texts, authors attempt to define spirituality and differentiate it from the concept of religion. If this were an easy task, we would have more clarity on those differences. The task is further complicated when authors, after making a valiant effort to distinguish religion and spirituality, suggest interventions that are usually associated with religion, such as prayer. We will most likely never have a clear differentiation of the concepts, partly because they overlap and partly because many people use them interchangeably. We do, however, need to be as conscious as possible when we are referring to religion (the formal institution, dogmas, rituals) and when we are discussing spirituality (a broader, personal, more inclusive concept). As a final note, currently there is a tendency to see religion as "bad" and spirituality as "good" (Pargament, 2007; Zinnbauer & Pargament, 2005). In reality, both can be adaptive, coping resources for clients and both can be harmful.

Definition of Religion

Among those who try to distinguish spirituality and religion, there is some consensus that religion is a formal, institutionalized set of beliefs and practices shared by a faith community and transmitted over time (Canda & Furman, 2010; Cunningham, 2000; Koenig, 2005; Sperry, 2001; Swinton, 2001). "Organized religions are rooted within a particular tradition or traditions, which engender their own narratives, symbols and doctrines that are used by adherents to interpret and explain their experiences of the world" (Swinton, 2001, p. 28). Religious beliefs usually center on "some conception of God" and are fundamental to the individual's view of himself (Swinton, 2001, p. 28). Doctrines, proscribed behaviors, and beliefs may be "authoritarian" and responsibility to the collective community is emphasized (Koenig, 2005).

There have been attempts by theorists to capture the essence of what we currently mean by spirituality or to distinguish "the public or institutional religion with its buildings, programs, clergy, theology, rituals and ceremonies" from the more "private or personal religion with its emphasis on nurturing the soul and development of one's spiritual life" (Elkins, 1998, p. 25). For example, William James differentiated between institutional and personal religion, Abraham Maslow referred to institutional religion as the "big R" religion and the personal experience of individuals as the "little R" religion, and Gordon Allport proposed the concepts of "intrinsic" and "extrinsic" religious orientation (as cited in Elkins, 1998, p. 25). Individuals with an extrinsic orientation are likely to adhere to the observable aspects of their religion, with little or no inner transformation, whereas those with an intrinsic orientation are likely to have religion infused in all aspects of their life (Swinton, 2001).

Definition of Spirituality

Regardless of variations in the definition of spirituality, it is in essence a broader, more inclusive concept than religion. It is a "personal quest" for meaning and understanding of life's ultimate questions (Koenig, 2005, p. 44) and a "frame that guides individuals in finding meaning in their lives and the events that occur" (Cunningham, 2000, p. 65). It provides a "sense of connectedness, meaning, peace, consciousness, purpose, and service that develops across the life span" (Derezotes, 2006, p. 3). Spirituality is an individual expression, whereas religious beliefs and practices are shaped by a community (Derezotes, 2006; Koenig, 2005). Many theorists propose that spirituality includes a relationship with the transcendent and sacred (Canda & Furman, 2010; Elkins, 1998; Koenig, 2005). For some this relationship is with God, whereas for others it is a connection with nature or some form of humanitarianism, and may not include a belief in an Ultimate Being (Koenig, 2005). The essence of spirituality is one's yearning for and "expression of living connection with everything" (Derezotes, 2006, p. 3).

As the understanding of the concept of spirituality shifted from the religious to the secular, its meaning broadened to "a more diffuse human need that can be met quite apart from institutionalized religious structures" (Swinton, 2001, p. 11). It is a universal, human phenomenon that focuses on our inner life and a longing for the sacred (Elkins, 1998; Pargament, 2007). Spirituality "relates to a universal and fundamental aspect of what it is to be human—to search for a sense of meaning, purpose, and moral frameworks for relating to self, other, and the ultimate reality" (Canda & Furman, 1999, p. 37).

Spirituality and the Soul

Spirituality emanates from the "unfathomable depths" of our being and refers to a longing "to touch and celebrate the mystery of life" (Elkins, 1998, p. 33). This deep place within us is called the soul. It is "our essence, our life force, our vitality" (Ingerman, 1995, p. 114), our deepest level of self (Cunningham, 2000). It is that which truly makes us human. Please note that my use of the word *soul* is not associated with its historical religious connotations. It is consistent with the work of Jungian psychologist Thomas Moore, who, in his widely popular *Care of the Soul* (1992), refers to the soul as our life force.

By definition, the soul, or life force, and therefore spirituality, would be associated with right-brain characteristics, such as being creative, intuitive, relational, and emotional, as opposed to left-brain characteristics, such as being logical, being analytically skilled, and having sequential thinking (Elkins, 1995, p. 88). The spiritual individual seeks the sacred (Elkins, 1998; Pargament, 1997, 2007), which is encountered in those moments "that fill us with a sense of poignancy, wonder, and awe" (Elkins, 1998, p. 31). Thus, spirituality exists whenever the "soul is stirred, nurtured and moved by the sacred" (Elkins, 1998, p. 31).

Transcendent Being

Elkins (1998) speculates on "the essence of spirituality, once all the religious trappings have been removed" (p. 27). He proposes that spirituality is a "multidimensional construct," which includes a transcendent dimension or belief in something beyond what we can know through rational thinking. For many this transcendent dimension is God, the Divine, or a Higher Power. It can, however, be any force outside the self that gives life meaning and purpose (Elkins, 1998). So, although many spiritual individuals believe in a transcendent being, a contemporary understanding of spirituality includes those who do not believe in God (Cunningham, 2000; Elkins, 1998; Pargament, 2007). Some may believe in a higher good, such as truth, compassion, social justice, or feel a sense of connection to nature. Wakefield (1990) states that the poetry of Dylan Thomas expresses the essence of a nondenominational God: "The force that through the green fuse drives the flower/drives my green age" (p. 2).

Spiritual Attributes

The search for meaning and purpose in life is an important dimension of spirituality (Cunningham, 2000; Elkins, 1998; Pargament, 2007). The spiritual person believes there is some reason we are here and has a commitment to living life fully (Teasdale, 2001). She sees life "infused with sacredness" and often feels a sense of wonder and awe, even in nonreligious places (Elkins, 1998, p. 34). Spirituality involves a sense of connectedness to others and the interconnectedness of all beings (Teasdale, 2001) and emphasizes compassion and social justice (Elkins, 1998, p. 27).

Spiritual Path

Some individuals express their spirituality through a traditional religious path. Others choose alternative paths (Elkins, 1998). For a growing number of people, traditional religions "no longer speak to the soul" (Elkins, 1998, p. 21). Regardless of the path one chooses, the spiritual person often recognizes the wisdom inherent in the world religions and integrates it into his own belief system (Cunningham, 2000). Some seek newer forms of spirituality built on the foundation of traditional values, but ones that do not prescribe the beliefs and practices of specific religions (Elkins, 1998). One may express her spirituality through traditional practices such as prayer or in more secular ways like volunteerism. Many combine both expressions.

SPIRITUALITY AND CLINICAL PRACTICE

Clearly, the meaning of spirituality is personal and there are many variations in how one defines it. When we engage in research, we need to define terms in a way that allows for measurement; but in clinical settings, we can work with the client's understanding and meaning of the concept. Our attempts to define spirituality and generalize it to all often lead us through murky waters where we fail to capture what it means for our clients. They often are clear about what they mean when they say they are spiritual. According to constructivist theory, we assign meaning to phenomena, and that meaning influences our response (Mahoney, 2003). This approach allows for a subjective interpretation of what spirituality means (Gray, 2008). Each individual defines spirituality as it fits his or her beliefs and experiences. Our role then becomes that of a listener, allowing the client to teach us what spirituality means for her, rather than clouding the issue with our definitions or assumptions. In this text, I focus as much as possible on spirituality (a personal search for meaning, purpose, and the sacred) rather than religion (the institution, dogmas, beliefs, and rituals) because the former concept is broader and more inclusive. Spirituality, in its healthy forms, can be integrated into any formalized belief system, making treatment uniquely tailored to specific clients.

THE SPIRITUAL DEBATE

Concerns About Inclusion

Those who oppose the inclusion of spirituality in clinical practice treatment raise several important concerns, including the empirical basis for spirituality, potential for proselytizing, lack of role clarity, and therapist's competence in working with spiritual issues. In this section, we will discuss these concerns.

Empiricism

To strengthen the scientific basis of social work and increase accountability, social workers place increasing importance on empirical findings and evidence-based practices. This thrust raises concerns about the inclusion of the spiritual domain and its accompanying lack of clarity as a construct. Because it is difficult to articulate, it is difficult to measure. Some researchers use the concept of religiosity, which allows them to study observable activities such as attendance at religious services, prayer, or reading of sacred texts. Spirituality often focuses on the inner life of the person and the search to understand issues such as the meaning, purpose, and connection to the sacred. Spirituality is less focused on the number of times one might attend a religious service and more focused on the internal experience and meaning one encounters during that service. Although difficult to measure and research, these are important issues to understand and include in treatment. Randomized controlled studies is the gold standard in research, but not an appropriate method to explore many issues of importance related to spirituality. Methods that "demand a much more subjective approach" may be needed "if understanding and effective intervention are to be achieved" (Swinton, 2001, p. 67).

Although therapists recognize the importance of empirical support for the inclusion of spiritual issues in treatment, they also understand that quantitative methods (e.g., surveys or questionnaires) are more suited to understanding the role of religious or spiritual practices rather than the internal experience of an individual (i.e., how one feels or finds meaning during the practice). Qualitative methods (e.g., interviews or focus groups) may be useful in getting a more in-depth understanding of how people feel or make meaning from their spiritual experiences. However, even these methods are limited to those aspects of one's internal experience that can be articulated.

Proselytizing

One of the most serious objections to the inclusion of the spiritual dimension in clinical practice is the concern that therapists will proselytize or impose their own spiritual values, morals, or beliefs on clients (Canda & Furman, 1999, 2010; Richards & Bergin, 2002, p. 154). Proselytizing includes using spiritual interventions without client consent or implementing ones that conflict with clients' values or life choices (Richards & Bergin, 2002). Although a legitimate concern, proselytizing is a misuse of spirituality and an example of poor clinical practice. It violates the client's right to self-determination (Woods & Hollis, 2000). It is unethical to impose any of our beliefs or values on clients. But, because spiritual beliefs include how one finds meaning and purpose, imposition of therapists' beliefs may be especially detrimental. Inappropriate intervention may trigger a crisis of meaning for the client or be a form of oppression. One can include spiritual issues without imposing beliefs, morals, or values on clients. Opponents concerned about proselytizing raise the need for vigilance and supervision. Therapists must continuously reflect on their practice to ensure they are not imposing their own values and beliefs on clients. Supervision provides an excellent resource for self-monitoring and reflection. The objective perspective of the supervisor is often helpful in detecting subtle forms of proselytizing.

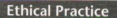

Ethical Practice

Practice Behavior Example: *Recognize and manage personal values in a way that allows professional values to guide practice.*

Critical Thinking Question: Discuss the ethical concerns of proselytizing when therapists include spirituality in their clinical work with clients. How do you think this may be complicated for therapists working in faith-based organizations? Elaborate.

Role Clarity and Boundaries

Issues related to role clarity and professional boundaries pose a potential concern. Unless sanctioned by a religious institution, therapists do not have spiritual authority (Canda & Furman, 1999; Pargament, 2007; Richards & Bergin, 2002). Therapists cannot perform authorized rituals (Canda & Furman, 1999, 2010; Pargament, 2007) or offer "absolute truth." We cannot claim with certainty the existence of a divine power or its nature (Pargament, 2007, p. 19). Nor are we able to interpret religious doctrines and sanction or admonish behaviors deemed morally right or wrong. We are not in a position to interpret dogmas, beliefs, or other issues directly related to the client's spiritual tradition, nor is it ethical to show disrespect toward or undermine the authority of the client's religious leaders (Richards & Bergin, 2002, p. 148). When clients are disappointed or angry with their religious leaders, one can be empathic without denigrating the latter (Richards & Bergin, 2002). This, however, can create a dilemma: What should therapists do when they feel clients' spiritual or religious beliefs or practices are detrimental to them? Canda and Furman (2010) suggest that one should help clients assess for themselves the extent of their satisfaction or dissatisfaction with a particular spiritual leader or community. They include a list of questions to help in this process (Canda & Furman, 2010, p. 275). Although this approach fits our social work ethics, it does imply that the client is able to determine if his spiritual community or leader is detrimental and is in a position to disengage when appropriate. Do you think that clients are always able to determine if their faith community or spiritual leader is having a detrimental effect on them? Do you think that it is easy, when they are aware that their spiritual community or leader is potentially harmful to them, for clients to disengage from that community or leader without support?

Competent Practice

Raising and addressing spiritual concerns when one is not equipped to do so is an example of practicing outside the realm of one's competence (Canda & Furman, 2010; Richards & Bergin, 2002, p. 166). Like any other area of therapeutic exploration, when one is not competent in the area, one needs to either refer the client to someone who is or take steps to prepare oneself to effectively address these issues in practice. Therapists who have not received adequate preparation to address clients' spiritual concerns may be tempted to draw on their personal experiences to guide clients. Personal experience can never take the place of formal training in spiritually focused therapy.

Benefits of Inclusion

Although the above-mentioned concerns about the inclusion of spirituality in treatment are real, there are many advantages to including the spiritual domain in our clinical practice. Spirituality is an important aspect of clients' lives and excluding it from treatment compromises a holistic approach to assessment and intervention. Spirituality is pivotal in the search for meaning and how clients interpret the events that occur. It is a coping resource for many; finally, some client problems are spiritual in nature or are exacerbated by spiritual or religious issues that need to be addressed in treatment.

Importance of Spirituality

Spirituality is a "vital" aspect of human growth (Sperry, 2001, p. 1). Many individuals believe there is something more to life than what we perceive through our senses (Miller, 1999). Swinton (2001, p. 7) states that although institutional religion may be on the decline, "the human quest for the transcendent remains as strong as ever." For many, traditional religions are no longer relevant, which has created a painful void and disconnection from the sacred. Attention to soul issues is critical for emotional health;

however, it is often neglected and "as a result, we find ourselves spiritually thirsty and drying up for lack of soulfulness" (Elkins, 1998, p. 3). Spirituality, often ignored by mental health professionals, "is in fact of central importance to many people who are struggling with the pain and confusion of mental health problems" (Swinton, 2001, p. 7). For those clients who are spiritual or religious, inclusion of the spiritual dimension in the therapeutic process is desired and seen as a necessary part of their therapy (Rose, Westefeld, & Ansley, 2001). Spirituality is implicit in many of our clients' difficulties, and if it is not made explicit, it becomes the proverbial elephant in the room (Pargament, 2007, p. 14).

Holistic Approach

Our profession values a holistic approach to clinical practice. We need to understand clients as biological, psychological, social, and *spiritual* beings. When we disregard the spiritual domain, our knowledge is incomplete (Miller, 1999), and we deny clients "a full spectrum of discovery, growth, and healing" (Gotterer, 2001, p. 187). Inclusion of the spiritual dimension highlights the complexities of our clients and their lives, reminding us that many clients want something more than relief from symptoms (Shafranske & Sperry, 2005). There is "a hunger to be understood as a whole person" (Miller, 1999, p. 10), and when we respond to this hunger, we move therapy from one focused on social adjustment to one that aims at a "cure of the soul" (Fromm, 1950, as cited in Faiver, Ingersoll, O'Brien, & McNally, 2001, p. 7).

Worldview

An important aspect of working with clients is our ability to understand how they view the world, how they interpret the events that occur, and how they find meaning and purpose. Historically, mental health professionals have focused on the cognitive aspects of these processes, omitting the influence of spirituality on the client's frame of reference and the search for meaning and purpose (Cunningham, 2000; Faiver et al., 2001). "Through the spiritual lens, people can see their lives in a broad, transcendent perspective; they can discern deeper truths in ordinary and extraordinary experience; and they can locate timeless values that offer grounding and direction in shifting times and circumstances" (Pargament, 2007, p. 12). Even if spirituality plays a minor role in making meaning, careful assessment is needed to understand our clients (Faiver et al., 2001; Shafranske & Sperry, 2005). Spirituality and its role in shaping the client's worldview are vital to understanding issues of diversity (Canda & Furman, 2010; Richards & Bergin, 2002).

Resource for Coping

Pargament (1997) defines coping as a "*search for significance in times of stress*" (p. 90, italics in the original). For some, spirituality is a means of strength and a resource for coping with the ordinary and extraordinary events of life (Canda & Furman, 1999, 2010; Gotterer, 2001; Faiver et al., 2001; Pargament, 1997, 2007). It is a source of "emotional consolation, inspiration, guidance, structure and security" (Gotterer, 2001, p. 188), an "essential" element in dealing with life's difficulties (Sperry, 2001, p. 1). Spirituality enables one to "transcend and embrace life situations" (Faiver et al., 2001, p. 2). It is a "distinctive resource," which allows one to feel a sense of control and therefore is well suited "to the struggle with human limitations and finitude" (Pargament, 2007, p. 12).

Spiritual beliefs and behaviors are a resource in promoting therapeutic change (Shafranske, 1996, as cited in Richards & Bergin, 2002, p. 9). "When spiritual and religious involvement has been measured (even poorly), it has with surprising consistency been found to be positively related to health and inversely related to disorders" (Miller, 1999, p. 11). In a review of the empirical literature on the relationship between spirituality/religion and mental health, Swinton (2001) concluded that the findings support the beneficial role spirituality plays in mental health. However, he points out there is still a great deal of ambiguity regarding findings and several methodology issues that continue to plague this area of inquiry. Richards and Bergin (2002) concur that research findings regarding the relationship between spirituality and mental health are inconsistent. One methodological issue they raise is the tendency of researchers to classify all "religious" participants as the same. They suggest looking at factors that distinguish individuals participating in studies such as religious orientation (intrinsic or extrinsic).

One potential concern with these research studies is the lack of clarity between religion and spirituality. As mentioned previously, some researchers use the concept of religiosity or some other observable phenomenon. Although the results about the positive role of religiosity in mental health are encouraging, we cannot assume the same outcomes are associated with the broader concept of spirituality. To understand the relationship between spirituality and the inner experiences of individuals, we need different research methods, such as qualitative approaches.

Spirituality, Religion, and Presenting Problems

Many of our clients' problems are spiritual in nature (Pargament, 2007, p. 14), especially those existential concerns such as the search for meaning and purpose. Clients' difficulties, including anxiety, guilt, loss of meaning, and grief, may be influenced by or even caused by spiritual issues (Richards & Bergin, 2002, p. 7). Cognitive-behavioral approaches alone may fail to capture their deeper concerns. "Underneath the depression, anxiety, and despair of many clients is a soul hungering for attention and care" (Elkins, 1998, p. 3). Benner (2005) states that many of the issues clients present reflect a "combination of soul suffering and spirit longing" (p. 292). Clients seek treatment not only to address problems "but also to deal with the spiritual malaise that at times underlies symptoms of depression, anxiety, or restless disquiet" (Shafranske & Sperry, 2005, p. 18). Therefore, spiritual resources may alleviate their suffering more fully than psychosocial approaches alone. Therapists can help clients explore and understand when their spiritual or religious beliefs are affecting their presenting problems or their lives in general and can encourage them to develop and use healthy spiritual resources to cope, change, or heal (Richards & Bergin, 2002).

Critical Thinking

Practice Behavior Example: Distinguish, appraise, and integrate multiple sources of knowledge, including research-based knowledge and practice wisdom.

Critical Thinking Question: In this chapter, many positives and concerns regarding the inclusion of spirituality in clinical practice are addressed. Critically analyze these issues and discuss how therapists can include the positives of spirituality while taking precautions to avoid the negatives.

Summary of the Debate on Inclusion

Shafranske and Sperry (2005) state that inclusion of the spiritual dimension in treatment is a "renaissance in psychological healing" (p. 24). Regardless of continuing arguments to include or exclude the spiritual domain in therapy many therapists are including it in their treatment with clients. The issue then is not whether spiritual issues should be included, but how to implement them effectively and in a manner consistent with our professional values (Canda & Furman, 1999; 2010; Coholic, Nichols, & Cadell, 2008). Regardless of the views of therapists on the role of spirituality, omitting spiritual issues when they are appropriate lessens our effectiveness in working with clients. However, such an omission is not as serious as inappropriately including spiritual issues when clients express opposition. Therapists who are ambivalent or opposed to discussing spiritual issues may refer clients to a spiritual director, clergyperson, or another therapist trained to deal with these issues. Clients may still raise concerns in the therapeutic process, and practitioners will need to develop strategies that allow them to meet clients' needs without compromising their own professional value system.

PRACTICE IMPLICATIONS

Client-Sensitive Terminology

The lack of clarity between religion and spirituality, as well as the variety of spiritual definitions, raises an important practice issue, namely, the terminology we use in our clinical conversations with clients. The words we use in treatment are powerful (Kahle & Robbins, 2004), and good therapists are sensitively attuned to the words, phrases, and metaphors a client uses as he tells us his story. For example, a client may tell you she is not spiritual, but as she relates her search to find meaning and purpose and speaks of her commitment to some higher good, you may believe the label *spiritual* fits her. However, to impose this concept on her narrative would be inappropriate. Likewise, if your client refers to a belief in a Higher Power, we need to use this same phrase. If she refers to God, and we talk about her Higher Power, we are not attuned to her experience (Kahle & Robbins, 2004). These are just a few examples of the importance of hearing the nuances of what clients relate to us. Currently, there is much emphasis on being politically correct. In an attempt to not impose our beliefs and values on clients, we may overcompensate, avoid using words such as *God*, *spiritual*, or *religious*, and miss the mark, leaving clients feeling misunderstood. Instead of political correctness, we need sensitive attunement. When we are unsure, we can engage clients in a discussion about which concepts are most suited to their experience and let them guide us. The important point is to allow the client to discuss his beliefs and spiritual concerns, rather than categorize them.

Healing Versus Cure

Inclusion of the spiritual dimension in practice potentially changes not only our approach to treatment but also our goals. Western perspectives on mental health place great emphasis on cure. Often, if cure is not obtained, treatment is deemed a failure. From a spiritual perspective, we recognize that cure is not always possible, but healing is. These concepts are related but not synonymous. When we focus on healing, it does not rule out cure, but shifts our attention from symptom removal to transcendence (Swinton, 2001) and unfolding of the soul (Mann, 1998, p. 24).

> Healing is a deeply spiritual task that stretches beyond the boundaries of disease and cure and into the realms of transcendence, purpose, hope and meaning that form the very fabric of human experience and desire. The aims and objectives of

healers are to enable a person to find enough meaning in their present struggles to sustain them even in the midst of the most unimaginable storms. (Swinton, 2001, p. 57)

Our goal is to help clients rise above their difficulties, even if they cannot be removed or resolved. We work to transform that which keeps clients from their True nature (Divine nature) rather than behavioral aspects alone. From a healing perspective we see a client affected by his difficulties, not defined by them (Swinton, 2001). For example, when we work with a dying client, we cannot remove the illness, but we can help her deal with her feelings, encourage her family to support her, help them cope with feelings of impending loss, and assist in a host of practical details that will allow her to die more peacefully. In an interview with Bill Moyers, Dr. Rachel Naomi Remen discusses the role of healing in her work with dying patients.

Healing is . . . the leading forth of wholeness in people. Sometimes people heal physically, and they don't heal emotionally, or mentally, or spiritually. And sometimes people heal emotionally, and they don't heal physically. (Moyers, 1993, p. 344)

Healing implies that the client is able to come to terms with his or her difficulty and flourish in spite of it. If good clinical practice aids healing, can it be considered spiritual even if spiritual issues are not explicitly addressed? If treatment helps clients learn to live the best life they can, even if they cannot overcome certain life circumstances, is that treatment spiritual?

Reflective Practice

As reflective practitioners, we need to be aware of the assumptions, attitudes, and biases we may bring to our work (Kahle & Robbins, 2004). It is essential that we reflect on the potential impact these assumptions may have on client treatment; when we include spiritual issues in our work we need to reflect on who we are in relation to the topic. Keeping a journal of your honest reactions, feelings, and thoughts is an excellent tool in your continuing professional development. Some areas for reflection include the following: Who are you in relation to the topic of spirituality? What does spirituality or religion mean in your personal life? Where do you stand on the issue of including spirituality in clinical treatment? What are your spiritual beliefs? How secure are you in those beliefs? How do you feel working with clients who have beliefs very different from yours? For example, if you believe in God and your client is an atheist? Or, if you are an atheist and your client is a devout member of a traditional conservative religion? What if your client engages in alternative spiritual practices, such as Wicca? When we think of ourselves as open to others' beliefs, are there any exceptions? Try to think about possible exceptions and how you would handle these differences in sessions with your clients. After identifying potential concerns in your journal, supervision is a

Professional Identity

Practice Behavior Example: Practice personal reflection and self-correction to ensure continual professional development.

Critical Thinking Question: In this chapter you have been asked to reflect on your own experiences with spirituality and/or religion and how they may affect your professional work. What issues have you identified? How can you implement the positive aspects of your experiences? What strategies are needed to ensure you use spirituality in a professional manner?

good resource to explore them further and reduce the likelihood they will negatively affect your work with clients.

CONCLUSION

After briefly setting the historical context for the relationship between the social work profession and the spiritual domain, we discussed various dimensions of the concepts of religion and spirituality. We included issues raised by opponents to and advocates for the inclusion of spirituality in clinical practice, along with practice implications. We ended with the importance of self-awareness and identification of potential personal pitfalls in discussing spiritual issues with clients.

In this text, when we use the concept of religion, we will be referring to the institutionalized, formal beliefs; dogmas; and practices to which followers of a particular spiritual path adhere. The concept of spirituality will be used in reference to the inner, more personal experiences of clients, especially the search for meaning and purpose. We recognize that one's spirituality may be expressed within or without the structure of religion.

Therapists who are opposed to including spiritual issues in treatment may decide to refer the client to another therapist, a clergyperson, or a spiritual director. Although a referral may be appropriate, it is important that the client's spiritual needs are not seen as pathological. Those who are opposed to or ambivalent about the inclusion may still encounter specific issues that raise spiritual concerns and will need to develop strategies to effectively deal with these situations. Each therapist needs to make decisions that fit his or her own professional values; however, if we choose to exclude spiritual issues in the clinical encounter, we may be denying our clients a safe place to explore those concerns. As stated above, some clients no longer find organized religion viable. If they cannot discuss their spiritual struggles in treatment, they may be left alone to deal with some of the most challenging issues they encounter.

PRACTICE TEST

The following questions will test your knowledge of the content found within this chapter and help you prepare for the licensing exam by applying chapter content to practice. For more questions styled like the licensing exam, visit **MySocialWorkLab.com**

---

1. Zachary is a 45-year-old business man who seeks social work services due to a mild, but persistent, depression. Upon exploration, he reveals that he no longer finds meaning is his relationships or work. His social worker should include spirituality in his treatment

    a. to discover the root of his loss of meaning.

    b. to find if there is a connection between his difficulty and spiritual beliefs.

    c. only if he is open to its use.

    d. because treatment will be ineffective if it is not included.

2. A client asks her social worker what her spiritual beliefs are. The social worker

    a. can share her beliefs because the client asked.

    b. can share her beliefs if the agency is faith based.

    c. can share her beliefs if they are similar to her client's.

    d. should not share her beliefs and instead explore why the client wants to know.

3. A client suffering from anxiety has asked the social worker to include spirituality in his treatment. This is appropriate if

    a. the root of the client's difficulty requires spiritually focused therapy.

    b. spirituality will bring solace to the client.

    c. the social worker is competent in the area.

    d. the client does not have a spiritual community.

4. John has been struggling with some spiritual dogmas related to his religious affiliation. The social worker should

    a. read about the dogmas.

    b. explore his feelings about a referral to a clergyperson.

    c. ask the client to explain his understanding of the dogmas.

    d. tell the client he is not familiar with the dogmas.

1. Discuss the dangers of proselytizing when spirituality is included in treatment. How is this complicated when social workers are employed by faith-based agencies?

2. Ethical dilemmas may arise in treatment when social workers and their clients have very different spiritual beliefs. What should social workers do to ensure ethical practice?

SUCCEED WITH

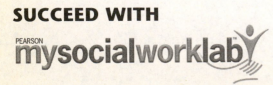

PEARSON
mysocialworklab™

Visit **MySocialWorkLab** for more licensing exam test questions, and to access case studies, videos, and much more.

3

Spirituality and Engagement

Advancing Core Competencies in This Chapter				
☒ Professional Identity	☐ Ethical Practice	☐ Critical Thinking	☐ Diversity in Practice	☐ Human Rights & Justice
☐ Research-Based Practice	☐ Human Behavior	☐ Policy Practice	☒ Practice Contexts	☒ Engage, Assess, Intervene, Evaluate

The foundation of clinical practice is the helping relationship. Our ability to create and maintain a safe environment allows clients to engage in the difficult work of therapy, to explore feelings, to develop insight, and to try out new behaviors. Spiritually focused treatment is no different. Without a relationship that "honors" both the client and the clinician, any discussion of spiritual issues is "empty" (Canda & Furman, 1999, p. 185). In this chapter we will discuss the importance of the therapeutic relationship in clinical work and how this concept can be reframed to reflect a spiritual context for therapy.

THE THERAPEUTIC ENVIRONMENT

Spirituality, especially concepts derived from Buddhist practice, provides a foundation for sound clinical practice. In chapter 2 we discussed the distinction between spirituality and religion. Buddhism contains many principles and values that one is able to incorporate into one's life without adherence to a formal religion. In fact, individuals often integrate Buddhist ideas into other belief systems, including an atheistic stance. Buddhism is "more about practices that align us with being awake, alive, psychologically healthy and intimate with the world than it is about adopting a set of beliefs" (Bien, 2008, p. 7). In creating a sacred space for clients, spiritual concepts help us reframe our view of clients and guide how we listen and attend to them and how we bear witness to their struggles and suffering. These concepts support our efforts to create and maintain a safe holding environment.

A SACRED SPACE

To integrate spirituality into clinical practice, we reframe the safe holding environment discussed in the clinical literature as the sacred space. The therapy session is viewed as "sacred ground"; a place "set apart" (Schoen, 1991, as cited in Faiver, Ingersoll, O'Brien, & McNally, 2001, p. 24). Sacred spaces are those that allow us to leave the secular world and have a "fixed point" and thus a sense of orientation amidst chaos (Eliade, 1957, p. 23). In sacred spaces, away from the everyday world, we are able to contact our inner selves, find a place of stillness, and listen to our deepest feelings and insights (Silf, 1999). In the sacred space, the clinician "not only offers her clinical tools to help the client, but also offers her life energy—her very self as a therapeutic tool" (Faiver et al., 2001, p. 24). We implement the sacred space with our professional view of clients and how we approach them in the clinical endeavor.

THE HOLDING ENVIRONMENT

The clinical literature stresses the importance of the helping relationship and the elements that characterize it. Woods and Hollis (2000) state that the relationship between the clinician and client is a "powerful tool" in treatment and without it treatment is most likely ineffective (p. 229). The helping relationship is characterized by the therapist's unconditional positive regard for the client, genuineness, warmth, empathy, caring, compassion, and acceptance (Bien, 2008; Gambrill, 2006; Rogers, 1989; Woods & Hollis, 2000). In the safe space the client is able to risk revealing herself and the struggles she is encountering. She is able to peel away the layers of her facades and discover who she truly is, the person she is meant to be (Rogers, 1989). Through our acceptance, she comes to accept herself. She is able to relax within a "safe house" (Fox, 2001). Like the time in the center of the labyrinth, clients are able to reflect, speak freely, and come to learn new ways of dealing with their life circumstances. She is able to find a place to test out new ideas and behaviors. Thus, therapy becomes not only a place of respite but also a place of discovery.

CREATING A SACRED SPACE

Providing a sacred space is a challenging task. A professional context that emphasizes outcomes, behavioral changes, and time restraints over transformation exacerbates the challenge (Applegate & Bronovitz, 1995; Bien, 2008). Although most clinical approaches acknowledge the importance of the relationship, most do not emphasize it as a goal in itself, but relegate it to the background, focusing more on assessment and intervention (Duncan, Miller, & Sparks,

2004). A spiritual approach to clinical practice recognizes that our clients need more than "technique or diagnostic driven approaches" (Bien, 2008, p. 5).

Spiritual concepts, which build on the clinical literature, shape our professional worldview and provide a different way for us to approach our work. This weaving of spiritual and clinical concepts informs how we view clients, how we approach them, and how we prepare for our encounters with them.

Unconditional Positive Regard: Loving-Kindness

In both traditional clinical practice and spiritually sensitive practice, the heart of the helping relationship is respect for the client. "Respect means encountering the client with a fresh mind, unhindered by presumption, and open to the mystery and possibility of the person" (Canda & Furman, 1999, p. 187). We acknowledge that he is the "expert" on his own experience (Woods & Hollis, 2000, p. 246). Spiritually, we view the therapeutic relationship as an encounter between two sacred beings. We value and cherish the individual before us just as he is. He is not a diagnostic category, not a presenting problem, not a treatment plan. He is a unique individual, entitled to the utmost respect and recognition of his dignity. We go beyond the concept of unconditional positive regard and client worth to view the client as sacred, a person whom we approach with respect, awe, and a sense of mystery. Kornfield (2008) states that in India, one bows before another saying *namaste*, which means, "I honor the divine within you." Thus, we recognize another's Buddha nature, the basis for a "sacred relationship" (p. 17).

Spiritually sensitive therapy suggests (either explicitly or implicitly) that human beings, along with their thoughts, feelings, and behaviors, have souls. Definitions of what a soul is vary, and some are associated with specific religious traditions. For therapeutic purposes, we need to conceptualize the soul in a broader fashion, avoiding specific religious connotations. Moore (1992) states that the soul "has to do with depth, value, relatedness, heart, and personal substance" (p. 5). He is careful to distinguish it from religious beliefs and associations with immortality or salvation. Soul is "our essence, our life force, our vitality" (Ingerman, 1995, p. 114). When we see clients as sacred beings we honor their souls and recognize that some of their difficulties are related to the loss of this life force.

The Buddhist equivalent of unconditional positive regard is loving-kindness, a quality that welcomes the client and her experience (Welwood, 2000). When we respect the client as a sacred being we respect who she is right now. We open ourselves to her suffering and struggles, rather than see the situation as something that needs to be fixed (Bien, 2008). We do not minimize our clients' difficulties, but rather along with their struggles we hear their resiliency, bravery, and heroism (Duncan et al., 2004). We may not agree with the choices our clients have made. However, the more difficult their lives have become, the more they feel a sense of guilt and shame about decisions made, the more courage they need to come for help. We view with deep compassion the circumstances that led to our clients entering treatment.

Engage, Assess, Intervene, Evaluate

Practice Behavior Example: Assess client strengths and limitations.

Critical Thinking Question: Discuss how clients who experienced interpersonal trauma may benefit from the creation of a sacred space for therapy. How would you create this safe space for clients?

Preparing the Sacred Space

We begin with the physical space that we provide for our clients. A sacred space is comfortable and private. Although Freud advocated for the therapist to act as a blank slate, this is neither desirable nor possible. Our office décor reflects our values, tastes, and personality. It should be professional, yet warm and inviting as well as spiritually neutral (Cunningham, 2004). Generic articles that have spiritual significance to us, such as plants, pictures from nature, or a shell from a walk on the beach, are appropriate. However, religious icons, sayings, or posters may create concern for clients. If there is a religious article or quote that inspires us, we might consider keeping it in a space that we can access, taking care to ensure it is not visible to clients (Cunningham, 2004).

In the sacred space, we minimize impingements. We hold phone calls, turn off electronic devices that signal waiting messages, we are on time for sessions, and, depending on our agency setting, we meet clients at a consistent time and place. We explain what clients can expect from treatment. We are clear and honest about agency policies that impact them, such as missed session policies, and we explain this in an unhurried manner (Applegate & Bonovitz, 1995).

Therapy as an Emotionally Corrective Experience

The most essential element in the creation of a sacred space is the way we present ourselves to our clients. Rather than adherence to a neutral stance advocated in the earlier days of our profession, the therapeutic relationship is now central to the treatment process (Applegate & Bonovitz, 1995; Cooper & Lesser, 2011; Fox, 2001; Woods & Hollis, 2000). "In fact, most change takes place in contexts of human relatedness" (Mahoney, 2003, p. 2). Drawing on the work of Winnicott, Applegate and Bonovitz (1995) state that the goal of the therapist is to create and provide a reparative relationship rather than the interpretation of unconscious conflicts designed for insight. Through the relationship with the therapist, clients are able to rework past hurts and move forward. The therapeutic relationship becomes a new template or prototype for their relationships outside therapy (Applegate & Bonovitz, 1995). Thus, the benefits of the time spent in treatment are realized in the clients' everyday lives.

The development and maintenance of the therapeutic relationship can be difficult. Like the labyrinth walk, this process can have many twists and turns. Clients, especially those who have experienced interpersonal trauma, may be reluctant to trust us. We may unintentionally misunderstand them or they us. However, this relationship is critically important and we need to consistently pay attention to it.

ELEMENTS OF THE SACRED SPACE

The most important characteristics needed to develop a sacred space for client treatment are our empathy, compassion, attentiveness, genuine caring, professional curiosity, and acceptance of the client and her story just as it is. We implement the sacred space by actively and attentively listening to clients. We present ourselves in a calm, unhurried manner and provide a receptive presence. We are nonjudgmental and warm yet professional. We make a consistent effort to understand, to learn who the client is, and we genuinely want to help. We are willing to open ourselves to the client's pain. More important than having a quick answer or clever interpretation is the need to just be there (Applegate & Bonovitz, 1995; Bien, 2008; Welwood, 2000). Clients experience a sense of safety when they perceive us as consistent and reliable. We will not judge or retaliate when clients feel the need to "test out" this new relationship. When we tolerate their strong affects, clients can begin to tolerate them as well and over time integrate them. This reduces the need to act on them (Applegate & Bronovitz, 1995).

Compassion

Compassion is key to understanding why therapists are able to present themselves as a container for strong negative client affect. "Compassion, according to Thich Nhat Hanh, involves our generous and resonating open heart as well as our willingness to *take action* to relieve pain and suffering" (Bien, 2008, p. 84, italics in the original). One quandary in spiritually focused treatment is the need to reconcile the idea of therapists as a container for strong client affect, such as anger, rage, and even hatred, with the belief that the therapist deserves respect. When we are encouraged to not retaliate or be defensive, how are we being treated as sacred beings? As therapists we accept our client's presentation, even when it might be personally painful to us. We compassionately reach beyond the words and behavior of the client to the pain that compels him to act as he does. Shea (1998) refers to "core pains" that motivate clients to resist our helping efforts or to act out inappropriately (pp. 215–219). Understanding what is behind problematic behaviors allows us to maintain our composure, our patience, and our empathy in the face of our clients' onslaught. "Skilled clinicians possess the knack of cutting through the complexities until the bare wounds, the core pains, are understood" (Shea, 1998, p. 215). Core pains include fears of unworthiness, being abandoned, or of the unknown (Shea, 1998, p. 216). When we are able to view the client's pain with compassion, we are able to place client need above our own. We understand why the client behaves as she does, and our goal is to help her understand what motivates her behavior. When she understands the reasons for acting as she does, she has a choice to approach others and us in a more productive manner. We are entitled to respect, but sometimes our clients are so badly hurt by their past experiences that we need to offer our acceptance and compassion until they are able to do better. Spiritual practices help us maintain our sense of composure as we compassionately tune into the pain behind our clients' behavior. Please note at no time should therapists ever allow any form of physical violence to be directed at them.

Engage, Assess, Intervene, Evaluate

Practice Behavior Example: Use empathy and other interpersonal skills.

Critical Thinking Question: Some clients have difficulty trusting. Discuss some of the challenges you might face when implementing a sacred space for your work with them? How would you address this?

Therapeutic Stance

The therapeutic stance refers to how we present ourselves to our clients. Spiritual concepts give us a different way to view our approach to clients and some techniques to implement the sacred space. They guide us in being attentive listeners and help us stay in the moment (mindfulness) and provide compassion and loving-kindness. They help us suspend judgment and allow the client's story to unfold in whatever manner the client is comfortable with.

Attentiveness

When we honor the sacredness of our clients, we empathically attune to their feelings and needs. This allows the client to feel a sense of being held in the clinician's full attention (Applegate & Bonovitz, 1995). Our encounter has the potential to be transformative when our comments "resonate with what the client already implicitly feels . . ." (Welwood, 2000, p. 95). We demonstrate our attentiveness through our well-timed and gently focused questions, comments, and unconditional presence (Applegate & Bonovitz, 1995; Welwood, 2000; Woods & Hollis, 2000). The client is our focus. We open our hearts and allow ourselves to be witnesses to their suffering.

It is easy to get caught up in what we should say or do with or for clients, but the most healing, yet most difficult, task is our attentive presence. It is our willingness to listen, our acceptance of them, our openness to being affected by their story, and our loving kindness that allow them to unfold and heal (Bien, 2008; Welwood, 2000). We allow our clients to have their own experience, accepting it as it is (Bien, 2008; Johanson & Kurtz, 1991). When we make every effort to understand and genuinely desire to help, we communicate to clients that they indeed are sacred beings. We create an empty space for them so they may discover who they are. And we create an empty space within ourselves to allow the client's experience to unfold without our assumptions and judgments. We are reflective and compassionate and our comments and actions emanate from a place of wisdom within, a place molded by theory and practice experience, but not limited to that alone. We create space so we may learn who our clients are and what they need, which is ever changing.

The Empty Space

The Buddhist concept of empty space encourages us to start with no preconceived notions (Johanson & Kurtz, 1991; Welwood, 2000). This allows the unfolding of the client's story in whatever manner she chooses. If we focus only on assessment and diagnosis, we shut down our clients' experiences (Welwood, 2000). We may have referral records, diagnostic materials, clients' school reports and medical records, or notes from previous workers. So, how do we balance being prepared for clients, our need to understand, and the concept of empty space? In clinical practice, whether it is spiritually focused or not, it is necessary to suspend our assessment until we have the necessary facts. Furthermore, our assessments are always in flux. As we get to know the client better and new information arises, our assessments need to change. It is difficult to resist the urge to fill the empty space with our words, interpretations, questions, and empathetic reflection or with actions. We struggle to be "a witness" who is "willing to observe, be receptive to, and learn from whatever arises" (Johanson & Kurtz, 1991, p. 13).

My client Mark returned to treatment when his elderly mother needed to be placed in a nursing home. Because I had not seen him for several years, I felt it was important to "engage" him. As he told me his story, I asked some questions and made reflective remarks. At the end of the session, he confronted me. When we had met in the past, I had allowed more silence (space). He had used this empty space to reflect on what he had shared with me and at times to add additional thoughts. This time around, he felt that I was "jumping in too quickly" and found this disconcerting. I did not need to engage him as a new client. He was a returning client and ready to pick up where we had left off in our relationship. My perceived notion that he needed to be engaged again led me to fill the empty space, when he needed that space for his own thoughts.

It is difficult for us to allow our client's experience to just be what it is. We may judge, even though we try not to, and we may cut off painful feelings. We may not be in touch with some of our own issues, which makes it more difficult for us to "hear" those experiences and feelings in others (Welwood, 2000). When we make a commitment to meet whatever unfolds, not knowing what will arise, we provide a receptive presence and create a sacred space. Here clients can begin to face their own painful feelings and struggles without harsh judgment. When we bring an authentic presence to our work, we invite the client to tell us her story, and we allow her to have her experience just as it is. This is "perhaps the greatest gift anyone can offer" (Welwood, 2000, p. 144).

Listening

Listening, which Stephen Covey calls the "magical habit" (Shafir, 2003, p. 65), is at the heart of being fully present to our clients. When we are attentive listeners, we are more interested in building a relationship than in achieving a goal (Covey, 2004). We are interested in learning the speaker's perspective (Shafir, 2003). Clinical practice literature stresses the importance of attentive listening (Fox, 2001; Gambrill, 2006; Woods & Hollis, 2000). Good listeners are able to focus on others. They are observant, able to hear the words the other uses, and notice his nonverbal behavior (Gambrill, 2006). Good listeners are able to observe the process, rather than focus on the content alone (Shafir, 2003). How the client tells her story is as important as what she tells us. Is she comfortable revealing the details, or is she reluctant and hesitant? We focus not only on what the client says but also on what she does not say. We hear beyond the words the client uses, to the meaning of her words. The good listener is able to "suspend assumptions" and acknowledges that what the other person is revealing is important (Gambrill, 2006, p. 417).

Listening and Beginner's Mind

Kadushin (1990, as cited in Gambrill, 2006, p. 417) states that we need to make an "assumption of ignorance" in order to truly hear what our clients are telling us. The Buddhists use the concept of "beginner's mind" to emphasize the importance of being in the moment and experiencing situations without preconceived notions (Siegel, 2007; Suzuki, 2006). This is difficult for us to do. It is easy and natural for us to worry about what we should say or do. We forget the healing potential of being with the client and listening to her, uninterrupted, uncensored. "The mind of the beginner is empty, free of the habits of the expert, ready to accept, to doubt, and open to all the possibilities" (Baker's introduction to Suzuki, 2006, p. xiv). "In the beginner's mind there are many possibilities; in the expert's mind there are few" (Suzuki, 2006, p. 2). When we get caught up

Engage, Assess, Intervene, Evaluate

Practice Behavior Example: *Collect, organize, and interpret client data.*

Critical Thinking Question: A challenge in clinical practice is remaining open to the client's disclosure of information. Discuss how the concept of "beginner's mind" can help the therapist avoid making premature assessments of the information clients disclose.

in "categorizing" (Langer, 1989, p. 11) what our clients tell us, we become distracted and are no longer listening. We become trapped by our categories, and we lose a sense of our client's uniqueness (Langer, 1989; Mahoney, 2003).

It is difficult for us to observe and not evaluate (Rosenberg, 1999). We may become focused on diagnosis; concerns about substance abuse, trauma, suicidal ideation; or a host of other important assessment issues, which make it especially difficult to stay present to the client. As we gain more experience and increasingly trust the process, we balance the need to stay in the moment with the client, while still making a careful assessment and planning appropriate interventions. In fact, when we can stay present, we increase the likelihood that we will make better assessments, as we are still open to the information the client is sharing with us, rather than making our decisions prematurely.

Mindfulness

To be attentive listeners, we need to develop skill in staying in the present moment. When we are distracted by personal feelings or pressing clinical questions, we are paying attention to ourselves, not our clients (Shafir, 2003). Mindfulness allows the therapist to concentrate without distraction on the client and his story. The therapist notes the thoughts and feelings that arise. And, accepting them, she neither pushes them away nor judges them (Bien, 2008). When we are mindful, we are in the present moment. We are alert and encounter reality as it is, without distraction (Carroll, 2004; Johanson & Kurtz, 1991; Welwood, 2000). Mindfulness is the difference between "*getting somewhere fast* to *being somewhere completely*" (Carroll, 2004, p. 8, italics in the original). It allows us to truly be with our clients (Bien, 2008).

When we listen in a mindful manner, we are absorbed by our client's narrative, his feelings, and how he experienced events. We are connected to the client and allow him to express what is in his heart, without evaluation (Shafir, 2003). We open our hearts and allow ourselves to be affected by the client's struggles (Welwood, 2000). When we approach our work with both our heads and our hearts, we respond genuinely to our clients, rather than automatically (Shafir, 2003; Welwood, 2000).

The Buddhists use the expression *monkey mind* to describe our experiences of jumping from thought to thought. This is a natural reaction, but one that is not helpful. In therapeutic work, monkey mind results in distraction, and we therefore emotionally abandon clients when they need us most. We may appear to be listening and interested, but the truth is we are listening to ourselves (Shafir, 2003). Mindfulness practice reminds us to not be harsh judges of ourselves when we do become distracted. We need to "note the thoughts," take a deep breath, and focus back on our client. It is easy to berate ourselves, but that only distracts us further (Bien, 2008; Shafir, 2003). When clients are in pain, the greatest gift—sometimes the only gift—we can give them is our presence. And when we are mindful, we provide our full presence.

PRACTICE THEORY

We need to make careful assessments, plan, and implement appropriate interventions. I strongly advocate theory-based practice and critical thinking. Theory provides a map that guides our practice. However, if we use theory rigidly, inappropriately, automatically, we risk shutting off our clients' experiences. We may hide behind our theories rather than accept the inevitability of uncertainty and our role as witness for the client (Carroll, 2004). When clinicians are mindful, they become more "alive, open, and unusually skillful" (Carroll, 2004, p. 8). This allows the therapist to tap into the wellspring of his or her innermost wisdom (Carroll, 2004). In treatment, mindfulness helps us to be in the moment, fully attentive to our clients and their here-and-now experience, rather than judging, assessing, critiquing, and planning what we might say or do. When we are mindful, we allow ourselves to not know, to "enter the confusion and mystery of whatever is happening with a curious, experimental attitude . . ." (Johanson & Kurtz, 1991, p. 13). We welcome, appreciate, and cherish whatever is. "We slow down, and let go of automatic reactions that normally tell us what something is and what it means" (Johanson & Kurtz, 1991, p. 13).

When we combine a strong foundation in theory with the practice of mindfulness, we learn to use theory creatively rather than ignore what is happening before us. This helps us to engage "our work precisely, genuinely, and directly as it constantly unfolds, moment by moment, without bias or pretense" (Carroll, 2004, p. 37). Whatever is, is. This goes against our tendency "to do something to move people beyond the place where they are stuck" (Johanson & Kurtz, 1991, p. 41).

PREPARING OURSELVES

Deep reflection begins with creating an empty space within the self, a receptive frame of mind (Johanson & Kurtz, 1991; Welwood, 2000). When we are authentic and able to remain calm and make a true connection to the client, "heartfelt interventions arise" (Bien, 2008, pp. 12–14). When we already know, there is no room for openness in our encounters with clients. There is a story about a Zen master (as cited Shafir, 2003) who continues to pour tea into the intellectual's cup even after it is filled. When the man tells him to stop because the cup is filled and no more can go in, the master comments that the mind is like the teacup: When it is already full, nothing more can go in. Likewise, if we are going to learn about our clients, we need to empty our minds so we can shift our attention to them and with warmth and appreciation invite them to tell us their story. The paradox is that to provide the empty space we must be well grounded in our practice theories. Only then can we use them flexibly and creatively. When we are unsure, we hold onto theory rigidly.

CONCLUSION

In this chapter we discussed the importance of providing a sacred space for spiritually sensitive practice. Providing this context allows clients to engage in the difficult work of therapy. Within the sacred space clients are able to discover who they are, allow genuine feelings to emerge, and share their experiences in a deeper, more intimate manner. This emotional space truly is sacred.

We implement the sacred space when we honor our clients as sacred beings and approach them with the utmost respect, allowing them to have their own experience. We present ourselves as attentive, receptive listeners, suspending our assessment so the client may truly unfold before us. We appreciate the client for who he is and compassionately attempt to understand the circumstances that brought him to treatment. We struggle to balance our theories with our need to remain open and flexible with what we encounter in the therapeutic encounter.

This chapter provides guidelines for integration of spiritual concepts into clinical work that can be used implicitly as well as explicitly. Viewing clients as sacred beings may help sustain our compassion as we struggle with sometimes difficult client situations, behaviors, and resistances. Unconditional presence and mindfulness are grounded in spiritual concepts, yet they parallel important principles from clinical practice, including listening, empathic attunement, and unconditional positive regard for our clients.

PRACTICE TEST The following questions will test your knowledge of the content found within this chapter and help you prepare for the licensing exam by applying chapter content to practice. For more questions styled like the licensing exam, visit **MySocialWorkLab.com**

1. When social workers use the Buddhist concept of loving-kindness it is most similar to
   a. gentle confrontation.
   b. unconditional positive regard.
   c. respect.
   d. authenticity.

2. Gary is working with a rebellious adolescent who consistently tries to get him angry. Which of the following techniques should Gary use to remind himself that his client is a sacred being?
   a. Loving-kindness.
   b. Unknowing to remind him that his client is the expert.
   c. Mastery to try to understand his client.
   d. Behavior modification to manage his behavior.

3. Which of the following actions should social workers do to listen attentively to clients?
   a. Gaze steadily at the client.
   b. Observe both the process and the content of client's communication.
   c. Focus on their own breathing.
   d. Refrain from interrupting the client.

4. Margot describes herself as spiritual. She attends 12-Step programs and often refers to her Higher Power. Her social worker considers himself to be spiritual but refers to God. In sessions the social worker can
   a. use either term because they both refer to an Ultimate Being.
   b. use the term *God* to be more authentic.
   c. use the client's term, *Higher Power*.
   d. use neither and try to agree to an alternative term.

1. Marcie works on a busy inpatient floor of a community hospital. Most of her clients are ambulatory. Marcie often has limited time to meet with clients and often little privacy. What are some things Marcie can do to create a sacred space for her clients in this environment?

2. The concept of mindfulness is used to describe being fully present in the moment. Discuss how social workers can balance being spontaneous in the moment with the importance of implementing theory-driven practice interventions.

SUCCEED WITH

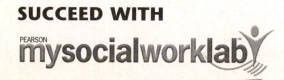

Visit **MySocialWorkLab** for more licensing exam test questions, and to access case studies, videos, and much more.

Carl is a 33-year-old white male who was physically and sexually abused by his stepfather when he was a child. Carl had repressed some of his memories, but after watching a television program on sexual abuse, he slowly began recalling some incidents of his abuse. These memories have left him frightened and confused and are interfering with his work and social life. He is especially concerned that he will continue to remember "more and more bad things." At the suggestion of a friend, who went for therapy several years ago to deal with her own abuse, Carl called a therapist. In the first few sessions, he haltingly began to share his story. He expressed reluctance to talk about the past and how he would like to "just forget about it all, like I did once before." When the therapist gently questioned him about his wanting to forget, Carl revealed that he had been aware for years that he was abused. During adolescence he experimented with drugs and drank heavily for several years. "The drugs did what I wanted them to, I forgot." Five years ago Carl began his recovery from substance abuse. "I would rather not remember, because I don't want to jeopardize my sobriety." He revealed that life since he began his sobriety has been "good." He had a job he liked and although he was not in a serious relationship, he dated several "interesting and nice young women." He reflected that even though a few of his friends have begun "to pop the question" he hesitated to make a permanent commitment to anyone "at this point in his life." He "doubted" whether he'd be able to love someone "forever" or that they would love him and "not hurt him."

Although Carl was gradually opening up to the therapist, it was an inconsistent process. He frequently retreated from the issues he found too painful to confront. In one session, he began telling the therapist about a summer picnic his family had attended when he was 10. Midway through the description of the event he stopped. After a few minutes, the therapist asked Carl if he could tell him the reason he hesitated. Carl shook his head and stated, "I can't say." The therapist waited quietly for a few minutes and then told Carl. "We know now that there is something about the picnic that is upsetting to you and when you feel comfortable we can return to it. It is most likely important, but we need for you to be comfortable enough to tell me what it is." Carl immediately began to relax. "No one ever did that," he replied. When the therapist asked him about his comment, he began to talk about how all his life he had felt pressured to answer when anyone asked him a question. He remembered his mother pressing him to tell her what was wrong when his stepfather was abusing him. "She knew something was wrong because I changed so much, she just didn't know what."

As the therapist talked to Carl about with whom and where he felt any sense of safety, Carl replied that he had a tree house in his backyard and when the pressure became too much, he would retreat there. It was "the one place I felt totally safe in the world." He smiled slightly and added, "My stepfather was afraid of heights." This led to a discussion of what the therapist could do to help Carl feel safe both in sessions with the therapist and in between sessions, without using drugs or alcohol.

1. Carl is hesitant to talk about the abuse he experienced. What obstacles or challenges can you anticipate in developing a therapeutic relationship and a sacred space for him? How will you address these challenges?
2. Carl experienced a sense of safety in his tree house. How can you use this as a metaphor to help him find safety as he explores his abuse experience?

4

Spiritual Assessment

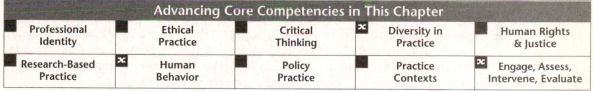

Advancing Core Competencies in This Chapter				
■ Professional Identity	■ Ethical Practice	■ Critical Thinking	✖ Diversity in Practice	■ Human Rights & Justice
■ Research-Based Practice	✖ Human Behavior	■ Policy Practice	■ Practice Contexts	✖ Engage, Assess, Intervene, Evaluate

The labyrinth walk, like the therapeutic process, is "a journey to the center of one's very being" (Houston, as cited in Foreword, Curry, 2000, p. xi). Entering therapy may feel like a "leap of faith" for clients, and encountering the unknown is perhaps the most frightening aspect (Curry, 2000, p. 57). In this chapter we will draw an analogy between the labyrinth's winding path to the center and the assessment process leading to intervention.

ENTERING THE LABYRINTH

According to Sands (2001), when you enter the labyrinth at Chartres Cathedral in France, the center appears to be just ahead. But as one begins to walk the twists and turns of the path he wonders if the center will ever be reached. In similar fashion, clients entering therapy often expect quick solutions or immediate relief from their suffering. Like the walk to the center, there is a process, one that takes more time than one might expect or wish for.

In the Foreword to Curry's (2000) book *The Way of the Labyrinth*, Jean Houston states, "During the walk inward, with its many surprising and disconcerting turns, one is invited to release: release old patterns, worn-out ideas and concepts, debilitating emotional memories, unhappy behaviors" (p. xi). Although the primary goal of the assessment process is to understand our client and her reasons for seeking treatment, we also invite her to release feelings as she relates her story, offering some beginning relief. We remember that treatment is not comprised of discrete stages, but a circular path. As we engage, we assess; as we assess, we intervene; as we intervene, we engage and assess. One of the most important lessons of the labyrinth for therapists is to honor the journey, rather than just the goal (West, 2000). And the journey of the assessment process includes engaging clients and beginning the intervention process.

When we explore the spiritual domain, we communicate to clients that we are interested in all aspects of their experience (Bien, 2008; Richards & Bergin, 2002; Sperry, 2001). Spiritual issues are often difficult to articulate and clients often welcome the opportunity to explore them with a caring professional (Bien, 2008). But exploration in this area is not appropriate for all clients, making assessment critical (Richards & Bergin, 2002).

SPIRITUAL ASSESSMENT

Spiritual assessment takes place over the course of treatment and is dependent on the development and maintenance of a therapeutic relationship (Pargament, 2007). Like the labyrinth walk, it is often a circuitous path, but a natural one. We gather information by engaging in conversation, guided by clinical wisdom. Richards and Bergin (2002) suggest routine questioning about the spiritual domain early in the assessment phase. However, Pargament (2007) argues that spirituality is often a personal, private matter that some clients are reluctant to share in therapy, especially early in the treatment process. He states that mechanical questions are inappropriate and ineffective. Some questions for your reflection: Should we ask routine questions about spirituality or wait until we "hear" issues emerging? What are the advantages and disadvantages to each approach?

Whether we ask routine questions about our clients' spiritual lives or wait until issues emerge in the course of treatment, we weave our questions with reflective comments and supporting statements. We explore the reasons clients seek treatment and assess their overall functioning. We respond to client comments and help him elaborate on the information shared. We notice what has not been said (Pargament, 2007). Our questions and comments come from genuine caring and professional curiosity. We do not have an agenda, and it is not our need to include spirituality in treatment. We are open to the possibility that spirituality is not a salient issue for our client, and even if it is, we respect his right to not explore it with us in treatment.

Although the goal of the assessment process is "finding unity in the face of apparent fragmentation" (Fox, 2001, p. 122), we initially suspend our evaluation of the information gathered. Like the walk into the labyrinth, this is a time for observation and reflection (Hogan, 2003), and it reminds us of the need to let go of expectations and remain open to what occurs (Hogan, 2003; West, 2000). We sit with a sense of mystery, allowing for uncertainty and unknowing. The process may feel like a meandering path, but it is a purposeful path, one that leads ultimately to the "center" of treatment. Despite the need for careful and complete assessments, the pressures of managed care and the emphasis on short-term treatment models often compromise this need and the effectiveness of our work. When we do not get to know our client and what is important to her, we may treat her like a case rather than a sacred being.

Assessing spirituality is a twofold process. We need to understand the overall functioning of our client and what role, if any, spirituality plays in his or her life. Secondly, we need a detailed picture of how spirituality is manifested in his or her life. When I was recovering from foot surgery, I needed to focus on each step. When I graduated from a walker to a cane, I ventured outside as part of my rehabilitation. It was autumn and as I gingerly took each step, watching for raised paving stones, holes, or cracks, I noticed the beautiful leaves scattered on the ground. However, not yet confident in my walking ability, I was not able to look beyond my immediate next step to see the trees overhead, ablaze with color, the falling leaves, as well as those lying on the ground before me. Thus, my "assessment" of my surroundings was incomplete. I was focused on the details, but not the big picture. Assessment of spirituality without an understanding of how it intersects with other aspects of the client's life is incomplete (Pargament, 2007; Richards & Bergin, 2002).

Although in this text we recognize the importance of assessing spirituality within the context of a complete biopsychosocial framework, we will limit our discussion to the spiritual domain. In this chapter, we highlight reasons to assess spirituality and outline content areas to explore. We recognize that cultural issues, including race, ethnicity, and religion, shape spirituality. I propose an approach to cultural diversity that emphasizes mystery, uncertainty, and beginner's mind. We end the chapter with a brief discussion of spiritual development models to understand changes over the course of the life span.

REASONS TO ASSESS SPIRITUALITY

A major goal of spiritual assessment is to determine if the client's spirituality is healthy (adaptive) or unhealthy (maladaptive). Is it a risk or a protective factor (Miller, 1999)? Is spirituality related to the presenting problems? Does it exacerbate them or pose a potential resource in resolving them (Pargament, 2007; Richards & Bergin, 2002)? Do the difficulties the client encounters negatively affect her spirituality (Pargament, 2007)? For example, does it create a crisis in meaning or initiate a dark night of the soul? We recognize that spirituality can differentially affect various aspects of one's life. Therefore, it may have positive effects in some areas and negative or no effects in others (Pargament, 2007).

AREAS OF ASSESSMENT

Spiritual History and Significance

We generally begin by assessing whether or not spirituality is a salient issue for our clients. We are interested in whether the client considers herself to be a spiritual or a religious person. If she considers herself to be a spiritual or religious person, we explore what that means to her and how it manifests itself in her life. Simply asking clients to identify their religion tells us little (Pargament, 2007; Sperry, 2001). "Most useful information is gleaned by examining how the client is spiritual, rather than the religious label attached to that spiritual system" (Sperry, 2001, p. 112). We need to assess the extent to which clients desire and are willing to discuss and explore spiritual issues in treatment (Matthews, 1998, as cited Sperry, 2001, p. 111).

Exploration of the details of the client's spirituality depends on the answers he or she gives to our initial queries. For example, if the client says spirituality is not important to her, we should suspend exploration in that direction unless the issue arises later in treatment. Pargament (2007) advises that at times spiritual issues arise implicitly. For example, a client may describe an encounter with nature that seems to reflect sacred content, including a sense of wonder and awe. Exploration may reveal a connection to something beyond the individual that implies a sense of the spiritual.

Spiritual or Religious Affiliation

One possible manifestation of spirituality may be current or past affiliation with a spiritual community (Pargament, 2007; Richards & Bergin, 2002). For many, their spiritual community is found within an organized religion. We need to know what this affiliation means to the client and whether it provides emotional support and facilitates spiritual and personal growth or if it is a source of conflict. If a client is currently involved with a religious affiliation, we would want to know how involved he is. Does the client's religious beliefs, practices, or affiliation contribute to or ameliorate his current problems (Richards & Bergin, 2002)? Susan, a practicing Catholic, experienced excessive guilt and shame after being divorced by her husband, whereas Martin found his spiritual beliefs about the afterlife a source of comfort in dealing with his partner's death from AIDS. In the first example, the client's beliefs exacerbated her pain, whereas in the second example the client's beliefs helped him cope with his grief.

Past Spiritual Affiliation

In addition to current religious or spiritual affiliation, exploration of past affiliations is also needed for accurate assessments, especially for clients who once belonged to a spiritual community but no longer do so (Richards & Bergin, 2002). Although clients may have left a particular spiritual community, it may still be a source of conflict and difficulty (Richards & Bergin, 2002). For example, Matthew was rebelling against his conservative Christian upbringing by breaking as many "rules" as he could. He claimed he was no longer a member of the community and did not share the community's beliefs. However, each time he broke a rule he experienced excessive guilt and anxiety. At this particular point in his life, leaving his spiritual community did not mean he was no longer influenced by it.

Although many clients with a spiritual affiliation belong to traditional organized religious communities, a growing number of people seek community through alternative spiritual paths. For example, clients may find community within a yoga or meditation group or an alternative spiritual group, such as Wicca, or other earth-based, pre-Christian spiritual movements (Canda & Furman, 2010; Yardley, 2008). These spiritual communities have the same potential to provide support or create conflict for members, and assessment is needed to understand the potential benefits or risks for a specific client.

Spiritual Beliefs and Life Choices

Richards and Bergin (2002) state that the "hallmark of healthy personality and spiritual development and functioning" is congruence between professed values and life style (p. 181). They distinguish *belief orthodoxy*, acceptance of the doctrines associated with a particular religion, from *behavioral orthodoxy* to describe adherence to moral teach-ings and religious practices. Lack of congruence can create guilt and anxiety (Pargament, 2007; Richards & Bergin, 2002). Here are some questions for reflection: Do you agree that congruence between values and lifestyle is the hallmark of a healthy personality? If so, are there exceptions? For example, if a client has a very "rigid" belief system and values and her lifestyle reflects this rigidity, there is congruence, but is it healthy? Perhaps another client may be moving away from beliefs and practices that no longer fit his life choices. Although there may be a temporary incongruence, if he is growing personally and spiritu-ally, is this incongruence unhealthy?

Exploration of the congruence between values and life choices is not limited to clients who follow traditional spiritual paths. Those who profess allegiance to New Age philoso-phies may or may not have congruence in these areas and experience similar conflicts, making assessment important.

Spiritual Coping Style

Pargament (2007) describes three approaches to spiritual coping: self-directing, deferred, and collaborative. The self-directing person attempts to solve her difficulties without any reliance on or involvement with the Divine, or, for those who follow New Age philoso-phies, a reliance on the Universe. This individual believes it is his or her responsibility to find solutions and that God/Universe grants individuals the freedom and resources to re-solve issues. Individuals who use a deferring coping style take no responsibility for solving their problems and rely on the Divine to solve them. Those who use collaborative coping style believe it is a shared responsibility between the individual and God. Mrs. Martin, an African American senior citizen, was very involved with her spiritual community. When her Social Security benefits were terminated for unknown reasons, Mrs. Martin asked the members of her church to pray for a successful outcome. Meanwhile, she asked a social worker from her local senior center to accompany her to a fair hearing. When the matter was successfully resolved, she attributed the outcome to her community's prayers that gave her the strength to "fight the system." This example demonstrates the collaborative style of spiritual coping.

Images of the Divine

Many believe in a Transcendent Being (God, Higher Power, the Divine), and an assess-ment of the client's image of this Being is important to understanding the client's spiritual health. Does the person believe in a personal, involved, benevolent, and forgiving God (Pargament, 2007; Wulff, 1997, as cited in Richards & Bergin, 2002, p. 179) or is the image one of an angry, punitive, impersonal deity (Benson & Spilka, 1973, as cited in Richards & Bergin, 2002, p. 179; Pargament, 2007). Some individuals profess they do not believe in a personal God, but in a concept such as the Universe or the Ultimate Force. In these cases, assessment of the benevolence or malevolence of this force, as seen by the client, is needed.

Kirkpatrick (1999) states that there is a relationship between religious beliefs and practices and an individual's attachment style (pp. 803–804). He contends that one's early relationships with significant attachment figures not only shape the individual's relation-ship with other people but also influence one's image of and relationship with the Divine. For example, if the individual had a secure relationship with his parents, he is likely to have a secure relationship with God; if he had an anxious or avoidant attachment style, he is likely to have an anxious or avoidant relationship with the Divine (Kirkpatrick, 1999). Citing the work of Kirkpatrick and Shaver (1992), Pargament (2007) states that there is some evidence that individuals with an avoidant or anxious/ambivalent relationship with the Divine are more likely to be lonelier, more anxious, and depressed and report less life satisfaction than those individuals with a secure relationship with God. Those who perceive their relationship with God to be uncertain experience more psychological distress (Kirkpatrick & Shaver, 1992, as cited in Pargament, 2007, p. 156). Images of the Divine as someone who is ever present, all knowing, and all powerful provide a sense of security for some and allow them to feel safe in this world (Kirkpatrick, 1999). Client perceptions of their relationship with God may provide a window into their interpersonal relationships with others (Richards & Bergin, 2002).

Worldview and Spiritual Beliefs

To work effectively with clients we need to understand experiences from their perspective. An individual's worldview is made up of the beliefs, assumptions, and thoughts she has about the world, herself, and other people. It provides a lens through which she views and interprets experiences. It evolves over the life course, is shaped by socialization and one's cultural group, and once established tends to be resistant to alteration (Castillo, 1997; Janoff-Bulman, 1992; Ibrahim, Roysircar-Sodowshy, & Ohnishi, 2001; Richards & Bergin, 2002). Spiritual beliefs and assumptions are an important part of the client's worldview but are often neglected in clinical assessment. Two important questions we need to ask ourselves during assessment are: Do the client's spiritual beliefs influence the problem? Does he use spiritual beliefs to understand the cause of his problem?

Important spiritual beliefs for exploration include the client's understanding of the origins of human existence, existence of a Transcendent Being, purpose of life, causes and existence of suffering and beliefs about the afterlife (Richards & Bergin, 2002). The ability to find meaning is essential for psychological health (Frankl, 1984; Yalom, 1980). In fact, "it is impossible to live" without meaning (Yalom, 1980, p. 420). When one searches for meaning, she seeks to understand if there is some cosmic plan, some design, a superior being who brings a sense of coherence to her life (Yalom, 1980). Those who find meaning in their suffering are more likely to survive and flourish (Frankl, 1984). Therefore, an understanding of the interplay between spiritual beliefs and meaning making as the client views it is essential to assessment.

Engage, Assess, Intervene, Evaluate

Practice Behavior Example: Collect, organize, and interpret client data.

Critical Thinking Question: Discuss the reasons to assess a client's spirituality. Address the importance of exploring clients' previous affiliation with a faith community even if they no longer consider themselves to be members of that community.

Healthy Spirituality Versus Unhealthy Spirituality

Spiritual health, like any other aspect of health, is on a continuum. Spirituality, as we noted earlier, has the potential to exacerbate or ameliorate client difficulties. Assessment is therefore needed on a case-by-case basis to understand if spirituality will create obstacles to resolving problems and impede the client's growth and development or be a coping resource (Richards & Bergin, 2002; Sperry, 2001). Excessive guilt may create anxiety or interfere with problem resolution (Richards & Bergin, 2002). Or, current difficulties can create spiritual difficulties, such as a crisis of meaning (Cunningham, 2000). Spiritual doubts may underlie client problems (Richards & Bergin, 2002). Alternatively, the client's spiritual beliefs and/or the spiritual community may be a source of support and thus a resource in healing (Richards & Bergin, 2002; Sperry, 2001).

Clinebell (1965, as cited in Richards & Bergin, 2002) outlines several dimensions for evaluating spiritual health. Beliefs and practices reflect a healthy spirituality when they help connect one to others; they strengthen the person's sense of trust in the universe, and they foster inner freedom and personal responsibility. Healthy forms of spirituality provide guidelines for ethical and moral behavior, without emphasizing the trivial, provide a process for moving from guilt to forgiveness, and allow for expression of emotions and needs, including sexuality and aggression. When one has a healthy form of spirituality she is encouraged to accept reality, is able to express spiritual doubts, and recognizes the complexity of life. Love and growth are emphasized, rather than fear (Richards & Bergin, 2002).

Some indicators of unhealthy forms of spirituality are scrupulosity, which often has an obsessive-compulsive quality and an overemphasis on sin and failure to comply with rules and regulations (Lovinger, 2005, p. 347), which creates excessive anxiety. Welwood (2000) uses the term *spiritual bypassing* to describe the use of spiritual practice to avoid emotions and human needs, or other unresolved personal issues. The person disguises old dysfunctional patterns with his new "spiritual" identity (pp. 11–12). For example, instead of dealing openly with difficult emotions such as anger, a person may suppress her anger because she believes positive emotions fit with her spiritual beliefs. Instead of dealing with her emotions in a healthy manner, she may express them in subtle, but destructive ways.

Criteria to distinguish mystical experiences from psychosis are important for assessment. When mystical experiences are accompanied by hallucinations, guidelines to rule out the possibility of psychosis, including an understanding of the fit between the content of the hallucinations and the client's religion and culture are needed. Another criterion is the extent to which the hallucinations are upsetting (Hartz, 2005). The cultural context is critical to determining the relationship between spirituality and psychological health (Loewenthal, 2007). For example, a spiritual system such as Espiritismo includes belief in the existence of benevolent and malevolent spirits who influence behavior. This example highlights the need to understand the cultural determinants of normative mental health (Castillo, 1997; Gotterer, 2001). Hallucinations associated with mystical experiences are usually positive, whereas those associated with psychosis are critical or threatening (Wulff, 2000, as cited in Hartz, 2005).

Therapists' Assumptions

When determining the extent to which a client's spirituality is healthy or not, we need to be vigilant about our own assumptions, beliefs, and feelings. The terms *healthy* and *unhealthy* imply judgment. It would perhaps be better to use the term *adaptive* for

Engage, Assess, Intervene, Evaluate

Practice Behavior Example: *Assess client strengths and limitations.*

Critical Thinking Question: Discuss the criteria for determining if a client's spirituality is adaptive or not. How does the therapist's own belief or assumptions create challenges in making this assessment?

beliefs and practices that allow clients to function at an optimal level and *maladaptive* for those that impede functioning. Because most of the literature refers to spirituality that is healthy or unhealthy I have used those terms as well, but I recognize that they can be pejorative. However, there are some manifestations of spirituality that are unhealthy, for example, scrupulosity. Our main concern is the human tendency to view beliefs and practice that are very different from those one is familiar with as unhealthy. Are there objective criteria to determine spiritual health? There is some evidence that individuals who are inwardly motivated (intrinsic orientation) demonstrate healthier forms of spirituality than those who engage in spiritual practices for external reasons, such as approval or safety (Elkins, 1998; Richards & Bergin, 2002; Swinton, 2001). Striving for a connection to the sacred indicates a healthier form of spirituality than being motivated by excessive guilt (Richards & Bergin, 2002).

THE SPIRITUAL DOMAIN IN TREATMENT

Assessment can help us determine if the client's spiritual issues should be part of treatment (Richards & Bergin, 2002; Sperry, 2001). Richards and Bergin (2002) state that if spiritual difficulties have a psychological basis, therapy is most likely the best place to address them. If they are based on conflicts around doctrines, rules and regulations, or religious practices, referral to a clergyperson is usually more appropriate. Of course, client preference must be considered. A client may be more comfortable discussing her spiritual concerns with a therapist, whereas another may prefer to discuss her psychological difficulties with a clergyperson. When Ms. Dubois's son died suddenly, she was referred for bereavement counseling to a mental health clinic. Child Protective Services investigated the case and even though investigators concluded that her son died from natural causes, they felt a referral for therapy was needed. Child Protective Services concluded that the client's grief was interfering with her ability to parent her other children. They thought therapy would enable her to deal with her own feelings as well as helping her children deal with the loss of their brother. She was adamantly opposed to talking with a mental health professional. She had a strong support group within her church community and chose to discuss her grief with church members and her minister.

SPIRITUAL ASSESSMENT TOOLS

Bullis (1996) recommends the use of a spiritual genogram and/or spiritual timelines to identify and highlight significant individuals and events instrumental in the client's spiritual development (see chapter 5). Therapists may decide to use spiritual measures as assessment tools. Miller (1999), however, cautions that there are differences between assessment and measurement, and many measures have not been validated for clinical purposes (Richards & Bergin, 2002).

CULTURAL DIVERSITY

Multiculturalism demands that we as therapists become skilled at working effectively with diverse client populations. To do this, we need not only knowledge but an "active appreciation" of our clients and their culture (Canda & Furman, 1999, 2010). One challenge in preparing to work with diverse populations is knowledge development of ways in which culture shapes spirituality, without categorizing clients based on generalizations about race, ethnicity, religion, or gender. Preparation often includes survey courses or texts that cover various religions and the spiritual experiences of different races and ethnic groups. This approach often implies that there is a typical experience for members of a particular cultural group, for example, African Americans, Buddhists, Irish Catholics, Lutheran adolescents, Hindu or Muslim men, or Orthodox Jewish women. Intergroup differences are stressed, whereas intra group differences are minimized. When we make assumptions about clients based on these generalizations we cut off their experiences and prevent them from sharing who they are (Griffith & Griffith, 2002, as cited in Pargament 2007, p. 203). It is important to recognize that "each individual has a unique relationship" to his religion or spirituality (Sahlein, 2002, p. 389). Swinton (2001) points out that spirituality is a universal phenomenon, shaped by one's culture and manifested uniquely by each person. Survey approaches tend to emphasize the first two characteristics (universal phenomenon and generalized cultural expressions) of one's spirituality but are less adept at preparing us for unique expressions of that phenomenon. Our goal is to understand the client's inner world, and we do this best when we allow her to "teach" us about who she is, rather than assuming we know (Pargament, 2007, p. 203; Swinton, 2001). Although we often focus on working with clients who are different from us, we also risk making erroneous assumptions about clients who are from the same religion, race, or ethnic group as we are. For example, we may expect their experiences or beliefs to parallel our own, minimizing intragroup differences and unintentionally minimizing clients' uniqueness.

Approach to Assess Cultural Diversity

In this text, I will propose an approach to working with diversity that emphasizes mystery, uncertainty, and beginner's mind. I do not survey the major world religions or discuss the generalized spiritual experiences of various racial and ethnic groups. There are several reasons for this. First, there are several other texts that focus exclusively on cultural groups. They provide more in-depth information on these issues. Second, summaries that highlight the most significant characteristics of each cultural group tend to increase the possibility of stereotyping. What we learn from such summaries may have little to do with the individual client who sits before us. Third, and perhaps most important, we do clients a disservice when we condense centuries of spiritual and cultural wisdom into a few brief paragraphs. I believe survey approaches trivialize the richness of clients' spiritual and cultural experiences and those of their ancestors. And finally, it is presumptuous to assume which cultural groups should be included or excluded. Marginalized groups and alternative spiritual paths tend to be omitted in surveys.

Encountering the Mystery

When we approach clients with a sense of mystery we acknowledge that despite all our theoretical knowledge, we do not know; nor can we ever fully know (Johnson, 2007). Mystery allows us to acknowledge each person's uniqueness. It challenges us to think in new ways (Attig, 2007). And because mysteries cannot be solved, "once and for all" we recognize that our understanding is always tentative rather than permanent (Attig, 2007, p. 45). We will get to know our client over time and in the context of an empathic relationship (Lantz, 1993b; Marcel, 1956; May, 1983, all as cited in Lantz, 1996). We acknowledge and respect her complexity, her sacredness. In the *Artist's Way,* Julia Cameron (1992) recommends we emphasize "mystery, not mastery" (p. 21). Mystery allows us to approach clients with openness, inviting them to tell us who they are. We engage their wisdom (Carroll, 2004) and acknowledge that they are the experts on their own experience. It is only through mystery that we can develop understanding; we cannot "learn from what we already know" (Johanson & Kurtz, 1991, p. 7). Mystery provides a needed balance to our assumption that we can know with our intellect alone (Lovell, 2001, p. 197).

We tend to see mystery as a puzzle to solve, one we can approach intellectually. Instead we approach mystery with heart, courage, and trust as well as our intellect. When we encounter mystery, it requires that we wait patiently for things to unfold and treasures to be revealed. We delve deeply into the unknown "and *allow it to lead us…*" (italics in the original) (Johanson & Kurtz, 1991, p. 5). What we seek to know does not quite have a name (Johansen & Kurtz, 1991, p. 4). It is full of surprises (Johnson, 2007), and when our work surprises us we need to become creative and innovative, rather than turn to familiar approaches that may not suit this new situation (Carroll, 2004). The mystery of each client can intrigue us and requires that we approach our work with curiosity rather than certainty. We do not try to force anything to happen; we act as witnesses to what does occur and learn as we go (Carroll, 2004, p. 211; Johanson & Kurtz, 1991, p. 7).

Uncertainty and Beginner's Mind

Uncertainty allows for an "unending adventure of exploration" (Johnson, 2007, p. 38). However, we may find that acknowledging uncertainty and dwelling in mystery to be challenging (Faiver, Ingersoll, O'Brien, & McNally, 2001, p. 25). Uncertainty reminds us that with each client "we are on entirely new ground" (Faiver et al., 2001, p. 25) and what worked with others may not work with this individual (Lantz, 1996, p. 302). We are required to "center ourselves on the ever-shifting ground" (Bien, 2008, p. 88). We may be uncomfortable with the need to relinquish control, but when we surrender, we do not give up; we become open to what is (Curry, 2000; Johanson & Kurtz, 1991). The concept of beginner's mind reminds us of the importance of experiencing situations without preconceived notions and being receptive to all possibilities (Siegel, 2007; Suzuki, 2006). We "accept that the waters of diversity are choppy and unpredictable and the journey is full of unknowns" (Bien, 2008, p. 88). Our client becomes our teacher. Although we are uncertain, we are curious to learn from him. It takes great courage to surrender to not knowing and uncertainty, to enter

Diversity in Practice

Practice Behavior Example: View themselves as learners and engage those with whom they work as informants.

Critical Thinking Question: Recognizing the role of culture in shaping our clients' spirituality is critically important. Discuss the challenges of developing knowledge of diverse cultural groups while avoiding the pitfalls of stereotyping. How does the concept of mystery help therapists avoid generalizations about cultural groups?

the unknown with him, asking him to lead the way. Yet when we do so, we treat him as the sacred person he is. Our theories anchor us, and that is helpful. But we need to hold them in suspension, to wait to see if what we think we know fits our client's situation or not.

DEVELOPMENTAL MODELS

Several developmental theories are helpful to assess the changes in spirituality over the life span of the client. These theories often propose progressive stages of development, with one stage of development building on and expanding on the previous stage. Growth is often viewed as a linear process, and the success of each stage is dependent on the successful completion of the previous stage. These theories help us understand the general progression of development but overlook its complexity along with the unique manifestations of each individual's development. In addition, many moral and spiritual stage theories are highly dependent on cognitive development theories, especially on Piaget's cognitive development model (Spilka, Hood, Hunsberger, & Gorsuch, 2003). Theories that propose step-like progressions have an inherent risk in that clients who do not fit the model may be negatively stereotyped. Of particular concern is the use of characteristics to label a client's spirituality as unhealthy or immature when it is in fact functional for her.

The complexity of individuals and their spirituality—a topic beyond the scope of this text—would be captured more effectively by understanding the intersection of the various stage theories. There is an interdependence of cognitive, social, moral, and spiritual development. For example, Erikson (1950, 1959, as cited in Goldstein, 1995, pp. 88–91) proposes that optimal psychological health is based on an eight-stage model of development. Each stage of development comprises a psychosocial task. The first psychosocial task is especially germane to understanding our clients' spiritual development. According to Erikson's model, the first psychosocial task individuals must accomplish is the development of a sense of trust. This task, accomplished in infancy, provides the basis for future personality development. Successful completion is dependent on the caretaker's ability to respond to the child's needs. If one is unsuccessful, she will experience a sense of mistrust. Success or failure of this task will influence the individual's relationship with others and will create a context for her life experiences (Goldstein, 1995). If an individual is unable to successfully develop a sense of trust, what implications does this have for his spiritual faith? Is not trust essential for faith and spiritual development? Another complexity of human development is that individuals may mature cognitively, socially, or emotionally at different rates, creating differential affects on spiritual development. For example, an individual may achieve social maturation but have delayed cognitive development. What impact will this have on his spiritual and moral development?

Stage theories are most helpful when used as a general guide. We must remember the importance of suspending judgment and allowing each client's experience to unfold. I now provide a brief summary of several stage theories helpful in understanding generally how individuals grow and develop over the life span. All these theories hold that progression is consistent with each phase building on the previous one. Important to our understanding is the reality that for some individuals, regression may occur due to a number of factors. For example, traumatic events may negatively affect one's stage of faith (see chapter 7, on suffering and spirituality). And, in chapter 10, I suggest that the spiritual development of women is often circular rather than progressive.

Piaget's Cognitive Development Model

Because many stage theories are based on cognitive processes, a brief understanding of Piaget's model of cognitive development is important. According to this theory, one's cognitive development is composed of several stages; it moves, in early childhood, from egocentric thinking, an inability to view things from another's perspective, to the ability to think logically about concrete matters (concrete operational thinking stage), and, in adolescence, to the capacity for complex abstract thinking (formal operational stage). Although Piaget's theory has been criticized, its important contribution is that it distinguishes children's thinking from that of adults, which is important in understanding children's spiritual development. The complexities and abstract concepts of most organized religions are beyond the cognitive abilities of young children (Spilka et al., 2003, pp. 76–77).

Kohlberg's Theory of Moral Development

Moral decisions for many are greatly influenced by one's spiritual belief system and dependent on cognitive development. Kohlberg's theory of moral development aims to understand the cognitive stages that provide the foundation for moral decision making (Spilka et al., 2003, p. 79). As the individual matures, moral decisions become "more complex, more comprehensive, more integrated, and more differentiated than the reasoning of the earlier stages" (Sapp, 1986, p. 273, as cited Spilka et al., 2003, p. 80). Moral choices in early childhood are marked by decisions that are seen as beneficial to the individual and are deemed moral or immoral based on whether one is rewarded or punished. As children develop, their decisions reflect their need for approval and the avoidance of disapproval. In adolescence, there is an increasing commitment to and a sense of responsibility for others and more emphasis on developing one's own conscience (Spilka et al., 2003). Thus, we can see that moral choices move from an extrinsic orientation to an intrinsic one. In adolescence and early adulthood, decisions are motivated by internal factors, rather than the need to avoid punishment or disapproval. Gilligan (1977) criticized Kohlberg's theory as being andocentric and proposes that moral decision making for women is often based on care for and responsibility to others. For men, morality is often more justice focused (as cited in Spilka et al., 2003, p. 81).

Fowler's Faith Development Model

Perhaps one of the most useful stage models for spiritual assessment is Fowler's faith development model. He proposes that from ages 3 to 7 children are in the intuitive-projective stage, which is marked by fantasy and illogical thought and is highly influenced by significant others. As the ability for logical thinking emerges (Piaget's concrete operational thinking stage), children begin to distinguish fact from fantasy. This initiates the mythic-literal faith stage. Children interpret moral rules literally and justice is based on reciprocity. Rigid perfectionism can mark this stage; however, the development of narrative in this stage of development helps the individual find meaning and helps her make sense out of her experiences. As the ability for abstract thinking develops (Piaget's formal operational thinking stage), usually in early adolescence, the literalism of the previous stage begins to disintegrate, ushering in the synthetic-conventional stage. In this stage, the individual has contact with and is influenced by those beyond family. The world becomes more complex and his spiritual orientation can help provide coherence amid these changes. Interpersonal relationships grow in importance, and beliefs and values, although deeply felt, are frequently not examined. Conformity is important and the individual is attuned to the expectations of others; autonomous judgments are rare. Many adults remain in this stage throughout their lives.

When one's beliefs and values clash with authority, he may question how they were formed and may be led to the individuative-reflective stage, when the individual takes increasing responsibility for his own choices, including his beliefs and lifestyle. Although this stage can begin in young adulthood, individuals reach this stage usually in their mid-thirties or forties. One must be able to critically examine her identity and ideology. For many, this stage is unsettling because they move away from what the group deems acceptable to what they believe is correct. The move away from conventional anchoring is distressing. There is a shift from reliance on external authority to internal guidance.

In the conjunctive faith stage, the individual can simultaneously see several sides to an issue and sees the interrelatedness of things. One begins to understand that his belief system and practices are limited to a particular group and are, therefore, incomplete. One becomes capable of encounters with other traditions and recognizes that his beliefs and practices may be influenced by other traditions. One is able to hold paradoxes and contradictions and feels an increasing commitment to justice for others. This stage of faith is rare before mid-life. The final stage proposed by Fowler is relatively rare. It is a mystical stage, one in which the individual feels oneness with God and focuses on the commitment to justice and eradication of oppression (Fowler, 1981).

CONCLUSION

In this chapter, we discussed reasons to include spirituality in our clinical assessments. We are especially interested in the extent to which spirituality is a salient issue for our clients. We discussed the importance of determining whether spirituality is part of the problem, whether it exacerbates it, or whether it is a coping resource in problem resolution. We addressed the important topic of cultural diversity and proposed an approach to working with diverse populations, which emphasizes mystery, uncertainty, and beginner's mind. We discussed several aspects of spirituality that are important to include in spiritual assessment and provided brief summaries of some spiritual development models.

PRACTICE TEST The following questions will test your knowledge of the content found within this chapter and help you prepare for the licensing exam by applying chapter content to practice. For more questions styled like the licensing exam, visit **MySocialWorkLab.com**

1. Donald, a 28-year-old, told his social worker that he had a mystical experience during which "God told him to bomb abortion clinics." How should the social worker assess this?

   a. It is a hallucination because the client is too young to have a mystical experience.

   b. It is a hallucination because the content is threatening and distressing.

   c. It is a mystical experience because he heard God's voice.

   d. It is a mystical experience because he was given a command.

2. Abraham strictly follows the moral dictates of his religion. The social worker should use the following criteria to determine if his religious behavior is adaptive:

   a. Abraham believes his behavior brings him "closer to God."

   b. He believes his behavior is expected and helps him avoid Divine retribution.

   c. Through his behavior he receives praise from his community.

   d. He loves his parents, and his behavior makes them happy.

3. Vincent identifies as a "former Methodist." His social worker should explore his former affiliation to

   a. determine if he wishes to return to his church.

   b. determine if he should be referred to a Methodist minister.

   c. understand his reason for leaving the Methodist church.

   d. do not explore this area; it is no longer important to him

4. Angelina works to overcome her life difficulties, but also prayers to her Higher Power for strength and guidance. The social worker should assess her coping styles as

   a. self-directing.

   b. deferred.

   c. overly reliant.

   d. collaborative.

1. A social worker is conducting a spiritual assessment. What areas are important for exploration?

2. Discuss the importance of developing a strong therapeutic relationship before making a spiritual assessment.

SUCCEED WITH

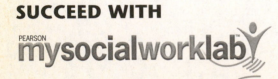

Visit **MySocialWorkLab** for more licensing exam test questions, and to access case studies, videos, and much more.

Esperanza is a 55-year-old Cuban-born lawyer. At age 6, when the Cuban revolution broke out, she, along with her parents and younger sister, fled their rural village and immigrated to a large urban community along the East coast of the United States. Throughout her life, Esperanza struggled with the trauma of immigration and had periods of profound depression. Esperanza eloquently describes her lifelong search for understanding and a sense of spiritual connection. She was always inquisitive and sought answers to the dilemmas life posed. As a young child, her family affectionately referred to her as "y porque?" ("Why?").

In Cuba, regardless of whether one was religious or not, it was the custom to baptize children in the Catholic faith. So Esperanza's parents followed this tradition even though there was no Catholic church nearby, and they themselves were not religious. As a toddler, Esperanza's aunt took her to a nearby Methodist church for Sunday services. When her family fled Cuba, Esperanza had no formal religious connections for several years.

Growing up in a largely Latino, predominantly Catholic, community, Esperanza observed many of the girls her age make their First Holy Communion. She longed to wear a pretty, white dress and a veil just like them. At age 11, she asked her parents if she could take religious instructions at the nearby Catholic church, so she too could make Communion. Her parents agreed and she, accompanied by her sister, began her formal training in Catholicism. During her training, she experienced the nuns as "mean" and felt they were "more concerned with donations to the church than spiritual development." This confused her. Her parents were on a tight budget, with little material wealth to spare. The nuns told the children that God would reward them for their generosity to the Church. She feared that God would not reward her parents and worried about what would happen to them. She struggled to reconcile the notion of a punitive, judgmental God concerned with sin that the nuns presented and her previous notion of God (that her parents had told her about) as a loving entity. Shortly after receiving her Communion, she stopped attending religious instruction.

When Esperanza left the Catholic church, she still had many questions and continued to search for something that gave meaning to her life and her spiritual suffering. One day, when she was a teenager, Esperanza answered the door to find a Jehovah's Witness, named Jackie. She and her sister accepted Jackie's invitation to study the Bible, but this, like her experience with the nuns, created a serious dilemma for her. According to Jackie, if Esperanza studied the Bible, she could be saved. Because her parents were not studying the Bible, she feared they would not be saved. She loved her parents dearly, and rather than risk separation from them in the afterlife, she and her sister decided they would "go down with" their parents and left the Jehovah's Witnesses.

Because religious institutions did not seem to help, Esperanza sought therapy to learn about herself and understand her suffering. She firmly believed that God did not want her to be miserable. Therapy was a tremendous resource, but she felt something vital was missing. She understood her feelings better, identified sources of conflict, and had a better appreciation of how her past influenced her current experience. But she still grappled with why she suffered and why anyone suffers.

After graduating from college, Esperanza was accepted at a prestigious school in the Midwest to pursue her dream of a Masters in Fine Arts (MFA). Here she began attending services at the Catholic Student Center and was introduced to Jesuit spirituality. She felt something click for her, especially the notion of finding God in one's everyday activities. By studying and writing, she could connect to something greater than herself. She was also drawn to the image of a God who wanted her to fulfill her dreams and be happy. Before she could pursue this further, however, she stopped attending the Center. On her way there one evening, a group of adolescent boys mugged her. Rather than continue to the Center, she went home and never returned. She says that in some way she questioned why something "bad could happen, if the Center had been right for her."

While finishing up her Masters in Fine Arts, Esperanza began to think seriously about what she wanted to do with her life. She loved school, so the thought of further education was appealing, but she also needed to know what she would do after school. She had always been attracted to the cause of social justice and found the idea of helping people appealing. She considered several options and finally decided to apply to law school. She was accepted at Harvard Law School and moved to the Boston area. After completing her program, she accepted a "plum position with a prestigious law firm" in the Midwest. She began her "quest" for partnership. Despite her success and exciting new position she continued to feel unfulfilled and confused. "This wonderful new world lay at my feet, waiting for me to take it and run with it, but I felt miserable." Therapy continued to "keep her afloat" but she longed to "thrive" and "be happy." She saw others around her and believed them to be happy. She wondered "what was wrong" and why she could not be happy. Although she had many close friendships, she struggled to find a lasting romantic relationship. She longed for a "life partner," a "soul mate."

She "muddled through" writing briefs and billing clients. She worked hard and diligently, but kept questioning "why" she was doing what she was doing. Over a long weekend, one of the few she took off, a visiting friend from California told her she wanted to go see a "spiritual healer" and invited Esperanza to come along. She agreed even though she felt it was a "terrible waste of time and money for such nonsense." Her friend was disappointed with the healer, but Esperanza was fascinated and continued to see her. The woman was known as a "reader" (another word for a psychic or an intuitive). She understood Esperanza. "She read me like a book." She pointed out her impatience, her tendency to overwork, and her anger. She talked about the trauma Esperanza experienced as a child fleeing a repressive regime and relocating in another country, her move from a warm, relaxed rural environment, surrounded by family to a harsher climate and to the more frenetic pace of an urban community. Esperanza was "hooked." Being goal driven, she decided this healer could help her in her search for a life mate, but her teacher talked about her need to "meet herself" and to get in touch with her center. She talked about her need to develop patience and taught her to meditate. Esperanza learned about "being in the present moment" (a difficult task for her). She began to study other belief systems. She embraced her spiritual discoveries, often sacrificing her pursuit of becoming a partner at the law firm. As she worked on her spiritual development, especially being present and working on her relationship issues, she realized that even if she was made partner at the law firm, she would still not be happy. What she had pursued all these years was internal, not external. The university degree, the fabulous job, the esteem of colleagues, all the things she sought would not bring her happiness. Instead, what she needed was a healthy relationship with herself and ultimately a relationship with the Divine. As she worked on these issues, she decided to leave the law firm. As her relationship with herself became healthier, she became ready to begin a relationship with a life partner. Ironically, he was an Episcopalian priest. She assumed when she told him about her spiritual experiences of the past few years that the relationship would end, but he was open to her and her beliefs. He was familiar with metaphysics and talked about how they dovetailed with his own beliefs as an Episcopalian. So while Esperanza expected to "blow him out of the water with her beliefs" he "blew her out of the water" with his openness to her and how she chose to practice her spirituality. He had no expectations that she be a "traditional pastor's wife" and did not even expect her to attend church services unless she chose to. She accepted his marriage proposal and moved back east. She began work in a small not-for-profit clinic that did advocacy work for those in poverty. Here she met some Jesuit seminarians and was reintroduced to Jesuit spirituality. She remembered her earlier connection to the Jesuit approach to spirituality and was eager to learn more. She quipped that she was "living with the Episcopalians and working with the Jesuits" while still meditating and following many practices one would categorize as "New Age." Esperanza continues to integrate "the best" from her New Age and Eastern philosophies with Jesuit spirituality and traditional Christian beliefs. She is able to "put it all together" in a way that works for her. She is now happy and believes that "finding the spiritual has opened up a fascinating world" for her. For her spirituality is "seeing with your heart, not with your head only. The meaning and purpose of life are beyond what is tangible."

What role has the search for spirituality played throughout Esperanza's life?

1. From Esperanza's perspective, many of her early associations with religious institutions were negative. What effect do you think it would have had on her if she had remained in any of these institutions?

2. Esperanza searched for a sense of sustaining spiritual nourishment both within traditional spiritual paths and those categorized as New Age. What are your feelings about her story? Are there any countertransference issues that may arise for you while working with her?

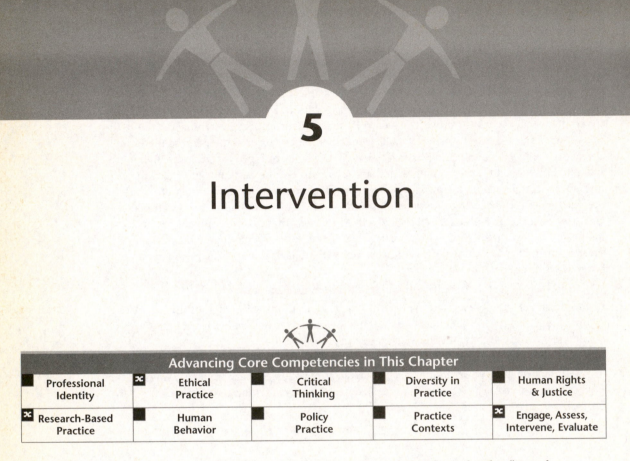

5

Intervention

Advancing Core Competencies in This Chapter				
Professional Identity	✂ Ethical Practice	Critical Thinking	Diversity in Practice	Human Rights & Justice
✂ Research-Based Practice	Human Behavior	Policy Practice	Practice Contexts	✂ Engage, Assess, Intervene, Evaluate

After the circuitous walk inward, we arrive at the center of the labyrinth. This "sacred destination" is a place to rest, a place to breathe, a place of stillness, a place of insight and discovery (Hogan, 2003, p. 10; Sands, 2001). Being in the center is "a time for contemplation," a time to think about the journey, the discoveries made, and insights gained (Curry, 2000, p. 71). The labyrinth teaches the power of process. By stepping into the unknown one can trust that truths will unfold (West, 2000). In this chapter we explore intervention techniques that can be used to integrate spirituality into clinical practice.

THE CENTER OF THE LABYRINTH

The center of the labyrinth is analogous to therapeutic intervention. The client moves from head to heart, from logic to intuition (Hogan, 2003). For some, therapeutic intervention, like the center of the labyrinth, represents the truth they seek, a place where they can connect with their authentic self or find "the still point within" (Curry, 2000, p. 70). Amid the twists and turns of life, the client finds sanctuary in the therapeutic session and learns that there is an accessible place of calm and wisdom within (Hogan, 2003). Curry (2000) states that along with the physical labyrinth walk there is a parallel process in which one navigates the "contours of the inner self" (p. 71). The therapeutic encounter, like the labyrinth walk, brings forth the innate wisdom that has always been in the person awaiting the right circumstances to emerge. Finding the stillness of the center amidst the twists and turns of the labyrinth reminds us that moments of wholeness and calm are surrounded by the "convoluted business of everyday life" (Sands, 2001, p. 66). So we engage clients in treatment and assess their needs, strengths, and limitations (the walk to the center). And now having arrived at the center, we encounter the heart of therapy, the intervention phase, which is a time and place of insight, discovery, change, growth, and healing.

SOUL AND SPIRIT

The words *soul* and *spirit*, although often used interchangeably, signify different concepts (Hillman, 1975, as cited in Elkins, 1998, p. 18). The soul is our center, which connects us to others, the Divine, and ourselves. Spirit, the animating force of life, on the other hand enables us to transcend, to move beyond the self (Malchiodi, 2002). Both soul and spirit are important for understanding spiritual life. The direction of the soul is downward, whereas the direction of the spirit is upward (Hillman, 1975, as cited in Elkins, 1998). Soul teaches us the importance of looking inward. Spirit allows us to focus on transcendence or rising above (Elkins, 1998).

The concepts of soul and spirit can provide a way for us to think about our interventions with clients. Interventions that are soul focused are designed to aid clients in going into the depth of their experiences, to face the difficulties of their lives. They are about finding internal stillness and thus wisdom. Spirit-focused interventions are about strengths and skills to rise above or transcend one's difficulties. Often clients need to do soul work before they can do spirit work. For example, soul work may be needed to face one's inner dragons and work through unfinished business. Once these problems have been dealt with, the client is able to, like the phoenix, soar above the ashes (Elkins, 1998) and embrace the fullness of life. Attempts to transcend without the needed soul work may be a form of spiritual bypassing. One would then be using spirituality to avoid life and one's difficulties rather than face them (Welwood, 2000) and then rise above them.

Soulful therapy appreciates the confusion and difficulties of life as a "mystery to be respected and explored rather than grasped and digested by our intellect" (Moore, 1995, p. 14). We encourage clients to engage in soul work to eliminate obstacles that impede authenticity, to allow a sense of connection to the self so one can heal (Arrien, 1995; Borysenko, 1995). The goal is to move toward wholeness and find meaning and purpose in both life and the circumstances that bring clients to therapy (Sperry & Shafranske, 2005).

Soul- and spirit-focused interventions are important and often complement each other. Interventions should be chosen based on client ability and the presenting circumstances. Is the client capable of doing the painful soul work? Will delving deeply into their experiences and feelings precipitate a crisis? Is the client willing to engage in depth work? Even if capable of doing the work, the client may choose not to. Although this may be a missed opportunity for growth, we must respect the client's right to forgo soul work. Naturally, some clients prefer to transcend the pain, rather than explore it. It is up to individual therapists and clients to decide whether this is appropriate or this is spiritual bypassing.

Soul-focused interventions are based on the assumption that in the midst of suffering there is usually a gift to be found, a lesson to be learned. By wrestling with difficulties one encounters the treasure. "Soul is always about coming back to the ground, about coming down, about descending into our depths. Soul is about learning the lessons that triumph and achievement cannot teach" (Elkins, 1998, p. 43). The spirit concerns itself with transforming, transcending, and ascending. At times, soulfulness enters after the spirit is crushed. "And in the cracks of our shattered life she plants the painful seeds of hope. This is the work of the soul . . ." (Elkins, 1998, p. 44).

The interventions described below can be used for either soul or spirit work. These concepts can guide therapists about the goal of a specific intervention. Are we encouraging the client to go inward or are we focusing on transcendence? However, neither soul- nor spirit-focused techniques eliminate the need for traditional treatment techniques. At times clients need hospitalization and pharmaceutical treatments along with traditional psychotherapy, including psychodynamic, interpersonal, or cognitive-behavioral treatment. Soul-focused treatment approaches remind us of the importance of depth work and that in the midst of suffering and illness there are gifts to be discovered and lessons to be learned. And, spirit reminds us of our clients' resiliency and capacity for personal and spiritual growth when they encounter life's greatest challenges and difficulties.

INTERVENTION

The benefits and harm of including spirituality can be as difficult to clarify as defining the term *spirituality* itself (Gorsuch & Miller, 1999). Before we outline specific interventions it is important to discuss some general guidelines, including some criteria that make spiritual interventions inappropriate.

Counter-Indications

There are several situations that preclude implementing spiritual interventions. For example, spiritual interventions should never be used with clients who indicate that they either are not spiritual or do not wish spirituality to be part of their therapy (Canda & Furman, 1999, 2010; Faiver, Ingersoll, O'Brien, & McNally, 2001; Richard & Bergin, 2002); Inclusion in such a case would be an ethical violation. Usually these interventions are inappropriate when clients have serious mental illnesses; strategies designed for transcendence are appropriate only for clients with well-established egos (Canda & Furman, 1999; Richards & Bergin, 2002). "Any practice, no matter how ordinary or common, can lead to unexpected and sometimes difficult experiences" (Canda & Furman, 1999, p. 292). This is especially true for clients facing imminent crises. Practices designed to raise awareness and contact deep feelings can pose hazards for some clients (Canda & Furman, 1999, 2010). Inappropriate use of spiritual interventions can bring about serious problems, including a psychotic episode and the need for hospitalization. Therapists should employ only spiritual strategies that they are comfortable with, have expertise in, and have personal experience with (Canda & Furman, 1999).

Integrating Techniques in Therapy

Although we recognize clients' difficulties and suffering, our spiritual interventions should draw on their strengths (Canda & Furman, 1999). Spiritually focused treatment approaches go beyond symptom removal (Sperry & Shafranske, 2005) and focus on wholeness and growth. However, to be helpful they need to be woven into sound clinical practice, which includes engaging the client, developing and maintaining a therapeutic alliance (sacred contract), assessment, and evaluating our practice interventions. Sometimes the importance of having a conversation about spiritual issues gets lost in the therapist's desire to use spiritual techniques. In the course of exploring clients' spiritual issues, therapists should use the same clinical skills as with any other presenting issue. They should gently word questions, make reflective comments, provide compassion and support, and listen attentively. They need to listen, hear, and understand the client's suffering (Sperry & Shafranske, 2005) in the spiritual domain. Content areas outlined in chapter 4 are all viable areas for exploration with clients.

Techniques or Gimmicks

To facilitate therapeutic conversations, therapists may ask clients to engage in exercises designed to help clients connect to memories or feelings about spiritual issues. These techniques have a place in clinical practice (we will discuss several), but when they are used without careful clinical thought and skill, they can be counterproductive and even dangerous. The founder of Gestalt therapy, Fritz Perls (1969), states that "a technique is a gimmick" (as cited in Fall, Holden, & Marquis, 2004, p. 234). Only when used appropriately do these techniques become powerful aids in facilitating therapeutic work. Following are some guidelines therapists can use in choosing spiritual interventions: What is it you hope to accomplish with the technique? Have you established a solid therapeutic relationship with the client? If the technique is designed to stir up strong emotions, is the client capable of handling them? Do you need to establish safety guidelines? For example, therapists may suggest that a client use a particular technique in session, so the therapist can help him process his emotions, rather than in between sessions when he is without therapeutic support. For some techniques, therapists may need to use lengthened sessions to allow sufficient time to process the exercise. With any techniques designed to stir up memories or emotions therapists need to ensure that the client is able to establish a sense of control and equilibrium before leaving the session.

Safety Concerns

Clients may complete exercises during their sessions with the therapist or in between sessions by themselves. Completing exercises between sessions allows more time in session to process information and keeps the client connected to the therapy during breaks. However, there are several concerns with this approach. Clients may have difficulty handling the strong emotions that may arise from the exercises when the therapist is not available for help. If clients are going to do exercises between sessions, those designed for containment and feelings of safety are recommended. For example, we discuss use of guided imagery designed to help clients envision a safe haven, which is usually more appropriate for in-between sessions than one designed to contact strong emotions that the client may have difficulty processing alone. It is important to note that even exercises that appear benign can stir up painful feelings. Therapists should discuss with clients some safety measures; for example, the client could contact the therapist if strong feelings emerged and use exercises that are more suitable for in-between sessions. Clients should also receive guidance on the type of exercises to be used during long breaks from sessions, for example, the therapist's vacations.

Assessment of client safety depends on the client's personality, as well as the nature of the exercise. Some clients are able to manage strong, painful affects; others cannot. Assuming that work between sessions is a universal positive may have unexpected and as unwelcome outcomes. However, as clients become more familiar with the exercises and as therapists have a chance to make informed assessments, work between sessions can facilitate the therapy and empower clients. With insurance companies restricting the number of sessions, techniques that allow the client to continue the work of therapy between sessions are desirable, provided client safety is not compromised.

INTERVENTION TECHNIQUES

Below are general descriptions of several exercises and techniques that may facilitate the discussion of spiritual issues. Although these strategies are used with other client issues, they lend themselves to work in the spiritual domain. In subsequent chapters we will discuss specific applications to spiritual content. Therapists should use only those techniques with which they are comfortable and those that they feel will be effective with their individual client and can be implemented safely. Techniques covered are the spiritual genogram and time line, journaling, mindfulness practice, guided imagery, and Gestalt techniques, such as empty chair and letter writing, dream work, and creative arts.

Spiritual Genogram

Therapists can ask clients to complete a spiritual genogram (Bullis, 1996), which is a diagram of the client's family members who are significant in the client's spiritual development. It can include several generations of relatives. Therapists can encourage clients to talk to other family members to fill in details that the client does not know. This process may also strengthen family ties and provide an incentive for families to discuss their spiritual history and specific spiritual issues. This is especially important when family members have cut off involvement with their spiritual community.

Arnold had never understood why when he was young his family never spent holidays with his mother's family. During the process of completing the genogram, he contacted an aunt who told him that his grandfather had been a strict Catholic. When Arnold's mother married his father, she rejected Catholicism and joined his father's faith. As a result, Arnold's grandfather would not allow anyone in the family to have contact with his mother. This information helped Arnold to not only understand family relationships but to also contact his feelings of fear in deciding to leave his religious community, which he felt was not nurturing his spiritual development. He was interested in contacting other relatives and possibly restoring relationships with them.

Spiritual Map

Bullis (1996) recommends a spiritual map, which often includes a time line. On this map, the client can look at significant turning points in several areas of her life, including her spiritual development. The overlap between her spiritual development and other aspects of life is important. Of particular importance is the relationship between significant life events and the increase or decrease in spiritual connection. For example, Marilyn, who sought therapy to deal with family of origin issues, knew that her family stopped attending religious services when she was 7 years old. However, after completing a time line, she realized that this change in her family's church attendance began a month after her father was diagnosed with brain cancer. She wondered if her parents had experienced a crisis in their beliefs. Because her mother was still alive, she decided to ask her about this time in her family's history.

Bullis (1996) states that the client can include photographs of significant events or people as well as mementoes or remembrances. Jason, an agnostic, reported that he considered himself to be a secular person, but felt something was missing in his life. During the course of his therapy he expressed an interest in completing a spiritual map. Between sessions, he went through a box of family albums and was very moved when he found a photo from his Bar Mitzvah. Even though he did not consider himself religious and felt no connection to Judaism as a religion, he was able to embrace the significance of this event in his spiritual development.

When completing the genogram or spiritual map, mere identification of family members and events is not sufficient. It is important to understand their significance in the client's spiritual development (Bullis, 1996, p. 49). With both the genogram and the spiritual map, therapists can engage the client in conversation and exploration by asking about the significant individuals and events they have diagramed in the exercises. Clients can be encouraged to write in their journals while completing these tools.

Spiritual Journal

The use of a spiritual journal to accompany the process of working with spiritual issues is easy to implement and effective. "A journal gives the opportunity to pause and move down rather than out, to discover, clarify, see new aspects, explore fresh possibilities" (Edward English, Keeping a Spiritual Journal, as cited in Silf, 1999, p. 207). It is a safe place for self-discovery (Carey, Fox, & Penney, 2002).

Clients may express reluctance to write a journal, fearing that their writing style will be judged. Reassurance may be needed that this is not a writing assignment and does not have to be creative or a work of art. The goal is self-discovery and for some their relationship with the Divine. Clients should be encouraged to approach journal writing with a sense of curiosity and to refrain from editing or judging what they write. It is also helpful to leave an entry for a period of time, before reading it (Doucet, 2002).

For a journal to be useful, the client needs to be completely honest. She can write about her ideas, questions, feelings, confusions, reactions to sessions, and other events in her life (Silf, 1999). It frequently takes several pages of uncensored writing before the writer can begin to get to deeper feelings and reflections. Clients can leave a blank space at the end of each entry to add comments or further reflections at a later point (Doucet, 2002). Therapists can reassure clients that their journal is private and sharing entries is their choice (Doucet, 2002; Silf, 1999).

There are several techniques that help facilitate journal writing. One technique, *streaming*, encourages the writer to start writing and keep the pen moving. If the writer hesitates and does not know what to write, she can write her name or repeat the last sentence until another thought comes. After a few moments of what Moon (2001, p. 181) calls being "present" to one's writing, there is a shift and the process loosens up again.

In *clustering* (Carey et al., 2002; Moon, 2001), one writes any word in the center of the page and circles it. Carey et al. (2002) refer to this as the "nucleus" word. One adds associations to the nucleus word, like spokes of a wheel. The associations may be related concepts, feelings, phases, or images. One continues to associate with each association, creating a rather elaborate diagram. Like the journaling process, it is important to silence the inner critic and "be receptive to what comes" (Carey et al., 2002, p. 58). This process can lead to "unexpected and surprising revelations" (Carey et al., 2002, p. 54). Moon (2001) recommends that one write down associations, even if they do not appear to make sense. After the clustering is completed, she can create a sentence that seems to pull the exercise together (Carey et al., 2002) or engage in streaming from the ideas or feelings that emerged (Moon, 2001).

Carey et al. (2002) also recommend adding artwork to the spiritual journal, including doodling. *Shuttling,* moving back and forth between different art forms, is used when one encounters creative blocks. So when one is stuck in her writing, Carey et al. (2002) recommend artwork, such as painting, to free up the process. For addition techniques to combine art and journal writing, the reader is referred to *The Artful Journal: A Spiritual Quest* (Carey et al., 2002).

Mindfulness Practice

"Mindfulness means paying attention in a particular way: on purpose, in the present moment, and nonjudgmentally" (Kabat-Zinn, 1994, p. 4). Mindfulness meditation has been used in many ways but is primarily a spiritual practice (Sperry, 2001). "Paying attention in the midst of life is a sacred practice, a practice of the soul" (Kornfield, 1995, p. 134). Although it comes from the Buddhist tradition, most spiritual traditions have a form of meditation and mindfulness practice (Marlatt & Kristeller, 1999). For example, in the Christian tradition, centering prayer or contemplative practice is based on the same principles (Sperry, 2001). Mindfulness can be practiced without any formal belief system. Both atheists and theists can comfortably integrate mindfulness principles and practices into their lives.

The purpose of mindfulness is to open one's awareness (Welwood, 2000). One pays attention to understand; the mindful person is respectful and curious (Kornfield, 2008). The goal is to be fully awake to life and to develop an appreciation for each moment. Being is emphasized over doing (Emmons, 2005; Kabat-Zinn, 1994). When one is mindful, one is truly present in the moment, accepting what is without judgment (Kabat-Zinn, 1994; Kornfield, 1995, 2008; Marlatt & Kirsteller, 1999). "Connection to the present moment allows us to touch the sacredness of all things and to cherish our moment-to-moment life" (Bien, 2008, p. 50).

The individual becomes a "vigilant, but detached observer" (Marlatt & Kirsteller, 1999, p. 71). He learns to recognize thoughts and feelings, accept them, investigate them, but not overidentify with them or run away from them (Kornfield, 2008). One develops patience and courage and learns equanimity in the face of difficult emotions. Acceptance does not mean resignation. It simply means a clear acknowledgement that *what is happening is happening*" (Kabat-Zinn, 1994, p. 16). To do this, one accepts "the whole catastrophe of life" with a courageous heart (Kabat-Zinn, 1990; Kornfield, 1995, p. 133). With practice the client is able to see his thoughts as "just thinking" and his feelings as "just emotions" (Marlatt & Kristeller, 1999, p. 69).

Mindfulness can be practiced while engaging in daily activities. For example, one can focus on eating an orange, noticing its texture, and savoring each bite as well as its aroma. This is an example of slow eating (Germer, 2005), appreciating the experience with all of the senses, rather than mindlessly eating our food. When one is fully present and engaged in the moment, she is aware of and savors even the most ordinary of experiences. Clients can be encouraged to mindfully wash dishes, shower, or drink a cup of coffee. A common approach to combining meditation and mindfulness practice is sitting meditation. One sits on a chair or meditation cushion with an erect posture. The focus is on the breath, being aware of the rise and fall of the diaphragm. One is encouraged to notice whatever arises, but to not judge it (Germer, 2005).

Some clients may have difficulty with the stillness of sitting meditation; a better alternative for them may be walking meditation or "slow walking" (Germer, 2005). In walking meditation the spiritual and the physical merge (Curry, 2000). As one walks, one becomes conscious of the body, the ground beneath, the lifting of the leg, and the placing of it back on the ground (Baer & Krietemeyer, 2006; Germer, 2005). While one walks, she can be encouraged to focus on each of her senses and notice visual, auditory, and tactile sensations (Saakvitne & Pearlman, 1996).

Other clients may benefit from yoga, a spiritual practice that combines gentle poses, focused breathing, and relaxation (Farhi, 2003; Khalsa, 2002). The poses help release bodily stress, and the focused breathing exercises help clients "align [themselves] with the ebb and flow of life" (Farhi, 2003, p. 5). Deep inhalation teaches us to open to new experiences, whereas complete exhalation encourages us to release old patterns and experiences (Farhi, 2003).

Mindfulness: Depression and Anxiety

In the past few years, therapy approaches that combine mindfulness practice with traditional cognitive therapy have been developed (Orsillo, Roemer, & Holowka, 2005; Segal, Williams, & Teasdale, 2002). Although both mindfulness meditation and cognitive therapy focus on observation of thoughts, Marlatt and Kristeller (1999) distinguish the two. In cognitive therapy, the goal is to change dysfunctional thoughts. In mindfulness practice, the goal is to change one's relationship to the thought. In other words, rather than change the content of the thoughts, one changes her attitude toward them.

Depression

Based on Kabat-Zinn's mindfulness-based stress reduction technique, Segal et al. (2002) developed an eight-week model combining mindfulness practice and cognitive therapy. The goals of the program are to help people have a different relationship with their thoughts and feelings. One not only becomes aware of the thoughts that lead to depressive episodes; one embraces them, accepting them for what they are. The technique of "decentering" refers to "welcoming and allowing" thoughts and feelings, not just avoiding or "stepping away from" them (Segal et al., 2002, p. 58). This is an important shift, from the traditional cognitive approach of trying to "nip in the bud" negative thoughts to one that encourages embracing them and learning "to live in the midst of them" (Segal et al., 2002, pp. 61–62). Randomized studies support the effectiveness of mindfulness-based cognitive therapy (Coffman, Dimidjian, & Baer, 2006), although its efficacy has not been tested in clients who are in the midst of a depressive episode.

Anxiety

Orsillo et al. (2005) have developed a model for the treatment of generalized anxiety, which combines acceptance and mindfulness theories with cognitive-behavioral approaches. Because avoidance is the usual response to anxiety, the emphasis of mindfulness practice on acceptance of what is, may be beneficial to the anxious person (Roemer, Salters-Pedneault, & Orsillo, 2006).

> Mindful attention involves cultivating a compassionate, nonjudgmental, and accepting response to one's observation of events in the present moment. Clients are encouraged to observe internal and external experiences with an openness and curiosity, to use a "beginner's mind" to see things as they are, rather than as one believes them to be. (Orsillo et al., 2005, p. 22)

If the individual is able to notice his feelings and accept them with compassion, rather than judgment, and be aware that they are separate from the self and transient, the individual will be able to engage in life more fully, rather than characteristically avoid situations that create anxiety for them (Roemer et al., 2006). Clients are seen individually for 16 sessions (Roemer et al., 2006, p. 55). Although more extensive research is needed on the effectiveness of this model, preliminary findings are encouraging (Orsillo et al., 2005, p. 27; Roemer et al., 2006, p. 72).

Engage, Assess, Intervene, Evaluate

Practice Behavior Example: Help clients resolve problems.

Critical Thinking Question: Discuss mindfulness as a treatment intervention. What types of clients will benefit from these approaches? Discuss a mindful approach to the treatment of depression and anxiety. How does it differ from traditional models of cognitive therapy?

Guided Imagery

Guided imagery is a technique based on the assumption that beliefs and attitudes affect healing (Rossman, 2000, p. 7). It combines relaxation techniques and the use of powerful images. The technique helps the person focus inward and to tap into his internal wellspring of wisdom (Davenport, 2009; Naparstek, 2004; Rossman, 2000). Images are internal representations of experiences and provide not only a window into an individual's inner world but an avenue for transformation (Rossman, 2000). Guided imagery is a "purposeful use of the imagination," to bring about change in a gentle but potent way (Naparstek, 2004).

Why It Works

Although the actual reasons imagery is so powerful in healing are not known, brain functioning helps explain some of its effectiveness (Rossman, 2000). The brain is divided into two halves, the left and right hemispheres. This division allows us to achieve complex functioning (Siegel, 2007). The left hemisphere of the brain is responsible for analytical and logical thinking and language skills, including speaking, writing, and understanding language. Linear or sequential and literal thinking are functions of the left side of the brain (Rossman, 2000; Siegel, 2007). The right hemisphere, on the other hand, is visual, holistic, and emotional; it "thinks" in pictures, sounds, and spatial relationships (Rossman, 2000; Siegel, 2007). Whereas the left hemisphere takes things apart and analyzes them, the right hemisphere allows us to synthesize (Rossman, 2000). If we use the metaphor of looking at a painting, the left brain allows us to notice the brush strokes, the right to take in the picture as a whole. It is the ability of the right hemisphere to see the big picture, along with its connection to emotions, that allows for the healing effect of guided imagery. It enables one to see things in a new way and thus create new solutions (Rossman, 2000). Because imagery is processed through the right side of the brain, it bypasses linear, logical thinking and therefore resistance (Naparstek, 2004).

How to Implement

Through guided imagery, a state of relaxation is induced, which allows healing images to be taken in (Naparstek, 2004, p. 150). Therapists can use guided imagery in sessions with clients or recommend audio tapes for in-between sessions. As discussed above, if therapists recommend the use of audio-tapes between sessions, she or he needs to evaluate the client, the stage of healing, and the content of the guided imagery to ensure client safety. Images of safety are more appropriate than those designed to stir up powerful feelings or memories. However, even the most benign images can create distress in some clients. Journal writing is an effective adjunct to using guided imagery between sessions. Clients can record reactions and discuss them in their next session.

Therapists may decide that some clients will benefit from guided imagery designed to stir up strong feelings or reactions. If this is the case, therapists are advised to use the guided imagery in session with the client so he is available to help the client process his or her emotions. Therapists need to plan for sufficient time in the session if they wish to include guided imagery. The content of imagery is chosen based on the treatment goal in a particular session. If the goal is to contact significant memories or feelings, the exercise needs to be used early in perhaps a lengthened session. If the goal is to contain overwhelming feelings and provide a sense of safety, the exercise could be used later in the session, which will help therapists close up clients at the end of sessions when painful work has been done. In either case, sufficient time is needed to process the exercise, because although our intent is to comfort and bring a sense of safety to clients, we need to be prepared for an unexpected outcome.

Mario, a 45-year-old business executive, grew up in a violent home. As he explored his past, it was difficult for him to manage and contain his feelings between sessions. The therapist introduced a guided meditation of a place of safety based on the one place Mario felt safe while growing up. When the meditation seemed to help Mario, the therapist recorded it in her own voice for him to use between sessions. Mario reported that he was able to regulate his emotions better and his functioning between sessions improved.

Guided imagery can be used to create layers of protection in dealing with painful material. To begin, you may ask the client to envision a beautiful, safe setting, an "inner haven," as one layer of protection (Connors, Toscova, & Tonigan, 1999; Naparstek, 2004). A second layer of protection can be created by asking the client to envision herself being surrounded by protectors (Naparstek, 2004), or she may visualize a caring person, either from her past or from her imagination, as an internalized positive image to draw strength from (Walsh, 1999, p. 44). To give clients a sense of control over painful material, you can ask them to envision events as occurring on a television screen: They have a remote control and can switch the channel whenever they choose (Naparstek, 2004).

When therapists use guided imagery, it is important that the clients choose images that are meaningful and comfortable for them. There is no universal image of peace, serenity, or safety, and scripts are usually worded accordingly: "imagine you are in a beautiful setting" rather than "imagine you are sitting on a beautiful beach." A peaceful image for one client may be distressing to another. Some clients may choose images related to their spiritual tradition, but this should come from the client, not the therapist.

Gestalt Techniques

Gestalt techniques are grounded in existential philosophy and emphasize personal responsibility (Perls, 1992, as cited in Congress, 1996, p. 341; Fall, Holden, & Marquis, 2004). It is a holistic approach and views self-actualization as the primary motivation for human behavior (Congress, 1996; Fall et al., 2004). Gestalt techniques are based on the assumption that enacting problems expedites healing more than talk approaches (Congress, 1996) and are rooted in the belief that the interpretation of experience shapes meaning (Fall et al., 2004). The focus on the here and now allows for a good fit between Gestalt approaches and mindfulness practices. Both encourage receptiveness to whatever arises. Gestalt therapy "challenges us to sit in openness with feelings of not knowing, lack of meaning, or emptiness" (Williams, 2006, p. 9).

Empty Chair

The empty chair is perhaps the most well known of all Gestalt techniques (Congress, 1996). This technique facilitates awareness via a dialogue with various aspects of the self, which one often keeps hidden (Fall et al., 2004). For example, the client may dialogue with his inner critic. A variation on the technique involves asking the client to imagine a person with whom she has a conflict sitting across the room from her. The client expresses her thoughts and feelings to the chair as if the person were actually there. She speaks in the first person, which is more emotional than speaking in the third person. For example, it is more powerful if she says "you hurt my feelings" rather than "I would tell her she hurt my feelings." Therapists should not engage in a role-play during the empty chair technique.

Engage, Assess, Intervene, Evaluate

Practice Behavior Example: Help clients resolve problems.

Critical Thinking Question: Gestalt techniques such as the empty chair and letter writing are designed to stir up deep emotions. Discuss the guidelines to ensure client safety when therapists use these techniques. Are there clients for whom these techniques are inappropriate?

Letter Writing

Letter writing is a powerful technique for clients to express their thoughts and feelings about specific experiences or individuals in their lives. The intention is not to send these letters. Later, if the client wishes, a revised version can be sent. The purpose of the initial letter, like the spiritual journal, is to develop insight and understand feelings without censor. If clients can read letters out loud to the therapist, it is very beneficial. Sperry and Giblin (2005) state that Gestalt techniques such as the empty chair or letter writing can be used to help clients discuss and explore their relationship with the Divine (p. 528). Specific applications of Gestalt techniques will be included in chapters 6 and 7.

Dream Work

Although there are different dream theories, our interest is the role of spirituality in dream work. "Dreams are a call to consciousness—to awareness and action" (Savary, Berne, & Williams, 1984, p. 107). According to Sperry and Giblin (2005), dreams are "God's language" (p. 526) and, in our work with clients, they allow us access to both the unconscious and the spiritual aspects of the individual. According to the Talmud, "A dream that has not been interpreted is like a letter that has not been opened" (as cited in Taylor, 1983, p. 5). A dream does not "mask or hide but does its best to reveal" (Taylor, 1983, p. 35). Dream work, which is used to decipher a dream, is like "opening the letter, reading it, and responding to it" (Savary et al., 1984, p. 5).

Dream Principles

Jeremy Taylor's (1983, 1992) approach to dream work fits well with our interest in the role of spirituality in dreams. He concludes that there are several assumptions one can make about dreams. "All dreams come in the service of health and wholeness" (Taylor, 1992, p. 5). Taylor argues that even nightmares, although they seem to not be in the interest of wholeness, are designed to get our attention and make sure we remember the message they have to bring. The second assumption Taylor makes is that no dream is designed to tell the dreamer what she already knows (Taylor, 1992). There is always new information in the dream. He states the only exception is when the dreamer intellectually knows valuable information but has not acted on it (Taylor, 1992).

The third assumption, and perhaps one of the most important for us as practitioners, is that only the dreamer knows for certain what the dream means. Others may have some valuable insights into the meaning of dreams, but the insights must resonate with the dreamer, who confirms the rightness or wrongness of the observation or interpretation. Taylor believes the dreamer already knows what the dream means, and when she hears it spoken aloud, she recognizes what she already knows. This recognition is often accompanied by an unspoken "aha" (Taylor, 1992). It is particularly important to avoid the dream becoming an "instrument of tyranny" in the dreamer's life (Taylor, 1992, p. 22). Taylor (1992) states that when the dreamer relies on others to interpret the meaning of his dream, he becomes dependent on external forces. He cedes his power to another, the "expert" or "authority" (Taylor, 1983). The dreamer is the sole interpreter, and interpretation is "remembering" what he already knows, as he was the one who created the dream initially (Taylor, 1992, p. 16).

Layers of Meaning

All dreams have several layers of meaning, all of which are simultaneously true (Taylor, 1992). Interpretation of the dream is never complete. Taylor states that, when the messages in the dream seem to conflict, the dreamer's life is moving into a new phase and that previously "unquestioned assumptions and values" will be "reshaped" by new experiences (Taylor, 1992, p. 8). And finally, although an individual's dream is unique to her, all dreams use the universal language of metaphors and symbols and reflect her innate creativity in problem solving (Taylor, 1992).

Dream Techniques

Johnson (1986) recommends we initially unpack the meaning of the dream by making associations with the images in the dream. It is important that the associations come from the dreamer, without reliance on external sources, including dream dictionaries. The associations do not have to make sense. The dreamer and therapist can use a diagram similar to that used in clustering (see under "Spiritual Journal" earlier). The dream image is placed in the center and a circle drawn around it. The image in the center is likened to the hub of a wheel and each association to a spoke radiating from the center. The dreamer makes associations with the initial association, creating a chain of associations. According to Jung (as cited in Johnson, 1986, p. 56), one of the associations will click. It will either generate a great deal of energy or touch a place of woundedness or confusion. Therefore, "*go where the energy is*" (italics in the original) (Johnson, 1986, p. 56).

In the second phase of dream work, the dreamer links the dream images to the part of self that it represents. This inward focus is important and allows the interpretation to go beyond external events in the life of the dreamer. "Most dreams, in one way or another, are portrayals of our individual journeys toward wholeness" (Johnson, 1986, p. 66). One way of making this inward connection is to ask about the similarities between the dreamer and the dream images.

The third stage is to synthesize all of the associations gleaned from the first two steps and create a unified picture or coherent understanding of what the dream means to the dreamer. A question the dreamer can ask is "What is the single most important insight that the dream is trying to get across to me?" (Johnson, 1986, p. 87). And finally, dream work needs to be accompanied by a ritual or physical act. It may be symbolic, such as purchasing a small replica of a meaningful dream image, or a concrete step that affirms the message of the dream, such as attending to a broken relationship (Johnson, 1986, p. 97).

Some other techniques for dream work include dialoguing with a dream figure or image (Savary et al., 1984, p. 62). In this technique, similar to the Gestalt technique of the empty chair, the individual uses her imagination to converse with an image she chose from her dream sequence. In another approach, the dreamer entitles his dream. The title should emerge spontaneously. He then identifies the major themes in the dream, followed by the primary feelings he had both during the dream and upon waking. When these steps are completed the dreamer asks a question. Two variations of the question follow: "*What question would you ask of this dream?*" and "*What question does this dream seem to be asking of you?*" (italics in the original) (Savary et al., 1984, p. 23). An alternative question, "What is the dream trying to help me become conscious of?" may also be posed (Savary et al., 1984, p. 24).

Group Work

Taylor (1983, 1992) recommends that dream interpretations be done in groups. Within a supportive group, there is potential for multiple insights. It is important to recognize that when one interprets another's dream, it is a projection of the interpreter. In fact,

> *anything* that is said about the possible meanings in someone else's dream is *always a projection* [italics in the original], a reflection of the interior life and symbol dramas of the person making the comment, more than is it is a reflection of the possible "objective" significance of the dream itself. (Taylor, 1992, p. 135)

Therefore, Taylor (1992) recommends prefacing comments or insights with the phrase "if it were my dream" (p. 134). In a group format, he contends that even if the interpretation of the symbol is not useful to the dreamer, it will be to others in the group or the individual making the comment.

Creative Arts

Creative arts such as painting, writing, drawing, music, and making collages are powerful tools in working with clients and their spiritual issues. Engaging in arts is a spiritual practice (Farrelly-Hansen, 2001, p. 17). It awakens the soul and points to what needs attention, healing, and transformation (Malchiodi, 2002; McNiff, 2004). "Art is an authentic language of the soul and a mirror of the true nature of the soul's experience" (Malchiodi, 2002, p. 3). Parts of the self are more easily expressed through the arts than through words alone. It is as close as we get to "seeing our souls" (Malchiodi, 2002, p. 19).

Therapists need to approach the interpretation of client's artwork with caution. Lovell (2001) states that a sense of mystery is more important than analysis. McNiff (2004) cautions that when someone in authority interprets someone's artwork, the individual may not feel free to disagree with the interpretation. He recommends the process of interpretation be approached with a sense of humility and awe.

The client's approach to creative arts may reflect struggles in other areas of her life. For example, to find one's authentic voice in writing, one must write from the soul (Hagberg, 1995). Exploring the client's difficulties with finding honesty in her writing or other creative endeavors might reveal concerns that challenge her.

Clients can create collages of issues related to their spiritual development. For example, the therapist can ask a client to create a collage that depicts what spirituality means to him. Or the client can be asked to create a collage of what nourishes his soul. Writing about these issues can also be a vehicle to observe what emerges. McNiff (2004) recommends a Gestalt technique that involves talking to the images in a piece of artwork. This is similar to the empty chair technique but may create a sense of safety because the images come from the imagination. In the subsequent chapters we will discuss further applications of creative arts.

CONCLUSION

In this chapter, we drew an analogy between the center of the labyrinth and the intervention phase of clinical practice. Intervention is indeed the heart or center of the therapeutic encounter. We discussed guidelines for inclusion of spiritual interventions and counterindications to assess the appropriateness of spiritual strategies with clients. Although spiritual strategies can be powerful tools to facilitate discussion, without a sound clinical foundation, they are merely gimmicks.

Included in this chapter was a discussion of techniques designed to help clients focus inwardly and deal with depth issues. These techniques are soul focused, whereas strategies designed for transcendence are spirit focused. We proposed several intervention strategies that therapists can use to explore the spiritual domain. These include having a clinical conversation about spiritual issues; journal writing; mindfulness practice; guided imagery; Gestalt techniques, including the empty chair and letter writing; dream work; and creative arts. These techniques are not specifically designed to address spiritual issues but lend themselves well to the topic. Application of techniques to specific spiritual content will be covered in subsequent chapters.

PRACTICE TEST

PRACTICE TEST The following questions will test your knowledge of the content found within this chapter and help you prepare for the licensing exam by applying chapter content to practice. For more questions styled like the licensing exam, visit **MySocialWorkLab.com**

1. A social worker should not include spirituality in treatment if
   a. the client has a serious mental illness.
   b. the client has not had previous experience with spiritual interventions.
   c. the client does not belong to a spiritual community.
   d. the social worker is not spiritual.

2. A social worker is working on spiritual issues with a 35-year-old computer analyst. The social worker can use a spiritual genogram to identify
   a. patterns of abuse within the client's family.
   b. family members who influenced his spiritual development.
   c. family members who are spiritual.
   d. family members who are not spiritual.

3. A social worker is facilitating a therapy group for adults who grew up in homes with substance-abusing parents. She plans to use the empty chair technique to help members confront issues from their past. At what phase of the group should she implement the technique?
   a. The first session, so members know what to expect.
   b. The first session because the clients are likely resistant.
   c. When the group is cohesive and members can support one another.
   d. The last session, when members know each other best.

4. Social workers using mindfulness-based approaches to depression work with clients to
   a. welcome and allow all thoughts and feelings.
   b. replace negative thoughts with positive thoughts.
   c. avoid negative thoughts.
   d. help clients change their negative thinking.

1. Discuss the reasons why guided meditation is an effective tool in clinical work with clients. How can therapists create layers of safety for clients dealing with painful memories or feelings?

2. Alice, a recent graduate, is working with Raul in a mental health clinic. Raul recently lost his job and, while discussing this, began to sob during the session. Alice is uncomfortable with the intensity of his emotions. What should Alice do during the session to contain her own discomfort? What should she do after the session to ensure she works effectively with Raul and other clients like him?

SUCCEED WITH

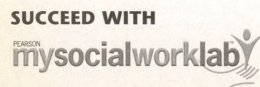

Visit **MySocialWorkLab** for more licensing exam test questions, and to access case studies, videos, and much more.

For sound clinical practice there should be a close link between our assessment of clients and our treatment interventions. Therefore, in this chapter, we will use the case of Esperanza (presented in chapter 4) to discuss treatment.

1. Based on your assessment of Esperanza, what treatment interventions are appropriate? Which are not? Support your answers with the information provided on Esperanza in chapter 4.

2. Esperanza is an intelligent, active, professional woman. Discuss why meditation or other mindfulness practices are appropriate for her.

6

Guilt, Shame, and Forgiveness

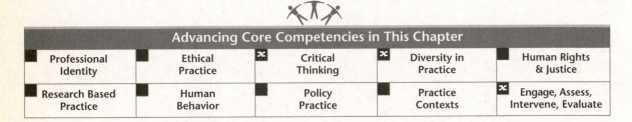

Advancing Core Competencies in This Chapter				
☐ Professional Identity	☐ Ethical Practice	☒ Critical Thinking	☒ Diversity in Practice	☐ Human Rights & Justice
☐ Research Based Practice	☐ Human Behavior	☐ Policy Practice	☐ Practice Contexts	☒ Engage, Assess, Intervene, Evaluate

The ubiquity of guilt and shame is reflected in the old joke, "My mother is a travel agent for guilt trips." Although clients do not often present with guilt or shame as their primary problem, in the course of therapy, issues related to these emotions frequently arise. And for some, the experience is so painful it may be what prompts them to seek help. The desire to avoid guilt and shame motivates individuals to engage in good behavior, inhibit the expression of unacceptable impulses, and avoid wrongdoing (Tangney, Wagner, Fletcher, & Gramzow, 1992). However, Tangney and Stuewig (2004) remark that research indicates that guilt and shame are not equally adaptive. To work effectively with clients who present with these issues, we need to be able to distinguish the concepts and understand the adaptive function of guilt as well as the maladaptive manifestations of excessive guilt and shame. In this chapter, along with the above topic, we will discuss intervention techniques that help clients process guilt and shame and address the role of forgiveness in clinical practice.

GUILT

Guilt is a painful feeling that occurs when an individual believes she has done something that violates either her own or others' moral standards (Albertsen, O'Conner, & Berry,

70

2006). It is associated with an individual's actions, inaction, or intentions and is based on the possibility that the person did something wrong (Baumeister, Stillwell, & Heatherton, 1994). Guilt is specific to the commission of wrongdoing, not a judgment about the individual who committed the action. The person may ruminate over his behavior and regret having done it, especially if others were hurt by his actions. However, rather than trying to avoid and defend, the guilty person usually seeks a way to apologize and make amends or in some way correct the situation. When reparation is not possible, the person may resolve to do better in the future. Thus, when adaptive, guilt is used to self-correct behavior (Tangney & Stuewig, 2004).

Causes of Guilt

The most common causes of guilt are failures of self-control(Geyer & Baumeister, 2005), and interpersonal transgressions (Baumeister, Stillwell, & Heatherton, 1994). Failures of self-control may include indulging in excessive behaviors and not conducting oneself in accordance with one's values or standards. Interpersonal guilt, which derives from one's belief that he or she has harmed another, is usually the healthier form (Albertsen et al., 2006). It derives from altruism, encourages one to avoid harming others, and evokes empathy along with the commitment to maintaining attachments, and thus leads to reparation and the resolve to avoid future transgressions (Albertsen et al., 2006; Geyer & Baumeister, 2005; O'Connor, Berry, & Weiss, 1999). Guilt teaches the lesson that to avoid painful feelings one needs to refrain from wrongdoing. Lack of guilt is a problem and an indication that one has an antisocial personality (Woods and Hollis, 2000, p. 147). It should be noted that guilt can be evoked in a maladaptive manner to manipulate another into doing what one wants (Baumeister et al., 1994).

Excessive or Irrational Guilt

"Excessive or inappropriate guilt may follow when individuals assume unrealistic demands or react in exaggerated ways to real or fancied transgressions rather than simply accepting appropriate levels of responsibility" (Faiver, Ingersoll, O'Brien, & McNally, 2001, p. 80). Healthy guilt enhances personal growth; excessive guilt impedes it. Excessive guilt interferes with the pursuit and achievement of life goals, and is often associated with anxiety, depression, and low self-esteem (Faiver et al., 2001; O'Connor, Berry, and Weiss, 1992; Albertsen et al., 2006).

Gordon (2000, as cited in Swinton, 2001, p. 162) describes "transgression guilt" as the justifiable guilt feelings that accompany wrongdoing. Thus, it is rational. One feels guilt because one did wrong. Guilt that is irrational is either extreme to the circumstances or occurs in the absence of wrongdoing. One may feel guilty for not living up to idealistic standards, whether internally or externally generated. Survivors of genocides, such as the Holocaust, often report guilt, which "appears to attach not to any particular action but merely to the inequity of one's outcome in relation to the outcomes experienced by" others (Baumeister et al., 1994, p. 252). Another example of irrational guilt is the distorted belief that one's success and happiness causes suffering to others simply by comparison. Furthermore, being different or separating from significant others is sometimes perceived as disloyalty and results in guilt feelings; sometimes, individuals feel guilt due to an exaggerated sense of responsibility to others (O'Conner et al., 1999).

The guilt clients report may sometimes be irrational, but it is real to them and requires sensitivity on our part. Although we do not want the client to needlessly feel guilt, we need to acknowledge that it will take time for him to understand the distortion in his thinking and to work through his feelings. Labeling clients' feelings as *irrational* at best minimizes their experience, and more likely leaves them feeling misunderstood and even disrespected. We need to gently explore her beliefs and the reasons why she feels responsible for what happened and slowly challenge her distorted thoughts. This is more effective than telling her she is not responsible for what happened.

Bloomfield and Goldberg (2003) highlight several thought distortions related to irrational guilt. These include the individual's belief that when anything goes wrong she is responsible. She may believe that her wrongdoing is worse than others' transgressions, and she may engage in either-or thinking, in which she sees things as right or wrong with nothing in between. In clinical practice with those who seem to experience irrational guilt, it is important for us to remember that self-blame can be adaptive. For example, after traumatic experiences, survivors may find self-blame preferable to the vulnerability that accompanies random acts. This gives the survivor a sense of control (Janoff-Bulman, 1999).

Constructive Guilt

Although guilt is always painful, it does have an adaptive function. Guilt helps individuals refrain from failures of self-control and interpersonal transgressions, which enhances relationships and benefits society (McCullough, Bono, & Root, 2005). Healthy or appropriate guilt can enable clients to think about the disparity between their behavior and the type of individual they strive to be. When painful guilt feelings are accompanied by this reflection, constructive changes can occur, for example, the avoidance of guilt-inducing behaviors. Furthermore, guilt may be a sign of personal growth for clients who previously disregarded the impact of their negative behavior on others. Guilt is adaptive only to the extent it allows self-reflection and reparation (Woods & Hollis, 2000). "Honest acknowledgment of appropriate guilt can shift a person from self-defeating preoccupation with mistakes to constructive acts of acceptance of self, correction of mistakes, and restitution" (Canda & Furman, 1999, p. 306).

Religion and Guilt

For assessment purposes it is important to distinguish appropriate and inappropriate guilt. Because one's perception of wrongdoing is based on one's expectations and beliefs regarding right and wrong, religion and spirituality can influence guilt. We need to explore the relationship between the client's guilt and his spiritual or religious worldview. For example, are issues such as sexual orientation, birth control, abortion, and lifestyle choices, including dietary choices, shaped by the client's spiritual or religious beliefs?

According to Albert Ellis (1980, as cited in Alberstein et al., 2006, p. 67) guilt is destructive and an unnecessary consequence of religion. Some religions overemphasize moral perfection, which results in excessive guilt (Miller, 1973, as cited in Spilka, Hood, Hunsberger, & Gorsuch, 2003, p. 529).

It is a sad commentary on modern religion that there is far more humiliation than humility in our pulpits and pews. All too often, institutions that were intended to lead people to the peace, love and freedom of the Divine have, instead, herded them into cages of guilt, shame, and fear. In the cacophony of contradictory messages—unconditional love versus harsh judgment; forgiveness versus punishment; mercy versus wrath—the punitive chorus has outshouted the music of love. (Bloomfield & Goldberg, 2003, p. 147)

When one experiences guilt for not adhering to the moral standards of his religion, assessment is needed to determine whether he suffers from maladaptive and excessive guilt or whether his guilt is appropriate to the wrongdoing and thus enhances prosocial behavior. For some, excessive guilt and an emphasis on strict control of one's thoughts and behaviors are associated with religiosity; however, Luyten, Corveleyn, and Fontaine (1998) found that religious subjects are more likely to use guilt constructively. Some individuals are more likely to feel guilty (Tangney et al., 1992). Albertsen et al. (2006) state that because spirituality values interconnectedness, those who are spiritual may be more likely to experience interpersonal guilt. Religion may also create a sense of guilt for those who believe they have offended God by their behavior (Geyer & Baumeister, 2005). Clients with excessive guilt often view God as an unrelenting taskmaster, judge, or police officer; only perfection is good enough. They may be scrupulous and consistently worried that they have done something wrong (Sperry, 2001).

In some religions, there is a shift from the recognition that one is capable of wrongdoing to an emphasis on being born "in sin" (Faiver et al., 2001). Religious institutions may use guilt to motivate congregants (Narramore, 1974, as cited in Faiver et al., 2001). There is a discrepancy between the teachings of the sacred texts associated with the religion and the messages some clergypersons convey by tapping people's fear of punishment and rejection, which leads to the development of a punitive sense of self and excessive guilt (Faiver et al., 2001). "When guilt is inappropriate, transgressions can be neither forgiven nor atoned for, since they essentially exist solely in the heart and mind of the supposed transgressor" (Faiver et al., 2001, p. 83).

Due to certain religious experiences that create excessive guilt, some are attracted to Eastern religions that emphasize the innate goodness of the individual (e.g., one's Buddha nature). From this perspective, mistakes are seen as natural missteps along the path of personal and spiritual growth. Others find the lack of judgment in the 12-Step programs an appealing alternative to an emphasis on wrongdoing and guilt. In these programs, one is seen as powerless, not evil (Bloomfield & Goldberg, 2003). Although we focus here on traditional religious experiences with guilt, we cannot assume that those who follow New Age practices are free from experiencing guilt: They too may experience guilt when they perceive themselves as violating the ethics and values of that movement. Likewise, individuals who are spiritual but not religious are vulnerable to guilt when they violate the ideals and values that are meaningful to them.

In assessing the role of guilt, we need to understand the extent to which it helps the client become a better, more responsible, and loving person engaged in ethical or moral behavior and to what extent it impedes his growth and ability to lead a happy life. Does it prevent him from experiencing inner peace and a feeling of self-worth? Is the guilt chronic and pervasive or is it limited to a specific event and time? Does the client experience excessive guilt, for too

Engage, Assess, Intervene, Evaluate

Practice Behavior Example: *Collect, organize, and interpret client data.*

Critical Thinking Question: Discuss the factors that distinguish constructive guilt from irrational guilt. What are the benefits of healthy guilt?

long, for too many reasons? Is it specific to one area of her life, for example, sexuality, or religious adherence (Bloomfield & Goldberg, 2003)?

SHAME

It is important to distinguish guilt from shame. Although the terms are often used interchangeably, they are different phenomena (Tangney, 1990; Tangney et al., 1992). Guilt is painful, but shame is excruciatingly painful. One may feel worthless, powerless, and diminished and have a sense of self-loathing. Rather than make reparation, the shame-filled individual wishes to disappear, hide, or avoid. Guilt can be adaptive; shame is always maladaptive (Tangney, 1990; Tangney & Stuewig, 2004). Research indicates that "guilt motivates people in a constructive, proactive, future-oriented direction, whereas shame motivates people toward separation, distance, and defense" (Tangney & Stuewig, 2004, p. 329). Guilt prompts one to make amends, whereas shame creates a feeling of exposure and the desire "to sink into the floor and disappear" (Tangney et al., 1992, p. 670). Unlike guilt, the focus of shame is not on the transgression, but on the person who commits the transgression. It is a negative evaluation of the self (Albertsen et al., 2006; Luyten et al., 1998; Tangney et al., 1992).

Shame prevents one from engaging in honest introspection; it gnaws at the soul and makes pursuing a spiritual life difficult. Spirituality is about being authentic, but the shame-based person is invested in hiding the self. Shame causes the spirit to contract. It prevents one from opening to the Sacred or the Divine and interferes with one's ability to experience wonder, awe, joy, and reverence. Inner peace is impeded and one tends to avoid the spiritual out of fear that she is not worthy and that introspection will further reveal this (Bloomfield & Goldberg, 2003).

COUNTERTRANSFERENCE ISSUES WITH GUILT AND SHAME

Due to the ubiquity of guilt and shame, it is likely that most therapists have experienced the painful feelings of one or both of these phenomena. Therefore, working with these issues is likely to raise countertransference issues. Out of compassion for clients, therapists may work to eradicate these feelings rather than help the client understand what they mean and determine if they are constructive or destructive. Woods and Hollis (2000) point out that therapists may be tempted to reassure clients when they talk about painful issues of guilt. However, this can lessen the client's motivation to look at problematic behaviors and make constructive changes. Therefore, it is important to reflect on our own experiences with guilt and shame. How do you think these experiences will influence your work?

FORGIVENESS

The topic of forgiveness, once neglected in the social sciences, has received increasing attention in the past several years (McCullough et al., 2005). Forgiveness is a difficult topic for many people. How does one forgive and move beyond deep hurt and anger? What does it mean to forgive? Are their benefits to forgiving or not forgiving?

As an assignment in my spirituality classes, I ask students to keep weekly logs of their thoughts and feelings in response to class discussions and readings. They are asked to choose three logs (which they may edit) to hand in. Although the logs typically reflect reactions to topics that are significant to the particular student, it is remarkable the number of times students write about forgiveness. In fact, one semester every student in the class chose to submit a log on forgiveness. Students, like others, have strong reactions to the topic. At times, incidents reported in the media about a crime victim who forgave his perpetrator sparked class discussion. Some were inspired by and admired the one who forgave, whereas others were baffled or confused and even outraged that one would forgive some transgressions. Class readings on forgiveness ignite similar reactions.

In his book *The Sunflower: On the Possibilities and Limits of Forgiveness*, holocaust survivor Simon Wiesenthal (1997) relates the story of a dying SS officer who asks him to forgive the atrocities he committed. The officer appears to be genuinely remorseful, and Wiesenthal is chosen simply because he is Jewish. Wiesenthal decides not to forgive him, but years later wonders if he made the correct decision. The question posed raises important issues. Are there limits to the possibilities of forgiveness? Are there acts that are unforgiveable? Can or should the family of a murder victim forgive the murderer? Can we forgive if we are not the direct victims of the offense? Should a drunk driver be forgiven if she maims or kills someone? Can a terrorist be forgiven? Should victims of childhood abuse forgive perpetrators? Does intentionality of the offender influence the decision to forgive or not?

Wiesenthal asks if we have the right to forgive on behalf of others who may have perished in a shared trauma such as the Holocaust. Can we forgive if there is no acknowledgement of the atrocity committed? Can we forgive if justice is not done? Must we forgive if someone repents? Must one repent for another to forgive? Before we can even consider these questions we need to think about what forgiveness is and even more importantly what it is not.

Professional Identity

Practice Behavior Example: *Practice professional reflection and self-correction to assure continual professional development.*

Critical Thinking Question: In this section the question is raised about the possible limits of forgiveness. What is your opinion on this topic? What potential countertransference issues may arise? How will you address them so they do not interfere with your work with clients?

Misperceptions About Forgiveness

Misperceptions complicate our understanding of what forgiveness means. It is important to our understanding of the psychology of forgiveness that Christian theorists have conducted most of the work in this area. As a result, Christian beliefs about forgiveness permeate the recent literature on the clinical implications of forgiveness. Forgiveness is not limited to Christianity, nor is it necessary for one to be religious or spiritual to forgive. Can one be spiritual and choose to not forgive? Below are some common misperceptions about what forgiveness is.

Pardon

Forgiveness is not pardoning the offender, excusing wrongdoing, forgetting an offense occurred, or denying that it was hurtful or harmful (McCullough et al., 2005). Enright and Fitzgibbons (2000) relate that philosophers have concurred that forgiveness and pardon are different concepts. One does not have to forgive an offender who has been pardoned, nor does the offender need to be pardoned to receive forgiveness. Forgiveness is the decision of the victim of wrongdoing, whereas a judge, in a court of law, grants a pardon (Enright & Fitzgibbons, 2000).

Reconciliation

Some are reluctant to forgive out of fear that they will make themselves vulnerable and open themselves to be hurt again. Forgiveness differs from reconciliation (Enright & Fitzgibbons, 2000). To reconcile, one must feel a renewal of trust and sense of safety within the relationship, which may be impossible. For example, if an individual is a victim of sexual abuse or interpersonal violence, attempts at reconciliation may put the individual at risk for further harm, even possible death (Enright & Fitzgibbons, 2000). Forgiveness occurs internally, within one's heart, whereas reconciliation is "an overt, behavioral process of two or more people working out an existing difficulty" (Enright & Fitzgibbons, 2000, p. 42). According to Enright and Fitzgibbons (2000), forgiveness is necessary for reconciliation, but reconciliation is not needed for forgiveness; they state that this gives the offender too much power, leaving the one harmed "trapped in unforgiveness until the injurer decides to make amends and change" (p. 42). On the other hand, Schimmel (2002) states that although reconciliation is not necessary, in the Christian and Jewish tradition, it is ideally the goal of forgiveness. He further states that forgiveness is not required for reconciliation.

Forgetting

The person wronged may think that forgiving an offense means he forgets it occurred. In fact, some clients may wish to forgive prematurely hoping to be able to forget painful experiences (Enright & Fitzgibbons, 2000). At times individuals naturally forget offenses committed against them. However, reminders of the wrongdoing can easily stir up old anger and resentment. Forgiving does not imply that one should forget the wrongdoing (Enright & Fitzgibbons, 2000; Schimmel, 2002). Schimmel (2002) points out that even if forgetting is possible, one must first remember. Remembering is important to avoid repeating the offense. This principle is reflected in Holocaust survivors' refrain, "never again." We must not forget or ever allow such atrocities to occur again.

Justice

There is a tension between the desire for justice and the decision to extend mercy to the offender (Enright, 2002). Schimmel (2002) cites Aristotle in suggesting that when anger is justifiable, "absence of anger at injustices toward oneself or others is a vice rather than a virtue" (p. 53). One can decide to forgive, but testify against an offender. For example, one can testify against a molester in order to prevent further harm from being done. "Legal justice may not satisfy an angry heart, but mercy can set a person free even if the offender remains unrepentant" (Enright, 2002, p. 32). Some argue for forgiveness based on the understanding that because we all commit offenses we should be able to forgive wrongdoing in others. Schimmel (2002) responds to this by stating, "To advocate forgiving *all* offenders and *all* offenses because everyone commits *some* offenses blurs all distinctions between degrees of sin, evil, and crime" (italics in the original) (p. 56). He relates an account of a Catholic nun, who, in the 1980s, was brutally attacked, but would not press rape charges against her assailants, who were then charged with a lesser offense. He expresses outrage at this breach of justice and argues that, from a societal standpoint, her decision was morally wrong because it may have allowed her assailants to harm others. Schimmel (2002) further argues that Judaism places more emphasis on justice than on forgiving unrepentant evildoers.

Healing Benefits of Forgiveness

"Forgiveness sees wisely. It willingly acknowledges what is unjust, harmful, and wrong" (Kornfield, 2002). In the Buddhist tradition forgiveness is not a commandment, but "a way to end suffering, to bring dignity and harmony to our life" (Kornfield, 2008, p. 346). We do not forgive for others' sake, but to release the pain that accompanies the anger and resentment we feel when we have been wronged (Kornfield, 2008). Before one can even consider forgiveness, she must acknowledge that she deserves respect. Denial of the negative impact of the offender's wrongdoing is a "major impediment to forgiving" (Enright, 2002, p. 24). The one wronged needs to admit she has been hurt and her anger and resentment are understandable and justifiable. However, after acknowledging her feelings, she decides to relinquish her anger and resentment. The inner peace that comes from giving up one's justifiable anger is a gift to the one who forgives (Enright, 2002; Enright & Fitzgibbons, 2000).

Forgiveness is a prosocial, multidimensional process that includes thoughts, feelings, and at times actions toward a blameworthy transgressor (Schimmel, 2002). Worthington, Mazzeo, and Canter (2005) state that forgiveness is "one of the many natural relationship-repair mechanisms" (p. 235). It is a difficult, lengthy process and one usually vacillates between wanting to forgive and wanting to retaliate (Enright, 2002; Enright & Fitzgibbons, 2000; Schimmel, 2002). Enright (2002), drawing on the work of philosopher North, defines forgiveness as follows:

> When unjustly hurt by another, we forgive when we overcome the resentment toward the offender, not by denying our right to the resentment, but instead by trying to offer the wrongdoer compassion, benevolence, and love; as we give these, we as forgivers realize that the offender does not necessarily have a right to such gifts. (p. 25)

What are your thoughts about this definition? Are there elements that draw you toward the idea of forgiveness? Do some aspects of this definition challenge you? What are your feelings about showing someone who perpetrates harm on another mercy, benevolence, or love?

When one forgives, one's emotions change. It differs from pardoning or excusing wrongdoing. However, it does mean that one gives up anger and the desire for retribution or revenge (Sanderson & Linehan, 1999). In forgiveness, "people quell their natural negative responses to transgressions and become increasingly motivated to enact positive ones instead" (McCullough & Witvliet, 2005, p. 446). The benefit to the victim is that he is no longer controlled by his angry feelings toward the offender. The victim often suffers more from his hatred than from what the perpetrator did. Therefore, forgiving releases the one wronged from these negative feelings and brings relief and peace. One forgives for one's own sake, not for the sake of the offender (Enright, 2002). Kornfield (2002) relates the story of two released prisoners of war. The first prisoner asks the second if he has forgiven his captors. When the second responds that he will never forgive them, the first remarks, "Well, then, they still have you in prison, don't they?" (p. 22).

Forgiveness Process

Forgiveness is an internal process, a change of heart toward the transgressor. It is not an easy process and is often filled with grief, anger, and sorrow. The process of forgiveness requires that these feelings be acknowledged. As the individual allows himself to feel and express his rage and pain, "forgiveness comes as a relief, a release" (Kornfield, 2008, p. 346).

When one forgives, she does not need to face her offender, or even let him know she has forgiven him. She does not need to put herself in harm's way (Enright, 2002). She may decide to stop making disparaging remarks to or about the offender. Some believe that refraining from resentment is sufficient for forgiveness (McGray, 1989 as cited in Enright, 2002, pp. 47–48). Enright (2002) believes it is necessary to replace negative thoughts and actions toward the transgressor with positive thoughts and actions. The offender is offered an unmerited gift of compassion. Some questions for reflection: What are your thoughts on this? Do you agree that one must feel compassion toward one's offender to forgive? Or do you agree that giving up resentment and the desire for retaliation is sufficient for forgiveness?

Religion and Forgiveness

Forgiveness, a change of heart, and compassion are integral to the world's major religions. Each has sacred stories and models of forgiveness and rituals for believers to seek or grant forgiveness (Sanderson & Linehan, 1999; McCullough and Worthington, 1999, as cited in McCullough et al., 2005, pp. 396–397). Forgiveness is a skill that one develops and hones (Sanderson & Linehan, 1999). Although religions place emphasis on forgiveness, in chapter 9 we will discuss how religious beliefs and doctrines have been used to justify acts of revenge and retaliation (McCullough et al, 2005). Religion shapes one's worldview, which in turn influences how one responds to experiences. Continuing with the account of the dying SS officer discussed earlier, Wiesenthal poses his dilemma regarding the correctness or wrongness of his decision to rabbis, clergypersons, philosophers, writers, and political figures. Schimmel (2002) remarks that, with only a few exceptions, respondents differed with his decision based on whether they were Jewish or Christian. Although forgiveness is central to both religions, the teachings about the practice differ. In Judaism, the victim of the offense has the right to forgive, but others do not have the right to forgive for the victim. Furthermore, there is no obligation to forgive in the absence of remorse, confession, apology, and reparation. According to Christianity, on the other hand, individuals can forgive offenders even if they are not direct victims. This is especially true if the offender expresses remorse; but even in the absence of reparation or repentance, Christians tend to favor forgiveness. Schimmel (2002) states that in the Jewish tradition, forgiving can reflect injustice and demean the victims of the offender. Regret is not sufficient for forgiveness (Boteach, 2000, as cited in Schimmel, 2002, p. 8). However, in the Jewish tradition, if one is asked for forgiveness, one must grant it (Schimmel, 2002).

There are differences in the approaches toward forgiveness among the world's religions, particularly between Eastern and Western traditions. Forgiveness is explicitly addressed in Judaism, Christianity, Islam, and Hinduism and is central to the Christian and Jewish traditions. For followers of Judaism and Islam, reconciliation is not necessary for forgiveness, whereas Christian scholars emphasize reconciliation as a possibility (Rye et al., 2000). The research of Gorsuch and Hao (1993, as cited in McCullough et al., 2005,

p. 398) indicates that religious individuals report being more motivated to forgive, work more earnestly to forgive, are less oriented toward revenge, and are less resentful toward offenders than those who are not religious. However, there is no evidence that these differences are realized in reality. In contrast, the research of Tsang, McCullough, and Hoyt (2005) indicates that through the mechanism of religion–forgiveness discrepancy, individuals theoretically value forgiveness but when queried about actual transgressions are less likely to behave in a forgiving fashion. Regardless of differences, all religions share similar guidelines for the process of forgiveness. The offender must take responsibility, express sincere regret, make reparation when possible, promise to refrain from further wrongdoing, and request forgiveness (McCullough and Worthington, 1999, as cited in McCullough et al., 2005, p. 398).

Diversity in Practice

Practice Behavior Example: *Recognize and communicate their understanding of the importance of differences in shaping life experiences.*

Critical Thinking Question: Beliefs and values about forgiveness vary. How does one's spiritual tradition shape one's views about forgiveness? What obstacles may arise when you work with clients whose views on forgiveness are very different from your own? How will you address these differences?

Repentance and Self-Forgiveness

The literature on forgiveness most often focuses on an individual's decision to forgive another who has harmed him. Two other concepts related to forgiveness are repentance, seeking forgiveness from another for our own wrongdoing, and self-forgiveness, or forgiving ourselves.

Repentance

Repentance has not been studied as much as forgiveness of others. Judaism, Islam, and Christianity view repentance as the mechanism to seek forgiveness for wrongdoing against others or the Divine. Repentance takes courage and humility, and many people are reluctant to repent because they are hesitant to admit wrongdoing. Individuals may feel that repentance will make them vulnerable, and some are concerned about the consequences of admitting wrongdoing. This may include fear of incarceration, lawsuits, or other denials of their freedom and rights (Exline & Baumeister, 2000). Shame-based individuals are less likely to admit wrongdoing than guilt-prone individuals (Exline & Baumeister, 2000).

Self-Forgiveness

Although many are reluctant to consider forgiving others, self-forgiveness, ironically, can be even more difficult. How does one admit wrongdoing, acknowledge the harm one has done, but release feelings of guilt and shame? As with forgiveness of others, are there types of wrongdoing that make self-forgiveness impossible? When one suffers from guilt, who decides she has suffered enough and has now earned the right to forgiveness? How does one go about forgiving oneself?

Forgiveness "includes letting go of anger at oneself over limitations, imperfections, and errors" (Sanderson & Linehan, 1999, p. 211). Considering the negative consequences of excessive guilt and shame, there is a surprising scarcity of professional literature on self-forgiveness. Schimmel (2002) asks, "Is it *morally* appropriate to forgive oneself?" (italics in original) (p. 121). According to him, perpetrators of wrongdoing cannot forgive themselves. To receive forgiveness, one must ask the person one harmed for forgiveness (Marino, 1995, as cited in Schimmel, 2002, p. 121). Do you agree that one cannot forgive herself? Is there a need to distinguish between egregious offenses and the smaller missteps that most humans make fairly often?

Key to self-forgiveness is compassion for the self and the ability to understand the transgression within the context of the individual's entire life (Schimmel, 2002; Brach, 2003). Based on Enright's model of forgiveness, Schimmel (2002) points out that when one engages in wrongdoing, there is a need to assess the transgression, but to do so within the overall assessment of the worth of the individual. Self-forgiveness requires that the individual recognize the wrong he did and take responsibility for his actions and their consequences, and to also look at himself "with love and compassion" (p. 123). This allows him to ultimately release the guilt, shame, and anger he feels towards himself (Schimmel, 2002). Self-forgiveness is not analogous to pardoning, but a "coming home" to the authentic self and acceptance of the imperfection of the human condition (Enright, 1996, as cited in Schimmel, 2002, p. 124; Kurtz & Ketcham, 1994). Self-compassion does not negate taking responsibility for one's actions, but it allows the individual to relinquish feelings of self-hatred and frees up energy to look at life more clearly (Brach, 2003). In self-forgiveness, one allows the self to open to "experiencing forgiveness" (Kurtz & Ketcham, 1994).

Mass Trauma, Forgiveness, and Reconciliation

In this chapter we focused primarily on the role of forgiveness in interpersonal transgressions and, for many of us, this focus is appropriate for our practice. Although discussion of the role of forgiveness and reconciliation for victims of mass trauma and human rights violations is beyond the scope of this book, we briefly address this issue.

Violence, oppression, and atrocities against humanity have occurred throughout history and continue in the present time. The Holocaust, My Lai, the violence in Northern Ireland, slavery, atrocities against indigenous peoples, the genocides of Rwanda and Bosnia, and apartheid in South Africa are just some examples of human inhumanity toward others. These atrocities are often highly strategized and focused on the annihilation or elimination of another group of human beings. If forgiveness and reconciliation are difficult topics in the interpersonal arena, they are more challenging and controversial for these victims. Staub and Pearlman (2001) state that even those who are not victims of these injustices are horrified at the thought of forgiveness or reconciliation. Can or should these victims ever consider forgiving their perpetrators? Is it an atrocity to even consider reconciling with them and living in peaceful coexistence?

Why would victims consider forgiveness or reconciliation? Although difficult to do, reconciliation is not only important in the healing process, it is necessary to end the cycle of violence (Ellis, 2001; Staub & Pearlman, 2001). Healing is cyclical. Reconciliation begins the healing process. As the community heals, the members are more open to further reconciliation, which furthers the healing process (Staub & Pearlman, 2001). Conversely, if one continues to meet violence with violence, the horror continues and escalates. Forgiveness and reconciliation break the cycle of violence (Ellis, 2001). We need to take strong action against injustice, but violence gnaws away the human character and when we respond to injustice with violence, even when justified, we "become similar to those who we are opposing" (Ellis, 2001, p. 399). Reconciliation allows the community to accept the past without allowing it to define the future (Staub & Pearlman, 2001, p. 207). Political reconciliation is not a private matter. The arena is not the "confessional, but public policy and conflict transformation" (Helmick & Petersen, 2001, p. xvii). Readers who are interested in models and approaches to working toward global or political reconciliation may find ideas outlined in Helmick, R. G., & Petersen, R. L. (Editors). (2001). *Forgiveness & reconciliation: Religion, public policy & conflict transformation.* Philadelphia, PA: Templeton Foundation Press.

COUNTERTRANSFERENCE ISSUES WITH FORGIVENESS

Religion molds one's worldview in obvious and subtle ways. Therapists who do not follow a traditional spiritual path may be influenced by earlier connections to a specific religion, or even be affected by his or her parents' religious beliefs. They may also be influenced by Judeo-Christian values that permeate American culture. This poses several potential countertransference issues in working with issues of forgiveness. As mentioned above, the world's religions have different views on when forgiveness is appropriate and when it is not. As therapists, we may need to work diligently to ensure we do not assume that our philosophy regarding forgiveness is appropriate for our clients. Differences may include one party seeing forgiveness as an obligation and the other as an injustice. It may be tempting to see one's philosophical view of forgiveness as morally correct and therefore superior to another's.

The desire to forgive must come from the one offended. It is not the place of therapists to urge clients to forgive another's wrongdoing toward them. To work well with clients considering forgiveness, therapists need to carefully explore their own feelings and thoughts about this topic. In a particular instance if you are not inclined to think forgiveness is a viable option, what would be your reaction to the client who feels she must forgive some atrocity she experienced? If you believe forgiveness is necessary, how will you react if your client indicates that he would never consider forgiving? Pressure to forgive increases the difficulty of healing from an offense and increases the victim's distress (McCullough & Witvliet, 2005).

INTERVENTIONS

For guilt and shame, talk therapy alone is probably insufficient. Below are specific applications of techniques described in chapter 5 to the issues of guilt, shame, and forgiveness. Therapists should encourage clients to use their journal to record their reactions and feelings before, during, and after the use of these techniques.

Letter Writing

In chapter 5, I described the technique of letter writing in detail. In this exercise, therapists ask clients to write letters to identify and explore their feelings of guilt and/or shame. Clients may benefit from some of the following ideas.

Client Seeks Forgiveness

The client can be asked to write a letter identifying behaviors and interpersonal transgressions related to his guilt. In his letter he describes what he did in detail, tells the one he wronged how he feels about his behavior and what impact he feels his actions had on the other, and asks the other for forgiveness (Bloomfield & Goldberg, 2003).

If the client does not feel she is ready to write directly to the individual she harmed, she may decide to write to another relative or friend who she feels will support her in her guilt and forgiveness work. Clients can ask this third party for guidance and/or forgiveness regarding her wrongdoing (Bloomfield & Goldberg, 2003). Clients who believe in the Divine can write a letter to God asking for forgiveness using the same format described above (Bloomfield & Goldberg, 2003).

Clients can use letter writing work on both rational and irrational guilt. They need to be as honest as possible about their feelings and transgressions. Letters should be written in the first person, with the client taking responsibility for her own feelings and reactions. Initial letters should be written without the intention of sharing them with the person they harmed. Later, clients may decide to share an edited version of the letter.

Client Considers Forgiving

Clients who were harmed by another and are considering forgiveness can write letters expressing their anger and resentment and how they were hurt by the other's actions (Bloomfield & Goldberg, 2003). If he is ready, he can offer forgiveness and describe why he chooses to extend this gift to his offender. Clients can use this technique to prepare for forgiveness, and when appropriate, use the letter as a medium for confrontation rather than facing the perpetrator directly.

Letter writing is a particularly good technique when either the offender or the one the client harmed is no longer living or direct contact would be dangerous to the client. The benefits of each of these exercises are maximized if clients read the letters aloud to the therapist, use their journals during the process, and at times engage in an appropriate ritual. For example, if the decision is made that a letter to another should not be sent, the client may decide to bury the letter, reciting a few words that fit with her spiritual beliefs. This ritual may facilitate letting go of the residual guilt, shame, or anger.

Empty Chair

In a similar fashion to the letter writing exercise, the empty chair technique can be used to "apologize" to the wronged party or to seek support from a third party or confront an offender on wrongdoing directed at the client.

Peter, a 49-year-old father of two boys, had been angry with his abusive father as long as he can remember. Although he is a loving father to his sons, he feared that the hatred he felt toward his father might poison his relationship with his sons. Peter was in therapy with a group of other men raised by abusive or neglectful fathers. After talking about his father in several sessions with the therapist and these men, he felt ready to "confront" his father using the empty chair technique. Initially, he had difficulty talking "directly" to his father and used phrases such as "if he were here I would say." With the support of the group Peter eventually was able to shift his dialogue to the first person. He began to "tell" his father how he felt hurt by his actions. As he continued he talked of his terror growing up with a father who was enraged most of the time and frequently violent. Through his tears, Peter told his father,

"All I wanted was to be loved by you. I felt you hated me all the time." Peter began to sob. The therapist and the group members sat as witnesses to his pain, calmly and silently supporting Peter in his work. After several minutes Peter sobbed, "All my life I hated you and now I'm so tired of all this anger and hatred. It's eaten me up and I don't want to feel this way anymore. I just don't want to hate you anymore."

Guided Imagery

Using the technique of guided imagery or guided meditation (see chapter 5), therapists can lead clients to a safe haven where they can encounter the person they harmed or hurt (a third party, or a spiritual figure). They can relate their transgression and their feelings of remorse, and, when they are ready, ask for forgiveness. Like the letter writing or empty chair technique, guided meditation can be used to prepare the client for forgiveness work. If the client needs additional support in this work, she can visualize a network of individuals whom she feels can help and guide her.

Pauline, a recovering substance abuser, was filled with remorse that her children had been raised in foster care due to her inability to parent them. Her children are now in late adolescence, and Pauline has been thinking about reaching out to them. She is not sure how receptive they will be to her and is confused about whether seeing them would be in their best interest. After several months in therapy discussing her feelings and her conflicts, her therapist suggested a guided meditation. After a relaxation exercise, he asked Pauline to picture herself in a safe and beautiful place. After she had spent a few minutes imagining this place, the therapist asked her to imagine a wise person approaching her and engaging her in a conversation about her dilemma. After the meditation ended, the therapist began to process it with her. Pauline revealed that her grandmother, who died when Pauline was 19, was the wise person who approached her. In the meditation Pauline told her about her feelings, confusion, and fears regarding her children. She was able to pour out her grief and feelings of guilt and shame that she had not been a suitable parent to them. Pauline then shared with the therapist her grandmother's warmth and gentle guidance. She realized how much her grandmother had always loved her, regardless of what she did. In her recovery program, Pauline began to understand the connection between her substance abuse and her earlier experience of childhood sexual molestation. She told the therapist that during the imagery she made the connection in a deeper way. She said, "You know I think I'm beginning to get it. In my program they talked about not being responsible for what happened to you, but taking responsibility for what you do." Pauline decided that she was not ready to meet her children, but she became very motivated to deepen her work regarding the abuse she endured as a child, as well as discovering ways to eventually contact her children and ask them for forgiveness.

Toxic Dump

The toxic dump technique is especially effective with issues of shame and is best used in a group format. Therapists can precede the exercise with a discussion on shame and its toxic effect on human functioning. They may include information on how shame differs from guilt. After the discussion, each group participant writes down a shameful experience or troubling feeling. Each participant takes a turn crumbling the paper and tossing it into a large wastebasket or garbage pail marked "toxic dump." As the paper is tossed the client states her intention to be released from her shame (Saakvitne & Pearlman, 1996).

Collages

Clients can engage in creative arts, such as making collages, to deal with issues of guilt and shame. Therapists can ask a client to create a picture of what makes him feel guilt or shame. Or he may create a collage of his image of the Divine in relation to his guilt. Journaling is an effective adjunct to this activity. Clients can share their collages with the therapist or in a group and process the feelings and thoughts that accompany the images chosen. Therapists can keep the collages and take note of how the themes may change over the course of therapy. Have the client's feelings lessened? Has the client moved from a pervasive sense of shame to more crystallized feelings of guilt regarding specific acts of wrongdoing? Are there any indications that the client is beginning to show self-compassion?

Forgiveness Models

Worthington et al. (2005) and Enright and Fitzgibbons (2000) have developed similar stage models for forgiveness work. Worthington's model REACH comprises *recalling* the offense, *empathizing* with the offender, extending the *altruistic* gift of forgiveness, *committing* to forgiving, and *holding* on to forgiveness. Worthington et al. developed their model from their work with marital couples (as cited in Schimmel, 2002, pp. 100–108). Enright and Fitzgibbons's (2000) model comprises the *uncovering*, *decision*, *work*, and *deepening* phases. Therapists working with clients who are interested in focusing on forgiveness over a period of time may find these models helpful in structuring their work. Before implementing with clients, therapists should be thoroughly versed in the model chosen and be able to use flexibility in its application with clients. Therapists should also be aware that these models are based on a Christian perspective of forgiveness.

CONCLUSION

In this chapter we explored the constructs of guilt and shame and how they differ from each other. Guilt, when healthy and adaptive, helps individuals to reflect on their behavior, acknowledge wrongdoing, apologize, and when possible, make reparation. Shame is a more global condemnation of the self, whereas guilt focuses on a specific behavior. We discussed techniques to address these issues with clients.

The difficult process of forgiveness was addressed, including the benefits of forgiving, misperceptions about forgiveness, and cautions regarding the pursuit of forgiveness. Richards and Bergin (2002) state that therapists need to be sure that clients are ready to consider forgiving others and to take responsibility for their transgressions before encouraging them to seek forgiveness.

PRACTICE TEST

The following questions will test your knowledge of the content found within this chapter and help you prepare for the licensing exam by applying chapter content to practice. For more questions styled like the licensing exam, visit **MySocialWorkLab.com**

1. Davida is an 89-year-old Holocaust survivor. She frequently talks about feelings of guilt that she survived the atrocities while others perished. The social worker should

   a. tell her she should not feel guilty.

   b. help her understand why she was not responsible for what happened.

   c. help her understand that her guilt is adaptive because she cares about others.

   d. probe for underlying shame.

2. Andrew had an argument with his wife right before she died suddenly. He is having difficult moving past his guilt. The social worker can

   a. suggest that he see a clergyperson for forgiveness.

   b. tell him arguments are common and guilt is unnecessary.

   c. tell him his wife would forgive him.

   d. use a letter writing technique to help Andrew release his feelings.

3. Nick recently uncovered memories of childhood sexual abuse. He told his social worker he forgives his perpetrator because forgiveness is a virtue consistent with his spiritual beliefs. If you were his social worker, what would be your assessment?

   a. He is ready to forgive because he repressed the memories.

   b. He is ready to forgive because it is consistent with his spiritual beliefs.

   c. His desire for forgiveness helps him avoid the feelings about his abuse.

   d. Forgiving a perpetrator of sexual abuse is inappropriate.

4. Beverly feels guilty about an extramarital affair. She expresses remorse that she "violated her marriage vows" and feels a sense of anguish that she would hurt her husband if he found out. How would you assess her guilt? It is

   a. irrational because humans make mistakes.

   b. irrational because problems in the marriage probably led to her affair.

   c. a healthy reaction to behavior that is not consistent with her values.

   d. an unhealthy response to avoid telling her husband.

1. Working with issues of guilt and shame pose challenges for clinical social workers. Discuss some interventions that are useful in helping clients deal with these issues. How would you approach the issue if the client's guilt were irrational? How would you intervene if the client's guilt were rational?

2. Discuss the concept of self-forgiveness. What are some techniques therapists can use in helping clients who are working on self-forgiveness? What are some obstacles that may arise either for clients or for therapists when working on these issues?

SUCCEED WITH

Visit **MySocialWorkLab** for more licensing exam test questions, and to access case studies, videos, and much more.

Bridget is a 43-year-old, African American nurse, who was referred to an outpatient substance abuse program. She is facing criminal charges from her involvement in a fatal car accident she caused while driving intoxicated.

Bridget's family has a history of alcoholism. Both her parents were alcoholics, and her father died from cirrhosis of the liver when she was 10 years old. Her mother is still an active alcoholic, who often becomes nasty and emotionally abusive of Bridget when she is drunk. Her oldest brother, age 45, is an active alcoholic. Her younger brother, age 41, has been in recovery for 10 years. He sought treatment when his wife threatened to end their marriage if he did not stop drinking. And her younger sister, Cheryl, age 39, never drank.

Bridget was raised Catholic and attended a Catholic grade school. She attended two years of Catholic high school, but transferred to public school when her mother could no longer afford the tuition. After working as an administrative assistant, Bridget pursued a degree in nursing. She works in an emergency room and is described as a warm, caring, dedicated, and competent professional. She is not married, dates rarely, and lives by herself.

Bridget drinks sporadically, but on the night of the accident she went to a bar near the hospital after her night shift. She had been feeling depressed after a recent argument with her mother and the loss of a patient, who had appeared to be doing well but suddenly died. She left the bar after several drinks and "knew she shouldn't be driving" but rationalized that "she only had to drive a mile or so."

Since the accident, Bridget has stopped going to church. She questions whether "God can forgive her for what she did." In her latest session she revealed that she had a nightmare in which the accident victim called her a murderer. Family members surrounded the victim and echoed his remarks.

1. Bridget is responsible for taking someone's life as a result of driving while intoxicated. She feels a great deal of guilt. Assess the extent to which Bridget's guilt is healthy or unhealthy.

2. What clinical issues arise in working with Bridget? For example, do you think it is appropriate to help Bridget relieve her guilt feelings? Do you think self-forgiveness is appropriate in this case? Explain your answer.

3. Many individuals would have a strong negative reaction toward Bridget. As a professional social worker what are some of the obstacles you may have in working with her? How does the concept of unconditional positive regard or loving-kindness (see chapter 3) fit with this case?

7

Suffering and Spirituality

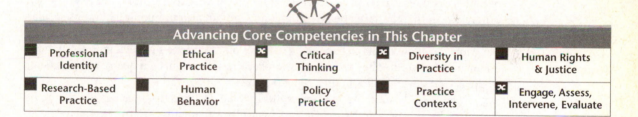

Advancing Core Competencies in This Chapter				
■ Professional Identity	■ Ethical Practice	✖ Critical Thinking	✖ Diversity in Practice	■ Human Rights & Justice
■ Research-Based Practice	■ Human Behavior	■ Policy Practice	■ Practice Contexts	✖ Engage, Assess, Intervene, Evaluate

When one encounters the tragedies of life, one may feel like the very ground beneath her has collapsed. She may ask, "Why?" "Why God?" Why is there suffering in this world? Why is there evil? In the unfathomable depths of unbearable suffering one can lose her sense of meaning and hope. And, as her world no longer makes sense, she may experience a dark night of the soul. Life tragedies strip some of a sense of the spiritual. For others, spirituality not only helps them face their suffering but also may allow them to transcend it and discover resources and gifts they did not know were possible.

In this chapter we will discuss suffering, including the suffering that accompanies some of life's greatest tragedies, traumatic events. Suffering is at times caused by malevolence, leading one to question why there is evil. Along with our discussion of suffering and evil, we will address both the potential for tragic events to disrupt one's spirituality, leading to a dark night of the soul, as well as the possibility that tragedies are a catalyst for transformation. Our challenge as therapists is, knowing that we can never erase suffering, to find ways to help clients discover the grace and courage to endure it and to face life in spite of it (Bloomfield & Goldberg, 2003).

SUFFERING

Suffering is inevitable given the human condition (Faiver, Ingersoll, O'Brien, & McNally, 2001). One may be plunged into the abyss of suffering without warning or it may encroach slowly over time. Suffering comes about in a myriad of ways. Natural disasters, such as hurricanes, earthquakes, or floods, wreak havoc and along with physical destruction bring mental anguish. Illness or death of a loved one causes grief. And, perhaps most challenging, we suffer at the hands of others. These include wars, murder, rape, child abuse, physical assault, and personal betrayals. When one suffers, he may cry out in confusion and anger. He may question the existence or nature of the Divine and wonder why such pain has befallen him. For theists, it may be difficult to reconcile the mystery and paradox of a loving, good deity existing alongside evil and suffering (Swinton, 2007). Nonbelievers may find that suffering and evil make belief in a Divine Being impossible. And for some, the world is meaningless; hence, evil and suffering are just part of how things are (Swinton, 2007).

Suffering may be a private, personal matter affecting an individual, a small group, or an entire community as a result of widespread, collective atrocities such as war or genocide. Johnson (2007) refers to the Holocaust and suffering inflicted on millions of Jewish men, women, and children. "It was an 'earthquake' that cracked open the ground of faith's confidence in God; an unbridgeable 'chasm' that spilt history and its supposed progress . . . . that shattered belief not only in God but also in humanity and its secular projects" (p. 50). She states that in the aftermath of such atrocities the proper question is not *why* God allowed this to happen or *how* can one reconcile such evil with God's governance of the world. The "proper question becomes the anguished query: *where* is God, where is God now?" (italics in the original) (Johnson, 2007, p. 51).

Along with the existence of God, suffering may lead one to question the nature of God. C. S. Lewis (1961) in *A Grief Observed* said, "Not that I am (I think) in much danger of ceasing to believe in God, the real danger is coming to believe such dreadful things about Him" (as cited in Doka, 2002, p. 51). One may conclude that the Divine is either powerless or cruel (Bloomfield & Goldberg, 2003; Johnson, 2007). Regardless of whether our clients believe in a Higher Power or not, they will struggle with these issues in treatment when they seek help with the tragedies of life. Because we as therapists share the human condition, we may struggle with the same existential or spiritual questions for which our clients seek our help.

WHY DOES SUFFERING EXIST?

In the wake of unbearable suffering, one asks, "Why does suffering exist?" Throughout the centuries, theologians, philosophers, psychologists, and sociologists have struggled to answer questions about the existence of suffering and evil. Faiver et al. (2001) cite the often-espoused message from the Old Testament that the righteous will receive blessings and the wicked will encounter evils. They comment that this view not only blames those who suffer for their own plight but also is a "simplistic" answer to a complex issue (Faiver et al., 2001).

The just world hypothesis (Lerner, 1980), which states that people get what they deserve and deserve what they get, is a modern and secular version of the same simplistic approach that blames the victim for her own suffering. Contrary to this hypothesis, those who do wrong often prosper, whereas the innocent suffer (Bloomfield & Goldberg, 2003). Matthew Fox points out that the Old Testament story of Job illustrates the fallacy of the above. Job was a righteous and God-fearing man, yet he suffered greatly (as cited in Faiver et al., 2001, p. 69).

In coming to terms with the perplexing problem of suffering, our own fears influence how we explain the suffering of others (Faiver et al., 2001). Although we do not consciously wish to blame others for the tragedies that befall them, doing so helps us keep the illusion that we are safe from harm. If we can find a "reason" for which they suffer, we feel a sense of control and do not have to face our own vulnerability (Janoff-Bulman, 1992).

> ### Engage, Assess, Intervene, Evaluate
>
> ***Practice Behavior Example:*** *Help clients resolve problems.*
>
> **Critical Thinking Question:** When clients are in the midst of unbearable suffering, they may ask questions such as "why did this happen?" or "why did God allow this to happen to me?" How would you intervene with clients who raise these questions?

EVIL

Life's tragedies raise questions not only about suffering, but at times about the existence of evil in the world. Remember that as social workers we often view those who engage in extreme wrongdoing not as evil but as suffering from severe psychopathology. The term *evil* at times denies the complexities of wrongdoing and is frequently dichotomized, that is, one is either good or evil. In this chapter, we will use the term *evil*; however, we will keep in mind that human behavior is a complex interaction of many factors and that psychopathology can lead one to engage in reprehensible acts. Peck (1983) believes that evil should be a diagnostic category. He distinguishes between the individual performing the evil act and the act itself. According to Peck, refusal to admit wrongdoing, along with persistent blaming of others, distinguishes evil people from their acts. Here are some questions for your reflection: What are your thoughts on this? Compared with *evil*, is *psychopathology* a more appropriate term? What implications does each have on how we view clients and their behavior? Are there positives or negatives to each of the terms? Which are you more comfortable with, and why?

EVIL AND SUFFERING

Although evil always causes suffering, not all suffering is due to evil. Suffering sometimes is due to tragic events. If we do not make this distinction, our understanding of evil is too broad and we dilute what we mean by it (Swinton, 2007). Intentionality is key to defining a piece of behavior as evil (Faiver et al., 2001). "*Evil consists in intentionally behaving in ways that harm, abuse, demean, dehumanize, or destroy innocent others—or using one's authority and systemic power to encourage or permit others to do so on your behalf*" (italics in the original) (Zimbardo, 2007, p. 5). In a nutshell, "evil is knowing better, but doing worse" (Sarnoff, cited in Zimbardo, 2004, p. 22).

Types of Evil

Russell (1988, as cited in Faiver et al., 2001, pp. 44–45) distinguishes natural evil, such as tornadoes, earthquakes, or diseases, from moral evil. Moral evil is the suffering that is knowingly and intentionally inflicted on one human being by another. It includes the failure of one to act to end the intentional suffering of another (Faiver et al., 2001, p. 45; Swinton, 2007, pp. 50–51). Moral evil always causes suffering, often innocent suffering (Swinton, 2007).

Baumeister and Vohs (2004) identify four "roots of evil." Violence may be used to achieve a goal. It may be used as a response to feeling threatened, or in a misguided effort to bring about something perceived as good. And finally, violence may be perpetrated on another to satisfy sadistic tendencies. Although sadism is relatively rare "it can lead to extremes of cruelty far beyond what the others produce" (Baumeister & Vohs, 2004, p. 96).

It is perhaps most perplexing when evil is the result of an attempt to bring about what is perceived to be a noble cause. Idealism has been the catalyst for some of history's worst atrocities (Baumeister & Vohs, 2004). For example, the Inquisition was an attempt to eradicate evil, yet it brought about the torture and death of scores of innocent people. "The terrible paradox of the Inquisition is that the ardent and often sincere desire to combat evil generated evil on a grander scale than the world had ever seen before" (Zimbardo, 2007, p. 9). When individuals use violence to bring about a desired end, they may justify it as a necessary evil, a "moral duty" and in the best interest of the general good. Killing others for the "cause" is justified as eliminating "a few bad people" in the interest of all (Baumeister & Vohs, 2004, pp. 93–94). To save the lives of unborn fetuses, some extremists have murdered abortion doctors or bombed their clinics. Those involved in these actions are somehow ironically able to justify killing to "protect innocent lives." Any clinic staff or innocent bystanders killed are seen as an inevitable cost for the cause. The perpetrator most likely rationalizes that the end (saving babies) justifies the means (killing others).

Explanations of Evil

There is little argument about the existence of evil. Explaining its existence is far more complicated. Some reasons proposed are spiritual or religious, whereas others are secular. Some are woven into the fabric of our society, and we may not be consciously aware of how they influence our thinking about suffering or evil. As we outline these explanations, reflect on how they shape your thinking. Do you agree or disagree with any of the explanations? How will these beliefs possibly affect your practice with clients?

Religious Perspectives on Good and Evil

Although good and evil exist on a continuum, religions tend to dichotomize them (Zimbardo, 2007). Reconciling belief in a Transcendent Being, the nature of the Divine and the existence of evil is a challenge for believers. *Theodicy* is an attempt to intellectually defend God, to maintain the view of God as all good and loving in the midst of suffering. From this perspective, evil, like any other problem, can be solved (Johnson, 2007; Swinton, 2007). Swinton (2007) states that when we ask questions about why there is evil or suffering we enter the world of ideas. We want an intelligent answer to the conundrum, but this approach takes suffering from the emotional level and makes it an intellectual activity. Evil is dealt with in the abstract, rather than looking at the problem from the practical experiences of real people who are suffering. The questions are inevitable and understandable, but we create problems when we try to answer them. In the face of unbearable suffering, "what answer could possibly help?" (Swinton, 2007). Many of the explanations offered are simplistic and insensitive, resulting in additional pain for those who suffer (Phillips, 2005). Therefore, theodicy, meant to explain suffering, creates problems, including the justification and rationalization of evil. Any attempt to explain evil ultimately becomes a way to "tame the evil, to dilute its terror, to give it, albeit unintentionally, a right to exist" (Johnson, 2007, p. 51). Rather than understanding evil, explanations "deny or fail to fully acknowledge the reality and horror of evil and instead attempt to spiritualize away the pain of suffering" (Swinton, 2007, pp. 19–20).

Free Will and Evil

One explanation given for why bad things occur is that humans engage in bad behavior (Swinton, 2007). Humans have the freedom to choose between good and evil (free will), and God rewards good behavior and punishes bad (Bloomfield & Goldberg, 2003; Johnson, 2007). In the choice between blaming the victim and blaming God, surely blaming the victim seems a safer route (Swinton, 2007). Any theodicy that proposes that God granted humans free will and humans chose to do wrong in essence blames those who suffer. Thus, the goodness of the Divine is preserved, but evil and suffering are blamed on the very humans who suffer. It denies the realities of suffering that not all humans suffer equally. Those who engage in evil, often prosper and those who are innocent, suffer (Johnson, 2007; Swinton, 2007). The result of this oppressive explanation is to "silence the voice of the innocent victim and choke the cry of lament" (Swinton, 2007, p. 26).

Theodicies then become instruments of evil because they intensify the anguish of those who suffer (Swinton, 2007). In recent times we have seen examples of this theodicy. In the aftermath of the September 11 attacks on the United States and in the wake of the horrific hurricanes Katrina and Rita, well-known televangelists attributed these tragedies to God's wrath due to what they consider immoral behavior of American citizens. This explanation implies that only those who suffered are responsible for the existence of that immorality. Furthermore, it trivializes the suffering of those affected by these events. And, as we will discuss below, attributing mass traumas to the behavior of individuals poses the possibility that they will be targets for violence in an attempt to eradicate the cause of widespread evil. For example, when televangelists blame tragic events on homosexuality, those who are homosexual may be scapegoated. When politicians or religious leaders blame specific groups for the ills of society, members of those groups can be targets of hatred or violence. At times, attacks on specific individuals may be a result of intentional cruelty, whereas at other times attacks may be enacted by individuals who are deluded into believing they are acting on behalf of the greater good. In either event ascribing evil to those individuals may bring about more evil.

Suffering as a Spiritual Tool

Some propose that suffering is a spiritual tool designed to help individuals learn what they need to learn to fulfill their life's purpose. Suffering draws one toward the sacred and away from the secular (Bloomfield & Goldberg, 2003) and tests one's character and helps her develop her soul (Johnson, 2007). Hick's theodicy (as cited in Swinton, 2007, p. 18) states that suffering is what is needed for "soul-making"; therefore, evil is not evil, but a way of achieving goodness. These explanations not only romanticize suffering but lead to questions about the nature of the Divine. When a theory explains evil as God's attempt to help us grow, it denies that evil exists or trivializes it (Johnson, 2007; Swinton, 2007). Johnson (2007) points out that to suggest atrocities such as the Holocaust "formed souls in virtue belies the fact that it literally destroyed persons and left survivors with a lifetime of physical, psychological, and spiritual struggle" (p. 52). Evil can never be conceptualized as good, and Hick's theodicy does not alleviate the rampant suffering of those around the world, nor does it preserve the nature of the Divine. It presents a deity with such little imagination that the only means the deity has to teach us to grow is "through the apparently random infliction of tragedies and atrocities on men, women, and children" (Swinton, 2007, p. 21).

Other Explanations

Others explain that suffering and evil exist because God left the world imperfect and challenges humans to heal it and bring it to perfection. Some believe that the Divine is not omnipotent. Others propose that suffering is a wake-up call and like physical pain indicates that we need to change something in our lives (Bloomfield & Goldberg, 2003).

Social and Psychological Theories

From a secular perspective one may be less inclined to question the existence or the nature of the Divine, but wonder how humans can perpetrate such suffering on others. Secularly, the question is, "Why do people, sometimes good people, do such bad things?" Zimbardo, a psychologist at Stanford University, distinguishes between dispositional and situational factors as a cause for wrongdoing. The dispositional explanation posits that the cause of wrongdoing lies within the individual, who may be influenced by psychological risk factors or genetics. The situational perspective focuses on external factors that lead to one's wrongdoing. According to this perspective under certain circumstances anyone is capable of engaging in wrongdoing, including violence (Zimbardo, 2004).

Zimbardo (2004) points out that the dispositional perspective can be an instrument in the perpetration of unspeakable evil. For example, as stated earlier, the goal of the Inquisition was to eliminate evil. However, individuals within the Catholic Church came to see witches as the intermediary for the devil (the personification of evil). To eliminate evil, one had to eliminate the source; thus the dispositional perspective allowed them a vehicle to achieve their goal, that is, blame the larger problem on specific individuals. Those who were marginalized, such as widows, the disabled, or those who were not attractive, were identified as witches and hunted with a vengeance. "The phenomenon of the Inquisition exemplifies the notion of simplifying the complex problem of widespread evil by identifying *individuals* who might be the guilty parties and then making them 'pay' for their evil deeds" (italics in the original) (Zimbardo, 2004, p. 23).

Situational factors that may lead to extreme wrongdoing include being given a reasonable justification for the action. For example, one may be led to believe violence is necessary to bring about a greater good. The use of euphemisms, minimizing negative consequences, and dehumanizing the victim all increase the likelihood that one will engage in reprehensible behavior (Bandura, as cited in Zimbardo, 2004, p. 31) (Zimbardo, 2004, 2007). When one blames the individual (dispositional perspective), one is able to distance himself from the possibility that he would engage in similar wrongdoing. The situational perspective, however, reminds us that "the barrier between good and evil is permeable and nebulous" (Zimbardo, 2007, p. 3) and not "an unbridgeable chasm" (Zimbardo, 2007, p. 6). Attributing the cause of evil to individual factors, such as psychopathology, ignores the reality that ordinary people at times engage in horrific behaviors (Swinton, 2007; Zimbardo, 2004).

Mass Evil

The same mechanism is used in war and genocide. A group of people is identified as the "enemy." Through stereotypes the enemy is dehumanized and depicted as worthless and as a threat to the ideals and values cherished by those who engage in violence against them. This very deliberate process of propaganda allows those who go to war to engage in killing and other atrocities against another group of human beings. To remove the threat, elimination of the enemy is justified. Thus, when we ignore the political, economic, and social factors we have an incomplete picture of what causes people to engage in perpetrating human suffering on others (Zimbardo, 2007). Zimbardo's (2004, 2007) theory fits well with our social work perspective of viewing behavior as the intersection of individual and environmental factors.

THE SHADOW

The Jungian concept of the shadow adds to our understanding of evil and why individuals or groups engage in intentional harm to others. According to Jung, we are complex beings and not always aware of all aspects of ourselves (Hollis, 2007). The shadow is made up of feelings, attitudes, and traits we disown and project onto others. Through this process the unwanted aspects appear to be external or "out there" instead of internal (Zweig & Abrams, 1991). This dark (shadow) side of individuals can manifest as evil (Faiver et al., 2001).

The shadow evolves naturally when as young children we learn which thoughts, feelings, and attitudes are acceptable to those in authority and which are not (Zweig & Abrams, 1991). Those that are not become those aspects that are disowned and projected onto others in order to control them. Usually, it is those aspects of ourselves that we find most repugnant that are disowned and projected (Faiver et al., 2001; Hollis, 2007; Surya Das, 1999; Zweig & Abrams, 1991). Through this unconscious process one is able to maintain a self-image of a person who does not have those unwanted traits. Thus, "the shadow is the underbelly of our bright public personas" (Surya Das, 1999, p. 64).

Although the shadow is the repository of unwanted aspects of the self, it is not evil in and of itself, but it may enable individuals to engage in evil behavior (Hollis, 2007; Zweig & Abrams, 1991). Because this process (disowning and projecting) is unconscious, we believe and act as if the unwanted trait is outside us and we may attempt to control the threat by engaging in questionable acts. We tend to despise in others what we have disowned in ourselves. This makes them potential targets for disdain, anger, and even violence (Faiver et al., 2001; Hollis, 2007). Those traits in others that trigger strong reactions within us are often a clue to our own disowned and projected thoughts, feelings, and behaviors (Surya Das, 1999). Hollis (2007) gives the example of the overly zealous religious person who spends excessive energy on a convert because of his own unacknowledged doubts. All aspects of the shadow, however, are not negative. We are equally capable of disowning positive aspects of ourselves, which we then admire in others. When we become conscious of them and access them, they aid our healing and journey to wholeness (Hollis, 2007, p. 9).

The Collective Shadow

Along with personal or individual shadows, there are collective shadows that operate within our social systems, including political and religious systems. The collective shadow is the dark side of our culture and like the personal shadow contains those unwanted aspects of our cultural group that are then projected onto other groups or nations (Hollis, 2007).

We see the results of the collective shadow in the Holocaust, the Rwandan genocides, racism, discrimination, homophobia, and other forms of irrational hatred. Along with our personal shadow, we each to varying degrees participate in the collective shadow (Hollis, 2007). Through the process of disowning unwanted aspects of our collective selves and projecting them onto other groups or nations, we are able to cast them in the role of "enemy" (Zweig & Abrams, 1991). We see them as inferior, less than human, and in some ways a threat to the rest of us. Similar to the point Zimbardo (2004, 2007) makes about the dangers of attributing wrongdoing to individual personalities, Zweig and Abrams (1991) remark that when nations project their collective shadow onto specific groups or other nations, grave injustices and atrocities may be justified in the name of righteousness. "And none of us are more dangerous than the righteous who uncritically believe they are right, for they are the least capable of knowing the harm they bring with them into this world" (Hollis, 2007, p. 20).

Political leaders often flame the perceived threat for political reasons (Hollis, 2007). For example, Zimbardo (2004) cites the example of the tactics used by the George W. Bush Administration to garner support for the war in Iraq. Drawing on the nations' fear and anxiety after the attacks of September 11th, the Administration convinced the public that Iraq was a threat to U.S. security because it harbored weapons of mass destruction. In the absence of credible evidence, they were able to convince a frightened nation that war was justified.

Throughout history various groups have served as the target of the collective shadow (Hollis, 2007). For example, during the Inquisition, witches were targets, in Nazi Germany innocent Jews were imprisoned and executed, in the United States staunch conservatives target the gay and lesbian population. Ultraconservative religious individuals and atheists or agnostics often pose a threat to one another. Thus, each may trigger strong negative reactions, including hatred, in the other. When we project unwanted aspects of our collective selves onto other groups or nations, they become "*the carrier of our secret life, and for this we shall hate them, revile them, and destroy them, for they have committed the most heinous of offenses. They remind us of some aspects of ourselves we cannot bear to see*" (italics in the original) (Hollis, 2007, p. 18).

Dealing With the Shadow

To decrease the potential harm we can unconsciously cause because of the shadow, we must confront it, both our personal shadow and our collective shadow. It is not easy to face those elements that were originally disowned because they were unwanted. In working with clients around shadow issues, we need to understand the difficulty of this work for them. In addition to our compassion for clients doing this work, we need to help them learn self-compassion as they face and integrate disowned aspects of the self. Shadow elements present the primary obstacle to spiritual development (Surya Das, 1999). "Our shadows can either become our allies and teachers or our assailants and opponents" (Surya Das, 1999, p. 65). Understanding our collective shadows is key to social justice and world peace.

THE DARK NIGHT OF THE SOUL

In the midst of suffering, one implores the heavens with gut-wrenching questions, "Why?" "Why me?" "What is the meaning of this suffering?" When these questions are met with silence or the answers bring no comfort, one may lose her way. She may feel abandoned and alone, adrift in a stormy sea with no port in sight. St. John of the Cross referred to this period of anguish as a "dark night of the soul." One may be plunged in a dark void, the "existential vacuum," or experience the "abyss experience" unable to find meaning in one's suffering or one's life (Frankl, 1988, p. 83). That which once brought spiritual nourishment and sustenance may now feel dry, shriveled, and unfulfilling (Roth, 1999). The dark night of the soul crushes the spirit and cracks open the soul (Elkins, 1998). It initiates a "period of spiritual wandering and transformation…" (Roth, 1999, p. 65). Some of the pain that accompanies the dark night comes from facing the unknown. There are no assurances; there are no guarantees that one will emerge from the dark, renewed and stronger (Moore, 2004). Joyce Rupp (2000) uses the metaphor of a cave, where one wanders in the "dark, unknown nooks and crannies . . . ." (pp. 41–42). Like the dark night of the soul, "the 'cave' is about darkness, depression, silence, pain, waiting, not knowing, fear, struggle, obstacles, and all those things one wants to avoid in life" (Rupp, 2000, p. 42). The dark night is a spiritual crisis that shakes us to the core. It is a soul time. A time when one plumbs the internal depths in search of meaning and, perhaps amongst the ruins, one finds unbeknownst strengths and gifts.

Search for Meaning

One of the most painful aspects of trauma is the loss of meaningfulness. As humans we need to find meaning and purpose in life (Brewin & Power, 1997). We need to see that the world is coherent, it makes sense, and there is a relationship between who we are and what happens to us. Key to a sense of well-being is the belief that life is not a series of random acts (Janoff-Bulman & Frantz, 1997; Yalom, 1980). Amid the horrors of the concentration camp, Victor Frankl (1984) observed that those who found some meaning in the senseless suffering were more apt to survive. He concluded that meaning is essential to existence. Life's tragedies create "a crucible of meaning—a crucible in which meaning is tested and transformed, and from which it may perhaps emerge renewed" (Landsman, 2002, p. 13). However, when one is unable to find meaning, he is left floundering in the senselessness of his suffering (Johnson, 2007; Swinton, 2007).

Spirituality and Meaning

During traumas, one is challenged to find a way to cope, which requires more than logic (Phillips, 2007, p. xi). One needs to find a sense of coherence when she suddenly finds herself in "a universe that has no meaning" (Yalom, 1998, p. 173). Spirituality often helps individuals find meaning, but are those meanings resilient enough, "sturdy" enough to sustain them through life's tragedies? (Doka, 2002; Yalom, 1998, p. 173). Does suffering shatter one's spiritual beliefs, or does spirituality provide a framework to guide one through the uncharted waters of the dark night? "Simply put, being able to comprehend tragedy—to make it meaningful—probably constitutes the core of successful coping and adjustment" (Spilka, Hood, Hunsberger, & Gorsuch, 2003, p. 483).

Practice Behavior Example: *Recognize and manage personal values in a way that allows professional values to guide practice.*

Critical Thinking Question: The search for meaning is a critical aspect of trauma therapy. What clinical issues arise during therapy with this population? How can we assist clients in this search without imposing our own values and beliefs on them?

Spirituality helps some endure their suffering and enables them to transcend the pain. Adversity may even strengthen their faith. But for others, life's traumas shatter their faith (Connor, Davidson, & Lee, 2003; Janoff-Bulman, 1992; Pargament, 1997). Some may assume a "simplistic view of religion or spirituality as a panacea for life's troubles" (Exline & Rose, 2005), but spiritual coping can have either a positive or adverse effect (Pargament, Ano, & Wachholtz, 2005). For example, if one concludes that he suffers because of Divine retribution, he most likely will cope negatively with his experience. And the belief that his suffering is a punishment adds an additional dimension to his anguish (Pargament, Ano, & Wachholtz, 2005). Theists, who question the existence of the Divine in response to trauma, may lose their faith when they most need it (Swinton, 2007). And the loss of faith during life's traumas may leave the individual without an anchor, shaken, and frightened (Cunningham, 2000).

Empirical Data on Spirituality and Trauma

There has been some empirical data on the association between spirituality and trauma. The findings on whether spirituality is shattered or enhanced from traumatic experiences is mixed and no definitive conclusions can be drawn from the existing data. In a community sample, Connor et al. (2003) found indications of higher spiritual belief associated with poorer outcomes in a sample of survivors of violent crime. Not surprisingly, researchers (Koenig, Pargament, & Nielsen, 1998; Pargament, Smith, Koenig, & Perez, 1998) found that those who used positive religious coping strategies had more favorable outcomes than those who used negative religious coping (e.g., saw the tragedy as God's punishment). In a study of survivors of childhood sexual abuse, Gall (2006) found that negative and positive forms of spiritual coping predicted survivors' current level of distress. In a study of African American women living in poverty, negative religious coping was associated with higher levels of posttraumatic stress disorder (Bradley, Schwartz, & Kaslow, 2005). Falsetti, Resick, and Davis (2003) found that those with posttraumatic stress disorder were more likely to report changes in their religious beliefs, becoming less religious, whereas Tix and Frazier (1998) found that religious coping was correlated with better psychological adjustment among those facing transplant surgery.

Resolution of Crises of Meaning

According to Doka (2002), one may resolve the spiritual crises that frequently accompany suffering in several ways. After a period of questioning and wrestling with these issues, she may reaffirm her previous belief system. For this individual, spiritual beliefs do sustain her and help her find a sense of coherence in her experiences. Others may abandon previously held beliefs, feeling they no longer make sense, but they are unable to find a suitable set of beliefs to replace them. For these individuals life no longer has meaning or purpose. This can be one of the most devastating and long-lasting consequences of trauma. Another possible outcome is to find an alternative spiritual belief system, and, finally, one may modify his belief system, expanding it to include the tragic. In this case, individuals are able to stretch their beliefs and develop a more resilient spirituality. Spiritual resiliency allows one to find meaning in life's most difficult moments (Doka, 2002).

SUFFERING AND SPIRITUAL GROWTH

"Responses to spiritual suffering can act as turning points, places in which faith can wither or bloom afresh" (Exline & Rose, 2005, p. 316). Although the dark night of the soul is excruciatingly painful, many come out the other side transformed (Exline & Rose, 2005; Paloutzian, 2005) and with strengths and blessings they could not have imagined. The first Noble Truth of Buddhism is that suffering is inevitable. The Buddha tells us that "life, by its nature, is difficult, flawed, and imperfect" (Surya Das, 1999, p. 77). Therapists try to "ease human suffering, accepting that they will never erase suffering from the human condition" (Faiver et al., 2001, p. 41). A natural response is to ask why, but the more important spiritual question is how one might use this dark night as a "catalyst" for personal and spiritual growth (Bloomfield & Goldberg, 2003, p. 132). In Buddhist thinking suffering is "a magical elixir" (Glaser, 2001, p. 132). It hones and shapes the soul, stretching us to be more. From unspeakable pain "the soul spins strands of gold and weaves a cloak of wisdom and depth" (Elkins, 1998, pp. 249–250).

This transformational power of suffering is reflected in several spiritual paths. For example, the Sufi mystic Rumi asks, "Till the bread is broken, how can it serve as food; till the grapes are crushed, how can they yield wine?" (as cited in Bloomfield & Goldberg, 2003, p. 131). In the Jewish mystical tradition, if one is to grow spiritually, one must learn to "navigate" the darkness (Frankel, 2003, p. 18). And just as creation emerged from darkness, those who suffer can emerge from the dark night and give "birth" to a new, more mature self (Frankel, 2003, p. 250). Christians believe suffering informed by grace is the "alchemy of the soul," which allows the pain to change one's imperfections (Bloomfield & Goldberg, 2003, p. 131). The main point of these perspectives is that by being cracked open from suffering, we discover grace and spiritual growth. Denying pain brings more suffering. "If, rather than hardening and shutting down, we allow ourselves to be softened by the force of suffering in our life, it will penetrate our heart and open a doorway to the wisdom and compassion within" (Glaser, 2001, p. 132).

It is important that we do not romanticize suffering. In spite of its potential for spiritual growth, no one welcomes it. No one wishes to suffer. Dark nights are always accompanied by anguish, fear, and confusion. "They are harsh, rugged paths to the sacred, full of jagged rocks that scar the heart forever" (Elkins, 1998, p. 249). But in the midst of suffering, one can choose to despair or use this unwanted pain for transformation and growth (Bloomfield & Goldberg, 2003; Elkins, 1998; Schimmel, 2002). Victor Frankl (as cited in Bloomfield & Goldberg, 2003), in his search for meaning amid the horrors of Auschwitz, states,

> In the last violent protest against the hopelessness of imminent death, I sensed my spirit piercing through the enveloping gloom. I felt it transcend that hopelessness, meaningless world, and from somewhere I heard a victorious "Yes" in answer to my question of the existence of an ultimate purpose. (p. 145)

Practice Behavior Example: *Help clients resolve problems.*

Critical Thinking Question: In the aftermath of suffering, some individuals discover newfound strengths. Discuss why some are able to transcend the traumas they face, whereas others are not. How can social workers remain empathic to clients' suffering and be supportive of their resilience?

Posttraumatic Growth Theory

The spiritual literature is full of references to the benefits of working through the unwanted dark nights, learning from them, and growing personally as well as spiritually. In similar fashion, posttraumatic growth theory proposes that after a period of mourning, many traumatized individuals are able to find a new sense of meaning and "rebuild a way of life that they experience as superior to their old one in important ways" (Tedeschi, Park, & Calhoun, 1998, p. 2). Thus, suffering becomes a "springboard" for transformation and growth (Tedeschi et al., 1998, p. 1).

TREATMENT

The questions we ask in the midst of suffering may not be rational or answerable, but they are understandable, perhaps even necessary (Bloomfield & Goldberg, 2003; Swinton, 2007). We may cry out in anguish, although the answer is often "a humbling silence" (Bloomfield & Goldberg, 2003). And, as mentioned above, our attempts to answer these questions trivialize suffering and often blame those who suffer for their plight. Instead of answers, we need to find ways to help clients develop "an ability to live with unanswered questions" (Swinton, 2007, p. 47). Our clients benefit more from practices that sustain them in the midst of their suffering than from "clever arguments" (Swinton, 2007, p. 47).

During the dark night and anguishing loss of meaning, our role is to witness the struggle (Doka, 2002, p. 52). "Bearing witness, thus, involves our capacity, both to clear our minds of preconceived notions and self-constructed stories and to be present for the range of possibilities that the client will present" (Bien, 2008, p. 127). When we work with suffering clients, it is a time for listening (Bloomfield & Goldberg, 2003). We need to accept that we cannot answer their existential or spiritual questions about suffering. The need to provide answers is ours, and when we attempt to answer our clients' questions, we leave them feeling isolated and abandoned. We need to find a way to stay with our anxiety and not knowing and be present (see chapter 3) to the client and his pain. Kornfield (2008) cites a Jungian analyst, "There is in life a vulnerability so extreme, a suffering so unspeakable, that it goes beyond words. In the face of such suffering all we can do is stand in witness, so no one need bear it alone" (p. 246). When we recognize the depth of pain clients encounter from the tragedies they endure, "recovery is nothing short of remarkable" (Janoff-Bulman, 2002, p. xii). From the abyss of meaninglessness, they find a way to endure, create new meaning, and continue on (Janoff-Bulman & Frantz, 1997). These new meanings are a tribute to the survivors' strengths and their ability to forge a new life reflecting hard-earned wisdom (Janoff-Bulman, 2002) shaped by the dark night.

TREATMENT TECHNIQUES

Many of the techniques described in chapter 5 (on intervention) are appropriate for our work with suffering clients. These include guided imagery, collage making, letter writing or empty chair techniques, and journal writing. However, keep in mind that being a witness to a client's pain is far more important that any technique. If you choose to use techniques, they should be chosen based on the stage of treatment and the presentation of symptoms associated with traumatic stress. For example, if the client is overwhelmed with memories, thoughts, or feelings about the event, techniques that help with containment are appropriate. If you use a guided meditation, you need to provide layers of safety, as described in chapter 5. Journal writing may include exercises about places where the client feels secure or people with whom he feels safe. If the client is having difficulty accessing his feelings about the trauma, exercises to help him contact those emotions may include letter writing to the perpetrator (if his trauma is interpersonal) or the empty chair technique. If you chose a guided meditation, after helping the client establish layers of safety, you may ask her to slowly begin to get in touch with her feelings about the trauma. This meditation should end with the reestablishment of safety. Because strong affect may be stirred up from this exercise, adequate time to process it is necessary. And finally, careful assessment of the client's ability and readiness to contact these painful feelings and memories is essential.

CONCLUSION

Throughout the life course, it is inevitable that individuals will suffer. When tragedy befalls people they may struggle with the meaning of life and the existence or nature of the Divine and question why there is suffering or evil in the world. We are challenged to assist clients through their dark night of the soul, knowing we can neither answer their questions nor erase their pain. However, as witnesses to their suffering, we provide a healing presence, which often aids our clients not only in enduring their suffering, but in helping them transcend the pain and grow both personally and spiritually. Like our clients, we are challenged by the same existential or spiritual issues when we face suffering in our own lives. Our own fear of suffering may prompt us to try to resolve the dilemma—rather than bear witness—for our clients. When we do this, we leave them feeling misunderstood and floundering alone in the midst of their turmoil.

Spirituality helps many individuals when they encounter some of life's most difficult events. For some, it helps them endure and at times transcend their suffering, becoming strengthened by adversity. But for others, the tragedies that lead to suffering lead to unanswered questions and a failure to find meaning not only in their suffering, but in their life. For some the dark night of the soul that accompanies the loss of meaning leads to transformation; for others, who are unable to transcend their experiences, it may lead to a permanent loss of meaning, hopelessness, and chronic depression.

PRACTICE TEST The following questions will test your knowledge of the content found within this chapter and help you prepare for the licensing exam by applying chapter content to practice. For more questions styled like the licensing exam, visit **MySocialWorkLab.com**

1. Patricia is an atheistic social worker who is treating John, a former Catholic who was sexually abused by a priest when he was a child. Patricia should

   a. reduce John's shame by discussing the prevalence of clergy abuse.

   b. support his strength in leaving his religion.

   c. encourage him to report the abuse to the police.

   d. carefully monitor her feelings about religion and abuse.

2. Paul, a practicing Christian, is working with Arle, who was recently diagnosed with cancer. Arle questions if there is a God. Paul should

   a. explore her concern and reassure her there's a God.

   b. bear witness to her doubts and help her talk about them.

   c. explain to her that her doubts are caused by her distress.

   d. share his past doubts and how he resolved them.

3. Anthony is a survivor of a traumatic childhood. As he faces his painful memories, he has difficulty managing his thoughts and feelings between sessions. The social worker should

   a. encourage him to use his journal to uncover memories.

   b. help him visualize his trauma to resolve it more quickly.

   c. help him visualize a place of safety.

   d. encourage him to read memoirs of other survivors.

4. Sarah, who was paralyzed in an automobile accident, asked her social worker, "why God allowed this to happen to her?" Her social worker should

   a. explain the accident report to her.

   b. explore her thoughts about why it happened.

   c. tell her she does not know why it happened.

   d. share the worker's belief that "we all invite experiences that help us grow spiritually."

1. Discuss the importance of being a reflective practitioner when traumatized clients raise questions about why suffering exists.

2. Discuss the ways in which clients may resolve a crisis of belief in the aftermath of a traumatic event.

SUCCEED WITH

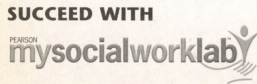

Visit **MySocialWorkLab** for more licensing exam test questions, and to access case studies, videos, and much more.

Marlena is a 33-year-old survivor of childhood physical and emotional abuse. She grew up in a rural area of the Northeast, the second oldest of six children. She was the oldest girl in the family. Her father was a minister, greatly loved and admired by his congregation. Her mother was sought after by congregants, especially on the area of marital and child-rearing issues. To the outside world, Marlena and her family appeared to be the "perfect Christian family." Both parents were outspoken advocates of corporal punishment, citing the Biblical phrase "spare the rod, spoil the child."

Although Marlena was a well-behaved child, who did well in school, she recalls frequent beatings for minor infractions. She also witnessed her siblings being beaten frequently. Strict discipline was enforced in the home, and the children were expected to be obedient, subservient, and quiet. They were expected to speak only when spoken to. Her parents were clear that they were a reflection of their father and his reputation was dependent on their good behavior. They were also admonished that what occurred in the home was to stay in the home.

Marlena's parents presented a picture of a loving, supportive couple, but their home life revealed a very different story. They argued frequently, and often violently. At times there were physical confrontations. In the midst of their battles it was not unusual for one of the children to be caught in the crossfire. One or both parents would lash out at the children for minor missteps, a spilled glass of milk by her youngest brother, a spot on her sister's blouse, or a misplaced item.

Marlena prayed that her parents would get along and that no one in the congregation would find out about the family's problems. She also prayed to "be a better girl" so she would not anger her parents or God. She prayed her siblings would also behave better. After a particularly violent argument between her parents, Marlena sought help from her teacher, a member of her father's congregation. The teacher was horrified at what she revealed and told her it was "wicked to lie about her parents." She told Marlena that she should pray that God forgive her for her lies. Marlena, who always had strong faith, became depressed and vacillated between questioning her beliefs and the conviction that she was "too wicked" and that was why her prayers were not answered.

As Marlena became an adolescent, she questioned her faith further. In college, she left the church and when asked about her beliefs stated she was an agnostic. For the past two years, Marlena has become aware of a void in her life. She has fond memories of the members of her congregation and cherishes the centrality of spirituality in the numerous holidays throughout the year. She longs to reclaim her "spiritual center." She believes that a formal religious affiliation is detrimental and has no interest in joining a church.

1. Discuss the effect Marlena's trauma has had on her spiritual development.

2. What interventions are appropriate for Marlena to deal with both her trauma and the effect her trauma had on her damaged spirituality?

3. What countertransference issues might arise for you when working with Marlena?

8

Death, Dying, and Grief

Advancing Core Competencies in This Chapter				
◼ Professional Identity	◼ Ethical Practice	✖ Critical Thinking	✖ Diversity in Practice	◼ Human Rights & Justice
◼ Research-Based Practice	◼ Human Behavior	◼ Policy Practice	◼ Practice Contexts	✖ Engage, Assess, Intervene, Evaluate

Yea, though I walk through the valley of the shadow of death, I will fear no evil.

PSALM 23

Humans are the only beings aware of their own mortality. Rabbi Kushner (2003) states, "It is not the fact of death, but the knowledge that we will one day die, that casts a shadow over our lives" (p. 86). Death is the "ultimate stranger" (Lesser, 1999, pp. 290–291). We do not know what to expect, when or how we will die, and what if any part of us survives. Thus, the prospect raises fear and anxiety, a state of existential angst (Spilka, Hood, Hunsberger, & Gorsuch, 2003). The fear of death is so widespread and common that most use a great deal of their life's energy to deny the reality (Yalom, 1998). It is unimaginable, unfathomable to most of us that at some future point we will cease to exist, at least in the form familiar to us. Does knowing our life will end make living absurd?

Faced with the reality that life is limited, humans struggle to find meaning and are challenged to live each day of their life to the fullest. For those who are young and healthy, death is a distant thought. Most are focused on pursuing educational, career, social, and life goals. But sooner than one expects, mid-life and advanced age come and, along with it, the unsettling thought that most likely more than half of one's life is completed. Illness and accidents threaten even the youngest of lives. And although the sages remind us that we are all in the process of dying, for those with terminal illness, the thought of dying may be a frequent companion. How does one find significance in life, knowing it will end? How does one continue to live with hope and dignity when dying is imminent? How does one go on after the loss of a loved one? In this chapter we will discuss the spiritual issues related to death, dying, and grief. Spirituality, an important resource in finding meaning, is a comfort for many in this final stage of life; for others, however, it may exacerbate death anxiety. In a variety of settings, especially hospices, hospitals, and nursing homes, social workers are confronted with clients who face imminent death. And in all settings, therapists may encounter clients who are grieving the loss of a loved one. Knowledge of how spirituality shapes the individual's experience of death, dying, and grief will enhance the quality of services to this vulnerable population.

DEATH AND DYING

"Death is a mystery that we must unravel." We are at a loss to make sense of it, yet it is a conundrum that taunts and challenges us (Spilka et al., 2003, p. 208). Kubler-Ross (1969), in her pioneering work on death and dying, found the denial of death in the American culture startling. She contrasts Americans' approach to death with her own experience. Having grown up in a rural European community, Dr. Ross states even young children were exposed to the realities of death and dying. In contrast, Americans are sheltered from death as their loved ones often die in nursing homes or hospitals. Children may be shielded from the impending death of loved ones by family members who wish to protect them or are too overwhelmed to include them in the process. Some hospitals do not allow visiting children, so children are not only excluded from the dying process but also denied the opportunity to say good-bye to loved ones. In the United States, often, professionals tend our sick and dying, and after death, with minimal involvement of family members, carry out funeral rituals. We certainly want the most advanced medical care for those we love and are often willing to pay the price of being excluded from the process. Likewise, those who are dying may be willing to endure isolation and a sterile environment in the hope that advanced medical care can prolong their lives or at least ease their pain and suffering.

It is not our intent to judge the "business" of dying, but to simply note that as a culture dying is not woven into the fabric of Americans' ordinary lives. It is an unwelcome, unexpected intruder. Being sheltered from death leaves us unprepared when we must face the death of a loved one or inevitably our own passing. It leaves those who are dying alone and frightened. Family members often do not know what to say to dying loved ones and are ill equipped to know what to do for them.

Fear of Death

"The fear of death plays a major role in our internal experience; it haunts as does nothing else; it rumbles continuously under the surface; it is a dark, unsettling presence at the rim of consciousness" (Yalom, 1998, pp. 183–184). Death reminds us of the transient nature of life, the impermanence of all things living (Rinpoche, 1994, as cited in Elkins, 1998, p. 253). Kornfield (2008) states that Westerners view death and dying as a failure and thus are loathed to reflect on it, whereas the Buddhists believe that, to face death, one learns wisdom and is motivated to live in the moment and appreciate each day.

Death and the Loss of Meaning

The realization that life is limited creates a sense of meaninglessness for some. Frankl (1986) observes that a frequent argument is that because life is finite there can be no meaning, for death ultimately destroys all. Yet, without meaning one faces the "inner void," the "existential vacuum," and encounters the "abyss-experience" (Frankl, 1988, p. 83). Individuals may keep busy with work or other distractions. They may view life as absurd and question the purpose of existence, suffering, and ultimately death. They may attempt to fill the void in their lives with material possessions and adventure, hoping to keep unsettling thoughts at bay. Yet, the challenging task for those who are dying is finding meaning in the face of imminent death (Nakashima, 2007, p. 46). The ultimate indignity in life is to die, believing one's life and death has no value (Sulmasy, 2002, as cited in Moss & Dobson, 2006, p. 286). If one cannot find meaning, one is likely to despair, bringing about mental anguish that may surpass even physical pain.

For some who previously found meaning and purpose in life, their belief system may be challenged when diagnosed with a life-threatening illness. Their belief and faith in a coherent world may be shattered. What once made sense and provided guidance has collapsed beneath them, and they are left staring into the existential abyss (Janoff-Bulman, 1992). The inability to find meaning in the face of suffering creates spiritual pain (Doka, 1993a).

Meaningfulness and Death

Contrary to the idea that death takes away meaning in life, Frankl (1986) contends that the realization we will die gives life meaning. "Doesn't the final meaning of life, too, reveal itself, if ever at all, only at its end, on the verge of death?" (Frankl, 2000, p. 143). Wrestling with impermanence helps us determine what is significant, establish priorities, and appreciate each moment we are alive (Frankl, 1986; Rinpoche, 1994, as cited in Elkins, 1998). If life were infinite, we might postpone living indefinitely. There would be no consequences to the failure to develop to our fullest capabilities. But by realizing that life is time limited, "we are under the imperative of utilizing our lifetimes to the utmost . . ." (Frankl, 1986, p. 64).

Drawing on the work of Heidegger, Yalom (1998) remarks that death awareness moves us from complacency to active involvement in life and provides the "catalyst" to live more authentically (pp. 185–186). Without the knowledge of death, life is less intense, less poignant (Yalom, 1998). It is not the length of one's lifetime that matters but rather the quality (Frankl, 1986). The challenge becomes learning to live fully with the time we have. The Buddha advises that reflecting on death reminds us to wake up (Fox, 2000). If we live life well, we most likely will die well and "learning to die well, is to learn to live well" (Yalom, 1998, p. 185). Dying does not diminish the life one has led. "Even when a torch goes out, its light has had meaning" (Frankl, 1986, p. 67).

From his work with cancer patients, Yalom (1998, p. 190) observes several themes. As a result of their terminal illness, patients are able to adjust their life priorities and de-emphasize the trivial. There is a sense of authenticity and freedom to engage in what is important to them, rather than feeling pressured to spend time on the trivial. Patients live more fully in the immediate moment rather than postpone life. There is an increased appreciation for life, including an awareness of the beauty of nature. They communicate more authentically, value their time with loved ones, and are more willing to take risks, not allowing fear to impede them.

Spirituality, Meaning, and Death

Questions about life's meaning and purpose and the reasons for death are spiritual questions (Doka, 1993a), and historically, spirituality and religion have dominated the way we understand death and dying (Spilka et al., 2003). Spirituality provides a way for individuals to "search for significance in the face of stressful life situations" and to negotiate those times in life when one has little or no control (Pargament, 2005, p. 217). It gives meaning to suffering and death, addresses concerns about the afterlife (Puchalski, 2008), and provides a counterbalance to hopelessness (Friedemann, Mouch, & Racey, 2002). Spirituality helps humans to find meaning in what does "not seem to be intrinsically reasonable" (Morgan, 1993, p. 6). Regardless of whether individuals engage in religious practices, spiritual beliefs contain impor-

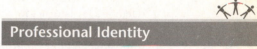

Professional Identity

Practice Behavior Example: *Attend to professional roles and boundaries.*

Critical Thinking Question: Discuss the role of spirituality in shaping an individual's understanding of death. What clinical issues may arise in this area? Address the possibility of the therapist's countertransference when the client's spiritual views about death differ from those of the therapist.

tant statements about life and death (Walsh et al., 2002, as cited in Kristjanson, 2006) and in the face of imminent death they become "particularly palpable" (Kristjanson, 2006, p. 194).

Empirical Evidence Related to Spirituality and Dying

In a study of 14 Australian hospice patients, McGrath (2003) explored the role of religious and spiritual beliefs. In the face of life-threatening illness, would participants embrace religion? A small number reported that religion was important to them prior to their diagnosis and that their illness strengthened their beliefs. However, some others, who had had religious beliefs, turned away from religion because of their illness. The majority did not turn to religion in the face of imminent death, but instead relied on broader spiritual beliefs. Often these were an eclectic mix of beliefs from several spiritual traditions. Spirituality was actualized by a connection to nature and significant others, a focus on the here and now, along with a sense of wonder and the mystical.

Nakashima (2007) studied 16 hospice patients who reported psychosocial and spiritual well-being. All were aware that they were dying and reported an absence of fear in the face of death. All indicated that it was their relationship to God or their faith that "gave them inner strength in confronting their mortality" (p. 49). Their belief that there is a God, who provides Divine guidance, allowed them to feel there was order to the universe and meaning in their dying. Levin (2002) studied the quality of one's relationship with God and its impact on distress. He concluded that those who perceived themselves to be in a loving relationship with the Divine experienced less psychological distress.

McCain, Rosenfeld, and Breithart (2002, as cited in Koenig, 2005, pp. 104–105) studied 160 terminally ill cancer patients with less than three months to live. Spiritual well-being lessened their sense of hopelessness, desire to hasten death, or thoughts of suicide. They concluded that spiritual well-being might protect dying persons from end-of-life despair.

Spirituality and the Afterlife

Those facing imminent death may ponder whether there is existence beyond the grave. The world's spiritual traditions speak to this concern; however, beliefs about the afterlife vary. Nevertheless, in spite of variations, most emphasize the immortality of the soul, which gives death significance and reduces death anxiety (Rosen, 2008; Spilka et al., 2003, p. 208). From a spiritual perspective, dying is a "sacred art" (Kramer, 1988, p. 2) and death is a transformation; the passage from earthly life to another form of life (Fox, 2000; Kramer, 1988). Our bodies may die, but our spirits live on. In Nakashima's (2007) study of hospice patients, there was a strong belief in some type of afterlife. For participants who were Christian, there was a belief in salvation, whereas for participants who were influenced by Eastern philosophy, there was a belief in karma and reincarnation. In all there was a remarkable lack of fear and a sense of hopefulness about their future. A sense of surrender was accompanied by a feeling of peace and trust.

Sulmasy (2002, as cited in Moss & Dobson, 2006, p. 285) states that any individual who seeks the ultimate meaning in life is a spiritual person. Some may not subscribe to any formal spiritual tradition, but may seek meaning through secular humanistic movements (Puchalski, 2008). When faced with the possibility of nonexistence, clients with no formal belief system may find meaning in reviewing how they used their time on earth and the legacy they will leave behind; this may be their children, those whose lives they touched, or their accomplishments. They may be comforted by the thought they will continue to live in the memories of those they loved (Doka, 1993a).

Frankl (2000) states that humans seek some "ultimate meaning," a meaning of the universe as a whole, or at least of their own lives. Irion (1993) discusses how even individuals who do not adhere to the beliefs of the world's great spiritual traditions seek ways to find meaning in the face of death. His description of secularists fits the broader definition of *spiritual* rather than *religious*. He cautions that it is a mistake to assume that these individuals are unable to find a sense of significance in their dying. They use a different language to talk about their beliefs than the Judeo-Christian language that dominates Western culture. Therapists working with such clients need to be sensitively attuned to their expressions of the spiritual, such as a connection to the beauty of nature (Irion, 1993) and may need to find creative ways to connect them with that which brings them peace. For example, if a client finds a sense of spirituality through nature and he is physically strong enough, you might consider having a session outdoors. If that is not possible perhaps there is a window with a view of the sunset or sunrise. And if none of these is viable, therapists can bring something from nature to the client, for example, flowers, a plant, or even a picture of the ocean. This may be as important for the spiritual client as sacred rituals are for religious clients. Responding to nontraditional needs not only reflects the therapist's respect for the client but also demonstrates the therapist's ability to be attuned to the client.

Ethical Practice

Practice Behavior Example: Apply strategies of ethical reasoning to arrive at principled decisions.

Critical Thinking Question: When working with dying clients the issue of an afterlife may arise. Discuss the role of therapists in addressing this concern. When is it appropriate to refer clients to clergypersons from their spiritual tradition? Discuss how you would address this issue with clients.

Spirituality and Death Anxiety

Although spirituality brings a sense of meaning to one's suffering and beliefs about the afterlife are a source of solace and comfort for many, for others it may exacerbate death anxiety. Murray, Kendall, Boyd, Worth, and Benton (2004) indicate that both initial diagnosis of terminal illness and the final stages of the dying process challenge one's spirituality. Additionally, some spiritual beliefs may be a source of anxiety (Doka, 1993a). For example, some individuals may feel abandoned by God or fear punishment in the afterlife; thus, spirituality may exacerbate the fear of dying (Moss & Dobson, 2006, p. 288). Unfinished business, especially the need for reconciliation with God or family members, may increase anxiety and guilt feelings.

Culture and Dying

Spirituality is shaped by one's culture. In fact, differences within spiritual traditions may best be explained by cultural influences. When working with diverse clients, therapists must understand how different cultures interpret death, dying, and grieving. However, when therapists approach each client with a sense of mystery and allow him to teach them, they honor the individual cultural expressions within groups (see also chapter 4).

For clients who are not part of the mainstream culture, we as therapists may need to use creativity to fulfill important cultural norms and still adhere to the restrictions of agencies, hospitals, or other settings. A hospice nurse, Julia was challenged in her work with a Native American princess who apparently died prior to the Julia's home visit. According to the princess's tribal tradition, only another member of royalty can touch the deceased body of a princess. Julia was required by state law to listen for the absence of a heartbeat before making a death pronouncement. She resolved the dilemma by asking a family member to hold the stethoscope to the princess's chest and then listened for her heartbeat. This is a beautiful example of cultural sensitivity. Julia was able to fulfill state requirements and also respect her client's cultural and spiritual norms. By Julia's thinking outside the box, the grieving family was able to draw comfort that an important dictum of their culture was adhered to.

Similar dilemmas may arise in our work with families who immigrated to the United States, when we are not able to follow certain rituals important to those who are dying or grieving. When possible, we need to advocate that their traditions be respected. When not possible we may need to find a symbolic way for them to fulfill their traditions or at least validate the importance of their rituals to them and acknowledge their feelings.

The Dying Process

Kubler-Ross (1969) outlined stages of the dying process, which scholars later adapted to the grieving process. In chapter 4 and later in this chapter we critique stage theories. An important criticism is the implication that there is a universal response to the dying process. Parkes (2002) indicates that each individual is unique and will deal with the dying process in his or her own way. And although he agrees with the criticisms of stage theories, he remarks that there is some value in them because they give us a sense of that process. Although family members may journey through a similar process, it is important that we do not assume they are simultaneously experiencing similar reactions.

In brief, the usual reactions to the end stages of illness are denial and isolation, anger, bargaining, depression, and acceptance (Kubler-Ross, 1969). In light of a terminal diagnosis, the usual response is disbelief. Clients may remark, "This cannot possibly be happening," "There must be some mistake." This defense is temporary and as the numb-ness and shock wear off, one is usually angry (Kubler-Ross, 1969). This stage is marked by questions such as "why me?" The question "Why?" can have many meanings. It can be a statement of guilt or rage. It may be a curse or a cry of anguish or helplessness. In working with individual clients, it is important to assess the meaning of the question for the particular client (Kauffman, 1993). Because the client may displace her anger on those around her, this is a difficult stage for family and professional staff. Her anger may be directed at the Divine (Kubler-Ross, 1969). Doka (1993a) points out that anger and rage at God can be a form of prayer. He refers to a woman he counseled who saw her ability to get angry with God as an indication of the strength of her relationship with God. For others, anger at God causes fear and anxiety. Client anger often subsides if family mem-bers and professionals use empathy and try to understand the situation from the client's perspective (Kubler-Ross, 1969). This allows them to "hear" what lies beyond the anger and respond with respect.

As the anger abates, the client may engage in "bargaining," making promises, (usually to God) in exchange for a cure. Clients may keep these promises private. When bargain-ing does not work, the client most often becomes aware of the extent of his impending losses, and becomes depressed. If the dying person is able to work through these stages, he is often able to accept the inevitable. Acceptance does not mean he is happy about his circumstances, but he achieves a sense of peace (Kubler-Ross, 1969). Dr. Remen (as cited in Mallon, 2008, p. 8) disagrees that acceptance is the final stage of the process. She be-lieves that gratitude and wisdom form the final stage of emotional healing for those who are dying.

SPIRITUAL TREATMENT FOR THE DYING CLIENT

Spiritual care is an essential aspect of the holistic care of the dying (Braun & Zir, 2001; Chochinov & Cann, 2005; Miller et al., 2005; Moss & Dobson, 2006; Murray et al., 2004; Puchalski, 2008; Steinhauser et al., 2000). In fact, some believe that spiritual care is as important as medical care (Kearney & Mount, 2000, as cited in Moss & Dobson, 2006, p. 286; Miller et al., 2005; Steinhauser et al., 2000) and omitting it compromises the quality of treatment (Moss & Dobson, 2006). Clients may be reluctant to express spiritual needs as they want to shelter family members and appear brave in their interactions with pro-fessionals. They may believe that professionals are too busy to discuss spiritual issues, but may welcome the opportunity to discuss if it is presented (Murray et al., 2004). Meaning-ful spiritual conversations can take place only within the context of a caring therapeutic relationship (Friedemann et al., 2002).

Assessment and the Dying Client

One should not assume that including spirituality in the treatment of the dying is wel-comed or appropriate (Moss & Dobson, 2006). Careful assessment is needed to under-stand if the client wishes to include it in his treatment and if he wishes to discuss this with his social worker, clergyperson, or both. In the face of distress, therapists do not need to solve all of the client's spiritual dilemmas, "but rather [need] to create an environment to nurture the patient's exploration whenever possible" (O'Connor, 1993, p. 136).

Margaret, an 84-year-old Catholic, was dying from cancer. She had been alienated from her church for over 40 years. In her talks with the social worker she indicated that she had been thinking lately about how in the past her faith sustained her and brought her comfort. She indicated that she longed to be reconciled with both God and her church, but she was afraid. After several discussions she agreed that she would like to talk to a priest, and the social worker made arrangements for one to meet with her. This brought Margaret a sense of peace, and she indicated that she felt ready to die. She also indicated that without her previous discussion with the social worker, she would not have been ready to talk to her priest.

Spiritual Needs of the Dying

Derezotes (2006, p. 252) indicates that the knowledge that one is dying provides a "powerful opportunity for transformation." By helping the dying person to be fully in the moment, the therapist ensures that imminent death becomes her teacher (Derezotes, 2006). Spiritual needs that emerge in the final stage of life include the need to find meaning and purpose in one's suffering (Galek, Flannelly, Vane, & Galek, 2005; Moss & Dobson, 2006), make peace with one's past (Derezotes, 2006), resolve conflicts, and reconcile (with God and/or others) (Braun & Zir, 2001; Friedemann et al., 2002; Galek et al., 2005; Moss & Dobson, 2006). Some have a need for self or other forgiveness, along with releasing anger, guilt, shame, and fear (Derezotes, 2006; Galek et al., 2005). Some want to prepare for their death, which may include a need to write a will or plan their funeral. Many desire to spend time with significant others and to say good-bye to them (Galek et al., 2005; Steinhauser et al., 2000). Social workers can help connect dying clients to a community of significant others and draw on their spiritual tradition to help prepare them for death (Derezotes, 2006).

Compassionate Presence

Death is a mystery, and when we work with dying clients we must honor that mystery. We need to be able to sit in silence, to be a compassionate presence as they "grapple with the unknown" (Puchalski, 2008, p. 42). Listening is the most powerful intervention in the face of this mystery we call death. To be effective we must suspend agendas and bring an open mind and heart "bowing to their experience, without any judgment" (Kornfield, 2008, p. 376). The greatest care we may give is to be present to dying clients in the midst of their suffering "without the need to have answers" (Puchalski, 2008, p. 43). When we work with dying persons the emphasis of our work is not on cure but on healing. We assist them in moving "from the chaos often associated with illness and crisis to a place of groundedness and peace within that chaos" (Puchalski, 2008, p. 39). Acknowledgment of spiritual angst is itself a treatment intervention (Chochinov & Cann, 2005). If we are willing to listen and ask open-ended questions, many are able to open up and talk about their life and their dying (Murray et al., 2004).

TREATMENT TECHNIQUES FOR THE DYING CLIENT

Although listening compassionately is the most powerful intervention in working with the dying, there are several other techniques that may help facilitate the need of the dying person to find meaning in life and to help prepare her and her loved ones for her death. These include a life review, an exploration of her family history, viewing family photographs, and listening to family stories. Any of these can be used to open issues for exploration (Doka, 1993a).

The life review interview can be recorded on a CD and, when completed, written into a narrative and given to the client, who may share it with family members (LeFavi & Wessels, 2003). Drawing on the work of Chochinov et al. (2005), Kristjanson developed the client's narratives into a "generativity document," which was given to the client. Early data indicate that this intervention was very effective in helping to prepare the client and her family members for her death. Steinhauser et al. (2000) conducted several focus groups with dying clients. An interesting finding emerged. Participants indicated their need to contribute to others, which, in addition to spending time with them, included sharing insights. The works of both LeFavi and Wessels (2003) and Kristjanson (2006) provide creative ways to fulfill this need.

In addition, if dying clients are physically able and interested, some creative art techniques may be appropriate. Creative arts, especially the use of music, drawing, painting, or collage, may provide an opportunity for clients to relay their experiences without the use of language. Thus, creative arts may be especially useful when working with clients who are having difficulty verbally conveying their emotions. For further descriptions of creative art techniques see chapter 5.

GRIEF

Permanent loss is unfathomable, throwing those left behind by the death of a loved one into a state of chaos. Suddenly, the world lacks meaning and coherence. The bereaved may feel adrift in a sea of sorrow, wondering how they will endure, how they will go on with their life. Their loss creates a "hole in the structure of significance . . ." (Pargament, 1997, p. 240). The bereaved, like those dying, query the heavens for answers to why this happened. They wonder about an afterlife and if the spirit of their loved one continues while they struggle to redefine themselves in his or her absence (Neimeyer, 2007; Worden, 2009). They may feel helpless or powerless along with "deep pain and anguish" as they experience their loss "as irretrievable and irredeemable," fearing their distress and suffering may be unending (Attig, 2007, p. 36).

Attig (2007, p. 37) states that grief is both a "soul pain" and a "spiritual pain." He refers to soul as that which makes one feel at home in one's everyday existence. When one is grieving he feels bereft, unable to find his way "home" or back to the way life was prior to his loss. Spirit is the ability to soar, transcend, and overcome adversity. As one mourns, one is often dispirited, feels no joy, and is motivated to do little. Life becomes "drained of meaning" (Attig, 2007, p. 37).

The Grief Process

Historically, the process of grief has been conceptualized as a universal, stage-like progression from shock and denial to acceptance (Kubler-Ross, 1969), with tasks in each stage (Worden, 2009). These theories provided an "authoritative road map through the turbulent emotional terrain associated with acute loss and grief" (Neimeyer, 2007, p. 2).

There is little empirical evidence to support stage theories in the grieving process (Parkes, 2002), and in recent years a new zeitgeist has developed along with new paradigms for understanding the grief process. This new wave of scholars criticizes existing grief theories that emphasize a universal and predictable pattern to grief with a clear endpoint for resolution (Attig, 1996; Neimeyer, 2007). To conceptualize mourning that does not follow prescribed stages as pathological is inappropriate and fails to recognize the complexity of grief (Attig, 2007; Neimeyer, 2007). Traditional theories do not make room for unique, individualistic, or idiosyncratic manifestations of grief. "Each person will grieve in their own way and their own time" (Parkes, 2002, p. 380). Spiritual and cultural beliefs shape mourners' reactions (Mallon, 2008). Rather than see reactions as an indication of pathology, new theories view them as significant indicators of the bereaved individual's struggle to adjust to a world in which the deceased is no longer present.

The Dual Process Model

As an alternative to stage theories, Stoebe and Schut (2007) propose a dual process model. To resolve grief, mourners oscillate between confronting and avoiding the reality of their loss. In *loss-oriented coping*, the bereaved makes adjustments to the loss (e.g., missing the person, expressing grief). In *restoration-oriented coping*, the bereaved learns new tasks and negotiates a new identity in the absence of the deceased. It is not possible to work on both tasks simultaneously; grieving individuals oscillate between the two foci (Stoebe & Schut, 2007). The dual process model fits well with our metaphor of the labyrinth walk. We can compare the oscillation of mourners between the two foci to the person winding first away from the center, then toward the center, and away again as one walks the circuitous path of the labyrinth.

The Search for Meaning in the Grieving Process

The ability to find meaning is essential to human existence (Park, 2005). Thus, the central task in mourning is the reconstruction of meaning for the bereaved in the face of their loss (Attig, 2007; Neimeyer, 2007; Worden, 2009). Finding meaning buffers intense grief (Ulmer, Range, & Silver, 1991; Schwartzberg & Janoff-Bulman, 1991), and if one is not able to find a sense of meaning, resolution of grief is unlikely.

Humans coauthor "their life stories, struggling to compose a meaningful account of the important events of their lives and revising, editing, or even dramatically rewriting these when the presuppositions that sustain these accounts are challenged by unanticipated or incongruous events" (Neimeyer, 2007, p. 263). In the wake of loss, the bereaved search to find new meaning in their changed personal world. Life patterns are disrupted, and the bereaved need to relearn "*how to be and act in the world*" (italics in the original) without the loved one (Attig, 2007, p. 41; Worden, 2009). This may include learning new roles and carrying out tasks once performed by the deceased.

Spirituality and the Bereaved

Spirituality may be an essential part of reconstructing one's worldview in the aftermath of loss (Neimeyer, 2007; Worden, 2009). Spiritual traditions have a dominant role in bringing meaning to death and dying, as well as the suffering that accompanies grief. Beliefs about the afterlife and immortality of the soul bring solace to many. A 48-year-old Muslim woman was bereft when her father died suddenly from a heart attack. She drew comfort from the hope that as a devout Muslim her father would ultimately be rewarded in the afterlife.

Death of a loved one may create a crisis of faith for those left behind. In the face of sudden, violent, or untimely death, mourners may question the existence or nature of the Divine (Doka, 1993b). This may leave the bereaved dealing with a dual loss, both of his loved one and his belief system. His faith may fail him when he most needs it (Swinton, 2007). Positive spiritual beliefs about the afterlife may bring comfort to mourners; however, negative beliefs may exacerbate grief. For example, if one perceives her loss as Divine retribution or fears her loved one will be punished in the afterlife, spirituality may impede the healing process (Doka, 1993b).

Spirituality may impede the expression of grief for some. Some mourners may believe that expressions of grief indicate a lack of or loss of faith.

> Faith alone rarely gives full-enduring comfort in the face of the reality of the loss. For many, the solace they hoped to find in their religious tradition is not there. Doubts that might have been intellectual before became existential for some. (Cullinan, 1993, p. 203)

If is helpful to determine if there have been negative changes in the person's spiritual beliefs or activities since the loved one's death (Doka, 1993b). "Perhaps even more important than the actual beliefs, or even religiosity of the given individual, is the certainty of their belief and faith themes around which people organize beliefs" (Doka, 1993b, p. 191).

Suicide and the Significant Other's Search for Meaning

When a loved one commits suicide, the search for meaning is usually more challenging (Mallon, 2008). Along with the usual grief, family and friends are at a loss to make sense of this unexpected tragedy. A 40-year-old businessman sought therapy to deal with the suicide of his younger sister. In his quest to find some sense of why his sister would kill herself, he commented that he hoped when the autopsy results came back he would learn that his sister had had terminal cancer. Upon exploration, he was able to say that a diagnosis of terminal cancer would mean he was going to lose his sister anyway and suicide spared her from a slow, painful death.

As indicated in chapter 7, challenges to one's belief system may be resolved in numerous ways (Doka, 2002). As a result of adversity, one's spirituality may mature and allow room for the complexities and complications of life, including the tragic. Others may, after a period of questioning, return to their previous belief system or search for and find an alternative spiritual tradition. The most painful resolution is when one's belief system is irrevocably shattered (Doka, 1993b, 2002). If one is unable to establish a new sense of meaning, resolution of grief is unlikely. Worden (2009) states most are able to reestablish some sense of meaning in the world, albeit it may differ from his worldview prior to the event.

Worden (2009) states sometimes it is impossible to find meaning in the usual sense of the word. However, some of these individuals find political or philanthropic causes to commit to in order to bring some sense to what appears senseless. For example, they may volunteer for a foundation dedicated to working with individuals who share the same diagnosis as did the deceased. Some who lost loved ones in drunk driving accidents may find meaning in joining an organization such as Mothers Against Drunk Driving. Working to provide a better world for others in memory of the loved one brings some meaning to their loss.

Funeral Rituals

Funerals, a ritual to mark the loved one's transition from life, are designed to facilitate grieving. As a public ritual, they provide the opportunity to remember the deceased and allow mourners to grieve within a supportive community (Mallon, 2008; Worden, 2009). Funerals "are a kind of punctuation in the life journey to show that something highly significant has occurred" (Mallon, 2008, p. 85). Although their purpose is to bring solace to mourners, funerals can be a source of distress (Doka, 1993b). For example, if the funeral is used by clergypersons to condemn a particular lifestyle such as drug use or homosexuality, mourners are more likely to experience anguish than comfort.

Doka (1993b) recommends that family members participate in and make personal funeral rites. This may include being a pallbearer, eulogizing the deceased, or displaying photographs or significant objects that symbolize the deceased's life. Religious institutions can either facilitate or impede family participation. Before my aunt and godmother died, she requested that I deliver the eulogy at her funeral. My family had quite a struggle with the clergy of her church, which had banned tributes by family members. Alternatively, at another funeral, family and friends were allotted time to pay tribute to the deceased. Some shared fond memories, or the favorite jokes of the deceased. One tribute included the recitation of the deceased's favorite poem, "Casey at the Bat." This service became a meaningful remembrance of the deceased and source of comfort to the mourners. Eulogies when delivered by family members or friends often provide a more personal perspective of the deceased. Clergypersons, who may or may not know the deceased personally, provide a spiritual perspective on the death. Both approaches are helpful to mourners processing their grief.

Ethical Practice

Practice Behavior Example: *Recognize and manage personal values in a way that allows professional values to guide practice.*

Critical Thinking Question: Social workers who treat grieving clients witness intense suffering and strong painful emotions. If you are working with bereaved clients who express anger at the Divine (God, Higher Power, Eternal Being), how would you address this issue? What potential countertransference issues might arise for you, and what steps would you take to ensure effective treatment?

Relinquishing Emotional Ties to the Deceased

Newer grief theories challenge the presumption that mourners must relinquish emotional ties to the deceased (Neimeyer, 2007). Theorists such as Worden (2009) posit that emotional ties must be broken for the mourner to resolve his grief. Stroebe (1992–1993, as cited in Mallon, 2008, p. 9) challenges this idea, stating there is little empirical evidence indicating this is necessary. Mallon (2008) remarks that the loved one can be remembered and those left behind can still invest in and enjoy life in his or her absence. Silverman and Nickman (1996, as cited in Mallon, 2008, p. 10) also argue that severing the emotional bond is not necessary to resolve the grief process and memories may comfort the bereaved (Hedtke & Winslade, 2004, as cited in Mallon, 2008, p. 10). Attig (2007) points out that the bereaved wish to continue to love the deceased, and similarly, the deceased would wish to be remembered after death. When the bereaved continue to love and remember the lost loved one, the deceased achieves "symbolic immortality" (Attig, 2007, p. 46). Bereaved family and friends may keep the deceased's memory alive by recounting stories, especially at family celebrations, beginning a scholarship in her name, or planting a tree in his memory. In this manner, the bereaved learns new ways to "reweave" the love of the deceased into the "complex fabric" of his life (Attig, 2007, p. 38). Another challenge to stage theories is the suggestion that there is a resolution stage in which one breaks ties with the deceased and achieves "closure"; rather, one may continue to have a symbolic bond with the deceased (Mallon, 2008, p. 10). Mallon (2008) quotes Attig (2000):

> We still hold the gifts they gave us, the values and meanings we found in their lives. We can still have them as we cherish their memories and treasure their legacies in our practical lives, souls and spirit. (p. 10)

TREATMENT TECHNIQUES FOR PROCESSING GRIEF

Like our work with dying clients, we need to be able to contain the grieving client's pain and anguish in the face of our inability to provide answers. If the central task of grieving is the reconstruction of one's life narrative, our role then is to assist in this complex process. Attig (1996) suggests that individuals seek counseling when they struggle with the loss of meaning. They seek a sacred place to tell and retell their loss narrative, depending on the therapist to bear witness to their pain without imposing simplistic assurances (Neimeyer, 2007, p. 264). Therapists often do not know what to say when faced with the deep pain and anguish of the bereaved. This requires that we become comfortable with not knowing and that we avoid platitudes. They are nothing more than attempts to quickly move clients out of their pain. They are rarely effective and usually result in the client shutting down his emotions. Platitudes include telling the client you know how she feels, suggesting that the pain will pass, "life is for the living," "he lived a long life," or "at least she is not suffering anymore" (Worden, 2009). When my father-in-law was dying, an overly zealous hospice volunteer commented to me that this was such a happy time because my father-in-law would soon be in heaven. I was horrified by his lack of sensitivity. Realizing that I found his remark offensive, he quickly backpedaled by saying, "Oh sad for us, but happy for him."

For some clients, grief is overwhelming, and they are unable to voice their feelings. Creative art techniques may help bypass the need for language and enable them to begin to express their grief through the medium of art (Mallon, 2008). The ultimate goal of these techniques is to help the client tell a coherent narrative of his grief experience, to enable him to tell his story. "In telling our stories we make a link to the larger stories that are found throughout the world and in doing so reduce our sense of isolation" (Mallon, 2008, p. 104).

Worden (2009) recommends that clients bring photographs of the deceased loved one to sessions. Therapists can ask about the events in the photos and the feelings attached to the event. This can lead to a discussion of the client's present feelings. Clients can be encouraged to keep a journal of their thoughts and feelings as they process their grief (Mallon, 2008; Worden, 2009). This provides a readily available outlet between sessions for clients to process thoughts and feelings as well as a record of their healing journey, which they may want to reflect on later. Clients can write letters to the deceased (Mallon, 2008; Worden, 2009). This is an especially effective technique in the case of sudden death, a missed opportunity to say good-bye, or unresolved issues with them. Therapists may suggest a ritual to accompany the letter writing experience. For example, the bereaved might decide to bury it near the grave of the loved one (Mallon, 2008). Collages, drawings, or paintings are another creative way to help clients express grief (Mallon, 2008) as they bypass the need for language. After the Pan Am jet was blown up over Lockerbie, Scotland, a Long Island mother of one of the victims created a beautiful sculpture that depicted her grief and anguish. This outlet allowed her to channel her grief and create a lasting tribute to her son.

Grieving family and friends may create a memory box or memory book (Mallon, 2008; Worden, 2009). It may include letters to or from the loved one, greeting cards sent or received, photographs, keepsakes, pieces of jewelry, or whatever the client feels would be helpful in remembering her loved one. Mallon (2008) also suggests planting a memory garden in honor of the deceased. This is especially appropriate when the deceased enjoyed nature, trees, or flowers. The continued beauty of life is symbolic of the lasting memory of the deceased in the hearts and minds of those who loved her.

For clients who are not interested in creative arts, bibliotherapy may be useful. Therapists can recommend either self-help books on the grieving process, fiction that captures the process, or memoirs of others' grief experiences. Before suggesting reading materials to clients, therapists should be familiar with them. They may also recommend that clients record reactions to the readings in their journal.

CONCLUSION

Working with dying or grieving clients is challenging for therapists. We are often at a loss when faced with the intense and painful emotions that accompany both processes. To work effectively with such clients, we need to be in touch with our own losses. What unresolved feelings of grief do we continue to carry? Our loss may be of a loved one to death, a significant relationship (romantic or otherwise), health, a job, an inability to have children, or even a loss of idealism. Whatever we grieve for, if unacknowledged, will impede our therapeutic work with dying and/or grieving clients.

In this chapter we outlined many issues that we may encounter in working with the dying or bereaved. We are particularly interested in the role of spirituality in our work, which may facilitate or impede both the dying or mourning process. Several techniques to facilitate our work with clients are included. Rather than see spirituality as helpful or an obstacle, we need to recognize the complexity of it in shaping the experiences of those who are dying or grieving. We need to understand to what extent and in what ways spiritual beliefs and activities help or harm clients during these difficult experiences (Pargament, 2002, as cited in Wortmann & Park, 2008, p. 728).

PRACTICE TEST

PRACTICE TEST The following questions will test your knowledge of the content found within this chapter and help you prepare for the licensing exam by applying chapter content to practice. For more questions styled like the licensing exam, visit **MySocialWorkLab.com**

1. Henry, an 84-year-old, is dying from Parkinson's disease. During his life spirituality was not important to him. As he faces the inevitability of his death he has become anxious about the possibility of an afterlife. As his social worker you should

   a. share positive beliefs about the afterlife.

   b. explore with him the appropriateness of a referral to a clergyperson.

   c. ask his family to share their beliefs with him.

   d. have a doctor discuss the expected length of time he has.

2. Kendra has been grieving for her grandmother who died six months ago. As Kendra's social worker, which of the following interventions would be appropriate?

   a. Refer her for a psychiatrist's evaluation for antidepressants.

   b. Ask her to make a memory book of her grandmother and use it in sessions.

   c. Gently suggest it is time for her to begin to move on.

   d. Explore underlying reasons for Kendra's grief.

3. Marilyn has begun to realize that the treatments she has been receiving for kidney cancer are not working. She has become depressed, sad, and angry as she faces the reality that she does not have much time remaining. As Marilyn's social worker you should

   a. try to help her find meaning in her death.

   b. refer her to an appropriate spiritual leader.

   c. create a compassionate presence for her as she grapples with the unknown.

   d. involve family members in helping her discuss her spiritual concerns.

4. Grace was having difficulty finding meaning in her life after her father died suddenly from heart failure. Which of the following would be the most appropriate intervention?

   a. Bear witness to her pain

   b. Point out to the importance of her spiritual beliefs in coping.

   c. Share your own beliefs to comfort her.

   d. Assure her she will eventually find new meaning in life.

1. Discuss the use of the life review technique with dying patients. For what types of clients would it be appropriate? In what ways can you involve family members?

2. Discuss the circumstances under which social workers, when working with dying clients, should involve or refer clients to clergypersons. Discuss the importance of self-awareness in whether referrals are appropriate or not.

SUCCEED WITH

Visit **MySocialWorkLab** for more licensing exam test questions, and to access case studies, videos, and much more.

Ralph, a 78-year-old Catholic, was shocked to learn that his wife Daniela was diagnosed with end-stage breast cancer with few treatment options. His wife decided to forego medical treatment and spend her final days with Ralph and their children doing the things she loved best. Although he was overwhelmed and upset, he acknowledged his wife's prerogative to refuse treatment that was unlikely to prolong her years and would most likely negatively impact the quality of her life. He was devastated by the thought of losing her but felt even more distressed that she would live her final days filled with treatments that would make her nauseous and exhausted. Ralph had always believed in God and occasionally went to church. His belief greatly influenced how he lived his life. He believed in fairness, kindness, and honesty in all his interactions with others. He felt a deep sense of gratitude for the blessings in his life. When Daniela was originally diagnosed, Ralph questioned God. Why should she suffer? Why should he lose her? But as the days went on and he accepted Daniela's decision to refuse treatment, Ralph realized he would probably never know why Daniela got cancer and looked to his faith for strength to help her through this time, rather than answers. Ralph tried to be strong in front of Daniela and not let her know about his grief. When they went on a surprise vacation to a lakeside community where they had spent many happy vacations, he was amazed at the sense of connection Daniela had to the lake and the surrounding area, which was abundant with autumn colors. As they reminisced and shared their favorite memories of previous vacations there, Ralph became overwhelmed and began to cry. Daniela cried along with him and expressed relief that he was finally able to share his feelings with her. She related her fears and concerns about herself, him, and their family.

After their return Daniela seemed "herself" for several weeks. Ralph began to think maybe the doctor's diagnosis had been wrong, but as the weeks passed, she became weaker. Ralph began to search for nontraditional treatments. He became angry and depressed when Daniela refused to consider them. One evening Daniela told him she called a local hospice program. He immediately felt a sense of despair, a belief that she had given up. She explained to him that this was how she wanted to do things. She did not want to die, but because she was going to, she wanted to be treated with dignity, to be as conscious as possible, to have her pain managed and to be with him and their family. She too had been doing some research, and the philosophy of hospice was what she wanted. She told him that a social worker from the program would be coming by in a few days to discuss the program.

Ralph had several sessions with the social worker. The social worker encouraged him to share his feelings with her. He was reluctant at first, but eventually talked about his anger that Daniela was dying and his anger with God. The social worker encouraged him to talk to his pastor, with whom he felt a strong connection. After meeting with him a few times, Ralph was more open with the social worker. He could not understand why Daniela was dying or imagine life without her. He expressed his fear that she was going to suffer. As he expressed more of his feelings, the social worker began to help him express his feelings to his wife. As he struggled to understand her choice to forego treatment, he also began to see her become more accepting of her impending death. She seemed peaceful and in very little pain. Although she frequently felt tired, she was alert when she was awake. She talked about her love for him and expressed gratitude to God for him. This enabled him to express his love and gratitude toward her. He grieved deeply after she died, but found a sense of strength drawn partially from the gifts she gave him in her final months and partly because of his deep belief in a loving God. Ralph continued to talk to the social worker for a few months after Daniela died. On what would have been their wedding anniversary, seven months after Daniela died, Ralph gathered his family at the lake and had a tree planted in Daniela's memory. Surrounded by the love of his children and grandchildren, in one of Daniela's favorite places, Ralph began to reconcile his sense of loss and sadness with acceptance. He stated to his son, "In this beautiful place, I am convinced that some day I will be with your mother again."

1. Discuss the impact Daniela's diagnosis and ultimate death had on Ralph's spirituality. As his reactions changed, how would you work with him?

2. Discuss the social worker's suggestion that Ralph speak with his pastor. Do you think this was appropriate? Why or why not? Do you think it was helpful? Why or why not?

9

When Religion and Spirituality Are Harmful

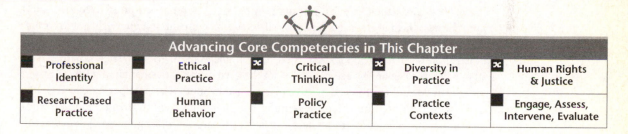

Advancing Core Competencies in This Chapter									
■	Professional Identity	■	Ethical Practice	✖	Critical Thinking	✖	Diversity in Practice	✖	Human Rights & Justice
■	Research-Based Practice	■	Human Behavior	■	Policy Practice	■	Practice Contexts	■	Engage, Assess, Intervene, Evaluate

"Religious ideologies and commitments are indisputably central factors in the escalation of violence and evil around the world" (Kimball, 2002, p. 4). Why is it that something that is beneficial to many becomes an instrument of harm and destruction in the hands of some? Religion and spirituality can be used to create excessive guilt and toxic shame. In the name of religion, abuse of women and children, hatred of those who are different, prejudice, bigotry, and even atrocities may be justified. Religion and spirituality intended for wholeness and holiness can be misused either consciously or unconsciously as instruments of control and fear, creating great harm.

Thus far, we have focused primarily on the benefits of spirituality, such as how it can help one find meaning, significance, and purpose in life. We have seen it as a healthy coping strategy. In this chapter, we will discuss the underbelly or shadow side of religion and spirituality, their potential for misuse, and the characteristics that may predispose them to cause potential harm.

In this text, we have attempted to distinguish religion and spirituality and when possible to focus on the latter. In this chapter, although we will address issues related to both, our primary focus will be on religion. Kimball (2002) has referred to religion as "the most powerful and pervasive force on earth." And though we recognize that religion has motivated and inspired many to strive for the betterment of themselves and the world, we must recognize the harm done in its name. "More wars have been waged, more people killed, and more evil perpetuated in the name of religion than any other institutional force in human history..." (Kimball, 2002, p. 1). Religion is uniquely poised to benefit or harm because of its power to shape meaning and provide answers to the most profound questions we have as human beings (Silberman, 2005a). It is imperative that we distinguish the destructive forms of religion and spirituality from those that are life affirming and authentic expressions of humans' search for meaning and connection (Kimball, 2002).

Religion, like other human institutions, can become corrupt and therefore needs a system of checks and balances. When a religion becomes destructive the structure no longer serves the purpose for which it was originally intended (Kimball, 2002). In other contexts, religion itself is not destructive, but some individuals distort it to serve their own purposes (Silberman, 2005a). It is not my intent here to denigrate religion or anyone's religious beliefs or practices, but it is essential to point out that in the hands of some, religion can be an instrument of harm.

IS RELIGION A DESTRUCTIVE FORCE?

Religion is a "double edged sword" that has been used for both peace and violence (Silberman, Higgins, & Dweck, 2005, p. 779). Through the ages, religion has "inspired individuals and communities of faith to transcend narrow self-interests in pursuit of higher values and truths" (Kimball, 2002, p. 1). It has been a salient factor in the lives of prominent individuals who worked endlessly to bring about social good, for example, Gandhi, Mother Theresa, and Martin Luther King, Jr. Religion has been a catalyst for the Civil Rights Movement in the United States, Solidarity in Poland, and the struggle to end apartheid in South Africa (Silberman, 2005a).

However, throughout history, religion has also been used to bring about destruction and harm. Some religious leaders and communities are willing to use violence in the name of "their god or convictions" (Kimball, 2002, p. 26). Examples include the Crusades; the Inquisition; witch hunts; and conflicts between the Catholics and Protestants in Ireland, the Hindus and Muslims in India, and the Jews and Muslims in the Middle East (Ellerbe, 1995; Hunsberger & Jackson, 2005; Silberman, 2005a). Clearly, throughout history religion has been both "hero" and "villain" (Silberman, 2005a, p. 530).

More recently, we see the shadow side of religion and spirituality in large-scale events that bring media attention, such as the Jonestown massacre; the September 11th attacks; religiously motivated genocides and ethnic cleansing; the bombing of abortion clinics; the murder of abortion doctors; parental refusal of medical treatment for their seriously ill children, attacks on gay, lesbian, bisexual, and transgendered individuals; and, in the privacy of some homes, the abuse of women and children justified by religious beliefs. It therefore behooves us to recognize that religion in the hands of misguided zealots can be a catalyst for unspeakable destruction and harm (Kimball, 2002).

Spiritual abuses may take place within traditional religious paths or alternative spiritual movements. When spiritual teachings and beliefs are rigid and followers are denied opportunities for growth, religion and spirituality become problematic (Kimball, 2002). Spiritual leaders may manipulate and control their congregants through the use of extreme fear and toxic shame. Spiritual beliefs may be used to blame those who are ill. Is there a difference between the Christian fundamentalist who believes that the gay population "deserves" AIDS and those in the New Age Movement, who rigidly adhere to the belief that one "creates her own reality" and thus she is blamed for getting cancer? In these contexts, religion and spirituality are instruments of suffering. In this chapter we recognize the awful truth "that spiritual beliefs and practices intended as doorways to wholeness can quickly become the gateway to hell" (Griffith & Griffith, 2002, p. 218).

RELIGION AND MEANING MAKING

To demonstrate how religion can be readily used for destructive purposes, let us focus on the relationship between religion and meaning making. Silberman (2005a) proposes that religion is a unique and comprehensive meaning system. It explains the entire history of the universe from its creation until the end of time. It gives meaning to one's individual life. Religion creates the lens through which we perceive what is sacred and what is not; it offers unique answers to the profound questions in life (Emmons, 2005; Pargament, Magyar-Russell, & Murray-Swank, 2005; Park, 2005). Thus, it can be used as a powerful instrument for creating either peace or violence (Silberman, 2005a).

COLLECTIVE MEANING SYSTEMS

Along with individual meaning systems, groups create collective meaning systems (Eidelson & Eidelson, 2003, as cited in Silberman, 2005b), which help to create a "shared reality" (Hardin & Higgins, 1996, as cited in Silberman, 2005a, p. 532) and a sense of shared conviction (Eidelson & Eidelson, 2003, as cited in Silberman, 2005a). Those with similar beliefs are part of the group (collective), and those who do not share these beliefs are excluded. Once developed, collective meanings rarely change and are viewed as the Truth (Eidelson & Eidelson, 2003, as cited in Silberman, 2005a; Silberman, 2005a). The values inherent in religious meaning systems may catalyze violence, prejudice, hatred, or hostility (Silberman, 2005a). These meaning systems may emphasize the "otherness" of those who are different or do not share the same beliefs (Martin, 2005; Silberman, 2005a). Thus, by designating what is sacred and what is not, religion can provide the lens through which one is seen as holy or evil, pious or sinful. It may determine who should be rewarded and who should be punished or shunned (Silberman, 2005a) and may leave those who are excluded as potential targets for violence, especially when their beliefs, values, or behavior are seen as threatening (Kimball, 2002; Silberman, 2005a). If we are to understand those who are different from us, we need to try to understand the world and events from the perspective of their meaning system.

WHAT GOES WRONG?

Why is religion, a source of meaning, hope, significance, peace, and joy for so many, a cause of distress for some and at times becomes a destructive force (Pargament et al., 2005)? To identify potentially abusive uses of religion, we focus on several characteristics that when present may create a context in which great harm may be done (Kimball, 2002).

Absolute Truth Claims

Each religion holds a set of authoritative beliefs, which serve as the foundation upon which the religion is based. They may derive from sacred texts, such as the Qur'an or Bible, or be initiated by a charismatic leader (Kimball, 2002). The belief that one's religion has the absolute and exclusive truth creates a mindset that can easily catalyze violence and other abuses (Allport, 1966, as cited in Hunsberger & Jackson, 2005; Kimball, 2002). Absolute truths set a clear boundary between those who believe and those who do not. The firm belief that one's worldview is the only one can lead to denigrating others' belief systems.

Doctrine of Election

The belief by a group that they have exclusive ownership of the Truth can be accompanied by the belief that they are among God's favored ones (doctrine of election). Schwartz (1997) proposes that the collective identity within monotheism (belief in one God) requires exclusive allegiance. Thus, one believes that one's God is the only true God, which highlights the thinking that God favors some and excludes others, posing the threat of violence toward those who are excluded. The elected may see others as "heathens" or "infidels, thus demonizing them" (Schwartz, 1997, p. xi).

Religion and Dehumanization

The likelihood of violence is greater when individuals or groups are demonized or seen as less than human. Using the concept of the collective shadow (see chapter 7), an entire group (nation, religion, or community) may disown unwanted aspects and project them onto others. Those who receive the projections may be viewed as the enemy, who may be despised for "possessing" certain traits (Zweig & Abrams, 1991). Thus, those who believe they exclusively own the Truth and are among God's favored may righteously justify punishing others if they engage in any behavior that is threatening to the collective (Hollis, 2007; Silberman, 2005a; Zweig & Abrams, 1991): Because God has rejected them, they are worthless and expendable (Zimbardo, 2007).

Gay marriages are viewed by some as a threat to Christian and family values. This can be used to sanction hate crimes against gays and lesbians, which is justified as necessary to preserve families, as well as religion. Some reframe violence and aggression as "holy wars" fought for the honor of God (Silberman, 2005a, pp. 536–537), so acts of violence are "religious battles" needed to enlighten those living in sin and to "bring truth and redemption . . ." (Selengut, 2003, as cited in Silberman, 2005a, p. 537).

Blind Obedience

"Authentic religion engages the intellect as people wrestle with the mystery of existence and the challenges of living in an imperfect world" (Kimball, 2002, p. 72). The demand for blind obedience limits intellectual freedom and requires that

Diversity in Practice

Practice Behavior Example: *Recognize the extent to which a culture's structures and values may oppress, marginalize, alienate, or create or enhance privilege and power.*

Critical Thinking Question: Suppose that you are working with a client who belongs to a spiritual community that believes they have exclusive ownership of the Truth and that those who are not part of the community are considered outsiders. How will you determine if this individual has the potential to use his or her beliefs in a destructive manner? What ethical obligation do you have to address this with him or her?

one not take responsibility for decisions but rely on religious leaders. There is often a zealous belief that one must relinquish his or her own integrity, uncritically accept the teachings of the collective, and blindly follow. This can easily become the "framework for violence and destruction" as members will blindly follow the orders of those in authority even if they are destructive (Kimball, 2002, p. 72).

FUNDAMENTALISM

"One of the most startling developments of the late twentieth century has been the emergence within every major religious tradition of a militant piety popularly known as 'fundamentalism' " (Armstrong, 2001, p. xi). The term *fundamentalism* varies by religion, and some have argued that the word is misleading. However, according to Armstrong (2001, 2002), it has become the best term to describe a particular pattern among religious groups, and it is difficult to come up with a more satisfactory term (Armstrong, 2002).

Altemeyer and Hunsberger (1992) define *fundamentalism* as

the belief that there is one set of religious teachings that clearly contains the fundamental, basic, intrinsic, essential, inerrant truth about humanity and deity; that this essential truth is fundamentally opposed by forces of evil which must be vigorously fought; that this truth must be followed today according to the fundamental, unchangeable practices of the past; and that those who believe and follow these fundamental teachings have a special relationship with the deity. (p. 118)

Armstrong (2001) states that, regardless of variations, all fundamentalist movements are "embattled forms of spirituality" that emerge in response to a perceived crisis. They view secularism as the antithesis of religion. "Fundamentalists do not regard this battle as a conventional political struggle, but experience it as a cosmic war between the forces of good and evil" (Armstrong, 2001, p. xiii). Altemeyer and Hunsberger (2005) view fundamentalism as an attitude toward one's beliefs, rather than a set of beliefs.

Fundamentalist beliefs have been used to justify violence, for example the September 11th attacks on the United States, the killing of abortion doctors, and even the overthrow of governments and assassinations of leaders (Armstrong, 2001). Fundamentalists are adamantly opposed to modernity, religious tolerance, multiculturalism, democracy, the separation of church and state, and free speech. They wish to establish the public role of religion and view secular pursuits as evil (Armstrong, 2001; Ruether, 2002). Fundamentalists view the world as divided into two sectors, those who are for and those who oppose God. The use of the tragedies of September 11th by Jerry Falwell and Pat Robertson to condemn secular behaviors and claim the attacks were punishment from an angry God is as much a distortion of religion as are the beliefs of the hijackers who attacked the United States that day (Armstrong, 2001).

Fundamentalists and Evangelicals

Not all conservatives are fundamentalists, nor are all evangelicals fundamentalists (Meyers, 2006). And though it is difficult to note the differences between fundamentalists and evangelicals, it is important to do so (Lovinger, 2005). Ammerman (1987, as cited in Lovinger, 2005) states that evangelicals are usually better integrated into mainstream society, better exposed to others' belief systems, and more willing to accommodate to the wider society. They do, however, believe that they are mandated to proselytize and convert others to their belief system (as cited in Lovinger, 2005, p. 339; Lovinger, 2005; Silberman, 2005a). Although historically fundamentalists have avoided contact with the larger society, more recently they are intersecting to further their political agenda (e.g., creationism, school prayer, censorship, opposition to abortion, and electing candidates who will represent their religious interests) (Lovinger, 2005, p. 338).

Fundamentalism and Women

A central feature of fundamentalism is the subordination of women. This is related to the literal interpretation of sacred texts, which originated within ancient patriarchal societies. Along with subjugation there is an element of misogyny embedded within fundamentalism (Reuther, 2002). The response of Westerners to the mistreatment of women in other parts of the world is to dismiss it in the name of cultural sensitivity. The Vatican, hoping to create a Muslim–Catholic front against birth control, abortion, diverse family constellations, and women's equality, "adopted rhetoric that pilloried Western feminists as assaulting the cultural traditions" of nonindustrialized nations of the world (Reuther, 2002, p. 5). Similar themes reverberate throughout fundamentalist Christian groups within the United States. Working mothers and sexually active single women are seen as the source of societal woes (Pollitt, 2002, pp. ix–xi).

RELIGION AND POLITICS

"The political and religious spheres are often tightly intertwined" and throughout history political leaders have used religion as a way to gain and maintain power (Donahue & Nielsen, 2005, p. 282) or to further their political agendas. The politicians' worldview, shaped by their religious meaning system, will likely influence their political policies and actions. It will affect whether they approach others (including other nations) in a peaceful or violent manner (Silberman, 2005a; Silberman et al., 2005). Religious meaning systems may also influence voting habits, so politicians may hesitate to support programs that are not in sync with the religious beliefs and moral values of their constituents (Silberman, 2005a).

Certainly, there are politicians who are authentically spiritual and closely identify with the beliefs and values of their particular religion. One would expect that religion would inform their opinions on important matters. However, as elected officials, they must uphold the Constitution of the United States, along with Supreme Court rulings and other laws of the land. Religious politicians have every right to support or oppose issues based on their beliefs as long as their religiosity does not lead to violations of the law. When motivated by their religious beliefs, politicians can violate the rights of others (including religious freedom and the right to no religion), abuse their political power, and misuse religion in a harmful manner. If they are honest in their campaigns about their beliefs and how those beliefs will affect their decisions when in office, the electorate can make an informed choice. The electorate may or may not like the election results, but at least they will know they were not consciously misled. Our concern in this section is not all religious politicians; it is those politicians and religious leaders who duplicitously use religion to advance a political agenda.

Separation of Church and State

Whatever happened to concerns about separation of Church and State? I remember during the Vietnam War, Daniel and Philip Berrigan, both Catholic priests, engaged in a series of illegal, but nonviolent actions to protest a war they believed was immoral. Because they were priests, some asked if their political activism violated the separation of church and state. Did they have the right as individuals to publically protest? Did they represent the Catholic Church because they were clergy? This example raises important questions. Can or should clergy preach about social issues such as poverty, injustice, oppression, discrimination, hatred, or racism? What if they preached to oppose gun control or to deny women's rights? Do clergy have a responsibility to use the pulpit to advance what they believe to be moral issues? When clergy partake in political or social action, do they act as private citizens or represent their religious institutions? Should clergy attempt to influence voting behavior? Are we as concerned now about separation of Church and State as we were in the 1960s? Should we be?

Clergy are strategically positioned to exert significant power (either directly or indirectly) with their congregants (Smidt, 2003). The Cooperative Clergy Research Project is designed to study the intersection of clergy and political activism (Guth et al., 2003). The research of these scholars indicates that ministers who are leaders in evangelical politics and who support political activism are likely to be conservative, members of Christian Right organizations, and motivated by a strong moral agenda. Among the evangelical ministers surveyed, the majority indicated that they preach on political concerns and encouraged congregants to vote (Smidt, 2003). Among rabbis, those who are Conservative or Orthodox are less likely to become politically active, and when they do it is over concern for Israel; those who are more liberal are usually more focused on civil rights (Djupe & Sokhey, 2003).

Religion and Recent National Elections

Since the 1980s and 1990s, evangelicals and fundamentalists have become increasingly involved in political activism. Meyers (2006) states that the Christian Right is a "broad, energized, theocratic voting bloc" (p. xiv). Television preachers support those they consider "God's candidates" and denounce all that is liberal as evil (Meyers, 2006, p. xiii). Religion figured prominently in the 2000 and, especially, in the 2004 National elections. During the presidential campaigns, including the debates, the candidate's religion, religious beliefs, and practices became an important focus in the media and for some voters. Some leaders of the Christian Right told congregants that a good Christian could vote only for George W. Bush (Wallis, 2005). Rozell (2003) states that the majority of political scientists believe that George W. Bush was motivated to reach out to Evangelicals because they provided an important base of support (as cited in Donahue & Nielsen, 2005), and many believe the Christian Right was a significant factor in the 2004 election (Meyers, 2006). Lerner (2006) and Meyers (2006) call the joined forces of the political Right and the Christian Right an "unholy alliance." Meyers refers to Jerry Falwell, one of many Christian Right leaders, who believed that voters had a "holy mandate" to vote for Bush. Wallis (2005) indicates that this is not only bad theology; it is a dangerous use of religion.

Need to Address Spiritual Concerns

The failure of the Left (liberal and usually Democratic) to discuss religion and articulate a vision for America that reflects people's spiritual longing allows the Right (conservative and usually Republican) to co-op religion and use it to promote their political agenda (Lerner, 2006; Wallis, 2005). Wallis (2005) states that the Right draws on the rhetoric of morality, but fails to support the values of social justice. The Right restricts religion to a "short list of hot-button social issues and [obstructs] its application to other matters that would threaten their agenda" (Wallis, 2005, p. xxii). Because the Democrats did not address the spiritual crisis voters were grappling with, the conservatives were able to "build a huge power base without worrying that the shabby ideas that they were advocating would be sufficiently challenged in the public sphere" (Lerner, 2006, p. 4). Meyers (2006) states that at the very time when "the virtues of true faith" were needed, Americans got "religion at its worst" (p. x).

Many liberals and moderates would welcome a vision of America that is congruent with their spiritual values of social justice and compassion but still allows for freedom of choice. Instead, religion is used by some to flame the fear of American voters. The world is presented as a dangerous place, where good and evil battle, where God seeks revenge, and where suffering is inescapable. Those who are in the "in" group are sanctified whereas those who are not are demonized (Lerner, 2006). The religious Right have co-opted "the name of a partisan God to fight crusades that pretend to be about moral values but are in fact about preserving and protecting wealth and power" (Meyers, 2006, p. xv).

RELIGION AND ABUSE

There are several issues related to religion and abuse, but Donahue and Nielsen (2005) indicate that there has been little empirical investigation of the interface between the two. Humans may suffer from abuse at the hands of religious leaders or from the use of religion in an abusive manner.

Abuse by Religious Authorities

Plante (2009) states that religious representatives are in a powerful position to harm individuals with either their words or their actions. They may create toxic shame in some because of lifestyle choices, for example, homosexuality, divorce, abortion, marrying outside one's religious group, failure to observe dietary laws, or having religious doubts. Individuals may be judged, ostracized, or victimized, especially when religious leaders are inflexible (Plante, 2009).

In recent years the sexual abuse of children by clergy, particularly Catholic priests, has received a great deal of media attention (Donahue & Nielsen, 2005). Clearly, this abuse of power is detrimental to the victims in many ways. The empirical evidence about the effect of clergy sexual abuse on victims is limited. What does exist, however, supports anecdotal data that along with the harmful effects any sexual abuse poses, abuse by clergy has a negative impact on the victim's spirituality. Abuse by clergy makes it almost impossible for victims to maintain a sense of trust in others and faith in God (Pargament, Murray-Swank, & Mahoney, 2008).

Physical Abuse of Women

There is often an assumption that, within conservative religious communities, religion is used to justify the abuse of women and children. Submission of women and dominance of men are prevalent in many patriarchal religions. Does this put women at greater risk for intimate partner violence? In a study by Manetta, Bryant, Cavanaugh, and Gange (2003) battered women believed that church teachings contributed to their abuse. Women seeking help from clergy may be reminded that they married "for better or for worse" and/or they should forgive their abusers. This may keep some women in abusive relationships (Manetta et al., 2003; Smullens, 2001, as cited in Manetta et al., 2003). Intimate partner violence among married couples is more prevalent when the male partner holds more conservative beliefs about the authority of biblical passages (Ellison, Barkowski, & Anderson, 1999, as cited in Manetta et al., 2003, p. 18). More research in this area will illuminate the role of religion in family violence. Although some may use religion to justify abuse, religion can be a powerful tool in reducing the incidence of abuse. Informed clergy can point out sacred text passages that admonish abusive behaviors and help congregants understand the need to settle disputes without violence.

Religion and Corporal Punishment

Biblical passages from both the Old and New Testaments have been cited to sanction the corporal punishment of children. Hamman (2000) argues that those Christians who believe in the literal interpretation of the Bible are the strongest advocates of physical punishment. One such passage states that "a child must be beaten in an attempt to break the will of the child, else immorality and sin would destroy the child's life, bringing shame on the parents of the child" (Hamman, 2000, p. 322). Although many social workers oppose the use of any physical punishment, Dyslin and Thomsen (2005) point out that it is important to distinguish corporal punishment from child abuse. Many parents who favor corporal punishment may oppose more extreme forms that constitute abuse.

Is there any empirical evidence of a relationship between religion and either corporal punishment or physical abuse of children? Numerous studies find a positive association between religious affiliation and the belief in corporal punishment (Dyslin & Thomsen, 2005, p. 291), with conservative Protestants favoring it compared to other denominations. Dyslin and Thomsen (2005) argue that although conservative Protestant child-rearing manuals advocate the use of corporal punishment they also establish limits on the manner in which the punishment is administered. They believe this discourages the escalation of punishment into physical abuse. In their study there was no association between affiliation and physical abuse.

Scholars reviewed research studies from the 1980s and 1990s and looked at the relationship between religion and parenting. The studies were limited to individuals of the Judeo-Christian tradition; participants in some of the studies were not parents. The finding of these studies indicates that religiously conservative parents emphasize the importance of having control over their children and that there is a modest positive association between conservatism and the endorsement of corporal punishment. Conservative parents were not only more likely to endorse corporal punishment but did so without feeling guilty (Mahoney, Pargament, Tarakesawar, & Swank, 2001). Danso, Hunsberger, and Pratt (1997, as cited in Mahoney et al., 2001, p. 81) found being an authoritative parent was more salient than whether one was conservative or not.

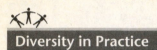

Diversity in Practice

Practice Behavior Example: *Recognize and communicate their understanding of the importance of differences in shaping life experiences.*

Critical Thinking Question: Address the ethical dilemmas that arise when therapists are working with families who use religious doctrines to justify corporal punishment. Discuss the difficulties of balancing respect for clients and their beliefs while adhering to your professional obligation to protect children from harm.

In general the empirical evidence does not support the conventional belief that religiously conservative parents overwhelmingly endorse corporal punishment. It does however suggest that religiously conservative parents, especially those who are authoritative, are more likely to use physical punishment. A major limitation of several studies is the use of participants who are not parents (Dyslin & Thomsen, 2005; Mahoney et al., 2001). Therefore, some of the findings may reflect attitudes toward corporal punishment rather than actual practices. Future studies need to use parent samples to clarify and strengthen findings. In addition, we need research to understand if there is a relationship between religion and physical child abuse.

RELIGION AND TERRORISM

Religiously motivated acts of terrorism have been perpetrated throughout the globe (Silberman, 2005a). Terrorism is fundamentally a psychological war aimed at creating a crippling fear in others so that the terrorists can achieve their goals (Ganor, 2002, as cited in Silberman, 2005a; Lavant, Barbanel, & DeLeon, 2004, as cited in Silberman, 2005a, p. 535). Some believe religion itself is responsible for religious terrorism. They argue that religious worldviews are outdated and irrelevant, that religion by its nature is divisive and destructive. When individuals hold differing worldviews, conflict is bound to happen (Kimball, 2002).

Others propose that it is the distortion of religion that leads to its destructive use. Armstrong (2002) states that although the Taliban were perceived to be the "quintessential Muslims," their regime violated critical Islamic values, reflecting a selective understanding of their religion (p. 15). This selectivity "perverts faith and turns it in the opposite direction of what was intended." Muslim fundamentalists, like all other fundamentalists, in their struggle to survive, may "make religion a tool of oppression and even of violence" (Armstrong, 2002, p. 16).

Religion remains an important part of people's lives; therefore, it is more helpful to understand how it molds behavior than to blame it for the world's woes (Kimball, 2002). Silberman et al. (2005) state that our religious meaning systems help to define what is sacred. Because these systems are highly malleable, we can change our positions based on a particular context. Thus, religious meaning systems influence how we interpret things, but the interpretations may not be consistent. For example, a group may espouse peace and nonviolence, yet under some circumstances favor violent activism (Silberman et al., 2005). Contextual issues such as poverty and oppression can be used to incite violence in individuals who ordinarily are pacifists (Silberman et al., 2005). Stern (2003, as cited in Silberman et al., 2005) states that individuals may engage in terrorist acts for either religious or nonreligious reasons. However, even religiously motivated attacks satisfy psychological needs as well as religious ones. These include the need to develop an identity and be recognized, the need to find meaning in one's life, and an outlet for one's rage.

One may believe that he will be seen as a hero for his actions. Therefore, those who wish to achieve a particular agenda can incite activism by playing on these psychological needs (Silberman et al., 2005). According to Kimball, the typical profile of a terrorist (suicide bomber, hijacker) is that of a poor, uneducated male who is lured into agreeing to commit violence with the promise that God will reward not only him but also his family. Once he agrees, he cannot reverse his decision (Kimball, 2002). Thus, a political, social, or economic agenda can be implemented in the name of religion.

The attacks of September 11th were proclaimed as a jihad or holy war against the "Western infidels." These attacks, however, violate the Qur'an. The Qur'an clearly admonishes suicide, and Islamic law forbids the killing of women, children, and noncombatants even in times of war (Kimball, 2002). On the night before the September 11 attacks, knowing their actions would lead to certain death for themselves, the hijackers (members of Al-Qaeda) were drinking and carousing with women, both violations of the Qur'an. Many question these unholy actions by a group of men who supposedly believed they were doing the work of Allah.

GURUS

Some gurus are undeniably spiritual teachers who possess attributes that make them role models and guides for other spiritual seekers. These individuals tend to influence others by example, which may be their compassion, their spiritual insight, or their holiness. Unscrupulous charismatic teachers or gurus, however, usually lure others through spiritual rhetoric. Claiming esoteric wisdom, they seek and thrive on the adulation of their adoring followers. They often convey the message that, unaided, the ordinary person cannot achieve spiritual enlightenment (Storr, 1996). Fitting with the theme of this chapter, our focus is the unscrupulous guru who misuses power and harms others in the process.

There are no training programs for gurus, no licensure to ensure that certain qualifications are met, and no standards to monitor practice. Gurus are self-selected (Storr, 1996). Rather than guide others, unscrupulous gurus are concerned with themselves. Claiming special spiritual gifts, powers, or insights they are often narcissistic, craving adulation, attention, and praise from others (Griffith & Griffith, 2002; Storr, 1996). To gain submission from their followers, gurus often "wrap their seduction in the language of spiritual enlightenment, righteousness, and the glorification of God" (Griffith & Griffith, 2002, p. 225). They claim they have received a personal revelation, often from a Divine source, that has transformed their lives and is universally applicable; therefore all should embrace the message (Spilka, Hood, Hunsberger, & Gorsuch, 2003; Storr, 1996). It is their ability to inspire hope or engender fear, along with their magnetism, that gives gurus a sense of authority, an authority they often abuse. Frequently, they display dominance through cruelty toward followers (Galanter, 2005; Spilka et al., 2003; Storr, 1996). Needing their followers' admiration to shore up their confidence, unscrupulous gurus do not tolerate criticism and see any disagreement as hostility; followers are expected to blindly obey (Kimball, 2002; Storr, 1996). As a form of

Engage, Assess, Intervene, Evaluate

Practice Behavior Example: Collect, organize, and interpret client data.

Critical Thinking Question: Discuss the guidelines you would use to assist clients in determining if their spiritual teacher is potentially abusive. How would you address this issue with your client if you thought the leader was unscrupulous? What ethical issues arise in this area?

social control, followers are often isolated from general society (Galanter, 2005). Isolation combined with the leader's grandiosity often leads followers to suspend their judgment and can in extreme cases lead to disasters, such as the Jonestown massacre (Galanter, 2005; Storr, 1996).

NEW AGE SPIRITUALITY

The New Age Movement provides opportunities for alternative spiritualities and an avenue to find meaning and connection for those who are not drawn to traditional spiritual paths. The New Age Movement is not exempt from the shadow side of spirituality; followers are as likely to deny the darker side of their belief systems as are those of any other religious institution (Zweig & Abrams, 1992). Followers may believe that "with the right teacher, or the right practice, they can transcend to higher levels of awareness without dealing with their more petty vices or ugly emotional attachments" (Zweig & Abrams, 1992, p. 130). This is similar to spiritual bypassing (Welwood, 2000, p. 11), the use of spiritual practices to avoid "unfinished business" and to transcend life's difficulties, rather than confront and deal with them. Spiritual teachers who have not dealt with their own issues (shadow) are likely to have a need for control and are intolerant of human weakness (Zweig & Abrams, 1992), making them detrimental to those who seek their guidance. Some spiritual teachers are "notorious for their angry outbursts; others for their authoritarianism" (Feuerstein, 1991, p. 148); still others are focused on the accumulation of wealth (Zweig & Abrams, 1992).

Barbs (1991) expresses concern about those followers of New Age philosophies who present themselves as willing to embrace all, but really believe they are right and others are wrong. Spiritual transformation begins within one's self. Only then can one reach out to others. However, these "New Age Fundamentalists" think their beliefs represent "the forces of light and goodness, while everyone else is duped by the forces of evil" (Barbs, 1991, p. 160). Barbs cautions that some approach life with a smoke screen of "thinly veiled" platitudes.

One prevalent New Age belief is that one creates his or her own reality, that one is responsible for everything that happens in one's life. The wisdom behind this belief is that one "invites" that which will be most helpful in growing spiritually. This belief, however, is often misused to blame individuals for all the negative things in their lives. Borysenko (1995) cautions against this "simplistic thinking" sometimes found among New Age followers. She is particularly concerned when the understanding of the mind–body connection is used to blame those who suffer from physical ailments or illnesses (p. 29). She remarks that some think that if one is "enlightened" one will never get ill. She refers to them as "mind body fundamentalists" and comments that this is a destructive and "self-punishing" path, a blame game that some fall back on as an alternative to "accepting the random mystery of the universe" (p. 27).

CONCLUSION

Whatever religious people may say about their love of God or the mandates of their religion, when their behavior toward others is violent and destructive, when it causes suffering among their neighbors, you can be sure the religion has been corrupted and reform is desperately needed. (Kimball, 2002, p. 39)

In this chapter we looked at the shadow side of religion. Currently, as well as throughout history, religion can and has been used to bring about great harm. The harm generated may be personal, like the person suffering from toxic shame, or it may be societal, such as hatred and bigotry. It may also be used for mass destruction, such as genocide or terrorist acts. Helmick (2001) states that it is important to study the relationship between religion and violence in order to determine what poisons the relationship. If we are able to engage in constructive dialogue, in a nondefensive manner, perhaps we could begin to sort out the negative and positive uses of religion. If we are able to do so, we would be in a better position to distinguish between healthy and unhealthy manifestations of religiosity on both the personal and global levels.

Characteristics that predispose one to the destructive use of religion are the belief that one has exclusive ownership of the Truth and that one is among God's favored. When individuals are willing to blindly obey and believe that any means justifies the end, unscrupulous leaders may incite them to violence and destruction. Religious meaning systems both personally and collectively shape what we view as sacred, secular, offensive, or threatening. They greatly influence whether we express ourselves in a peaceful or violent manner. Some argue that religion itself is the problem; others believe that it is the misuse of religion that leads to violence and harm. Kimball (2002) remarks that "arrogant confidence" that one's religious tradition is the only true one, along with the "condescending dismissal" of others' traditions, reinforces the belief of some that religion is inherently a problem (Kimball, 2002, p.27).

Just as religion can be used to bring about harm, it can be used to counteract violence. We chose in this chapter to focus almost exclusively on religion. Most religions are structured, sanctioned by the endorsement of their followers, and have existed over time. These characteristics allow religions to wield great power, which when misused can create widespread harm. These same attributes, however, can be utilized to condemn violence and the abuse of power and teach tolerance. Compassion that is not only preached but modeled by religious leaders is the best antidote to the potential misuse of religion. As social workers, along with our direct practice with clients, we can join and support organizations that advocate religious inclusiveness rather than exclusion, tolerance rather than arrogance and hatred, and peace rather than destruction. In this way, we may help to enhance the true message of the world's great religions, work to minimize the problematic, and protect those who choose to not follow any formal spiritual path. "Freedom *of* religion is a good thing. So is freedom *from* the religion others may wish to impose on those who differ" (italics in the original) (Kimball, 2002, p. 25).

PRACTICE TEST

The following questions will test your knowledge of the content found within this chapter and help you prepare for the licensing exam by applying chapter content to practice. For more questions styled like the licensing exam, visit **MySocialWorkLab.com**

1. Mrs. Marks, a member of a conservative religious sect, reports to her social worker that her husband uses corporal punishment to discipline their children. The social worker should

   a. tell the client this is wrong and make an abuse report.

   b. explore the details and determine if a report should be made.

   c. not report, because reporting may be insensitive to their sect's norms.

   d. help her protect her children from her husband.

2. Colin, a member in a group for parents raising children with emotional difficulties, states that his spiritual path is the only true one. The group leader should

   a. tell Colin that he cannot share his beliefs as other members may be offended.

   b. ask the others to share their beliefs.

   c. ask the other members about their reaction to what Colin said.

   d. tell Colin all spiritual paths are respected in the group.

3. Olivia reveals that she is contemplating making a commitment to a guru she heard speak at a New Age Philosophy conference she attended. Which criterion best indicates that her guru will not be harmful?

   a. Her guru influences others by how he lives his life.

   b. He claims special gifts or insights that are universally applicable.

   c. He has been granted authority to persuade others to follow him.

   d. An elected board grants licensure and monitors practice.

4. In a recently formed group for recovered substance abusers, Selene reveals that she was diagnosed with breast cancer. Emily, another member and devout follower of New Age Philosophy, tells Selene that her "negative thinking created this reality." The group leader should

   a. ask the group to respond to Emily's comment.

   b. ignore Emily's comment and focus on the session topic.

   c. ask Selene how she feels about what Emily said.

   d. explore what Emily was feeling when Selene shared her diagnosis.

1. Discuss some ethical concerns that may arise when social workers with different belief systems work with families who are affiliated with a very conservative religious sect. What issues may arise regarding sexual orientation? What countertransference issues may develop? What should social workers do when these issues occur?

2. Some religious belief systems do not endorse modern health practices. What issues may occur for social workers if parents refuse life-saving techniques for their children? Discuss how these issues may affect social workers working in medical settings. What should social workers do to address these issues?

SUCCEED WITH

PEARSON
mysocialworklab

Visit **MySocialWorkLab** for more licensing exam test questions, and to access case studies, videos, and much more.

10

Gender and Spirituality

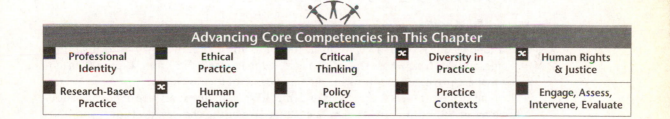

Advancing Core Competencies in This Chapter

	Professional Identity		Ethical Practice		Critical Thinking	✖	Diversity in Practice	✖	Human Rights & Justice
	Research-Based Practice	✖	Human Behavior		Policy Practice		Practice Contexts		Engage, Assess, Intervene, Evaluate

Sacred stories move us, tell us who we are, and call us to the Divine. Women's sacred stories have been suppressed, ignored, or subsumed under men's stories. Without hearing about women's experiences, we may assume that spirituality for them is the same as it is for men, that their spiritual development parallels men's. Likewise, some men's stories are privileged over other men's stories. We have only partial knowledge of men's spiritual experiences if those stories are not voiced. In this chapter, we will discuss the relationship between gender and spirituality. Because women's stories have often been overlooked, our primary focus is on women, their spiritual development, and the oppressive role of patriarchy in silencing the Sacred Feminine. However, we also include a section on the damaging effects of patriarchy on men's spiritual growth.

SACRED STORIES

"We live our lives immersed in stories" (Simpkinson & Simpkinson, 1993, p. 1). It is difficult to imagine life without them. They are the vehicles through which we explain and understand our lives (Stone, 1996). Those stories that move us deeply are sacred stories. They tell us who we are, where we come from, and about our relationship to the world and the Divine (Stone, 1996; Yolen, as cited in Simpkinson & Simpkinson, 1993). Although we may not consciously understand the meaning of the stories we hear, we somehow grasp the essence and make new discoveries (Yolen, as cited in Simpkinson & Simpkinson, 1993, p. 1).

Sacred stories are powerful vehicles for the imagination. They simultaneously transform us and connect us to others (Maguire, 1998; Stone, 1996; Yolen, as cited in Simpkinson & Simpkinson, 1993, p. 1), including our spiritual ancestors (Price & Simpkinson, 1993). We learn about their spiritual journeys, their struggles, and their faith and how they overcame obstacles. When we retell these stories, we remember them and allow them to guide us on our own faith journeys (Stone, 1996).

Sacred stories are pivotal to our rituals and ceremonies. As a community they enable us to celebrate and express reverence. In times of difficulty, they comfort and guide us (Maguire, 1998). A story is not sacred because of its content, but because of its power to inspire and transform us (Simpkinson & Simpkinson, 1993). Thus, the content need not be religious or spiritual to be holy (Happel, as cited in Simpkinson and Simpkinson, 1993, p. 2).

WOMEN'S SACRED STORIES

Some stories are privileged and become the dominant source of knowledge for a culture. That knowledge is often accepted as factual or as absolute rather than as relative truth (Epigg, 2008). Those whose stories are neglected may accept the "truth" expressed in stories that are privileged, not realizing the significance of their own truth.

The lack of women's sacred stories denies a woman the experience of hearing about the lives of those who are like her. She is unaware of the choices, decisions, and leadership of her female spiritual ancestors. In the wake of this loss, she is left only with men's stories and men's interpretation of women's stories. To understand her feminine soul, she must learn from other women, rather than allow those who are privileged to define her (Anderson & Hopkins, 1992; Fook, 2003, as cited in Suarez, Newman, & Reed, 2008).

Historically, men have told the sacred stories. They have written most of the religious texts and led the scholarly work that interprets their meaning. They have performed the religious rites and rituals (Canda & Furman, 1999, 2010; Chittister, 1998; Epigg, 2008; Plaskow & Christ, 1989). Thus, masculine spirituality has been the dominant spiritual discourse. Women's stories that are included in sacred texts are told by and interpreted by men. Men hold the power to tell women who they are and what their role in relation to the Divine should be. When traditional religion renders half the human race invisible it is oppressive and incomplete (Chittister, 1998). What happens when women's sacred stories are overlooked or given less importance? How do we understand women's relationship to the Divine if their stories are not told? How do we understand holiness or wholeness for women? What impact has this had on women and their spiritual development? What messages are women given from this neglect? What does it tell men about the importance of women's spiritual stories?

SPIRITUAL DEVELOPMENT AND GENDER

Although there has been an increasing understanding of the relationship between spirituality and mental health, there is a scarcity of literature on women's spirituality (Canda & Furman, 1999, 2010). Without specific knowledge of women and their spiritual development, the assumption that it is similar to men's spiritual development is likely to continue. Masculine models fail to address the nuances of women's spiritual experiences and development, especially women's search for the Sacred Feminine. The Sacred Feminine or Divine Feminine recognizes feminine aspects of the Divine and allows a woman to connect with her feminine soul (Kidd, 1996). It values a woman for who she is in her own right and not just as "an appendage or helpmate to man" (Peay, 2002, p. 3). In this chapter we will discuss that for some women the Divine is immanent rather than transcendent. Therefore, connection to her feminine soul and the Divine Feminine allows a woman to access the deep repository of wisdom that resides within her. She becomes empowered and is not reliant on others to define her or her spirituality (Kidd, 1996). Nurturance, connection, relationships, and interdependence are valued over autonomy and separation (Kidd, 1996; Peay, 2002).

In this section we will explore some of the general differences in the spiritual development of men and women using the metaphors of the ladder (masculine) and the circle (feminine). Both approaches to spiritual development are valuable and neither is superior to the other. However, these are useful metaphors to understand the general patterns and gender differences inherent in their development.

To avoid stereotyping, we need to keep in mind that the ladder is a more suitable metaphor for some women, just as the circle is more appropriate for some men. Some individuals may identify with both. At times they may be goal directed and focused on transcendence; at other times, they may be focused internally. The two metaphors are meant to complement each other, not compete or for one to supersede the other. When each is seen as valuable, men and women are able to respect one another's authentic path to the sacred (Borysenko, 1999).

MASCULINE SPIRITUALITY

Differences in the spiritual development of men and women can best be understood through the use of metaphors. Men's spiritual development is often conceptualized as a "ladder" or "staircase" (Borysenko, 1999; Harris, 1989). This implies that development is a step-like, logical progression with vertical and hierarchical dimensions. Each phase of development builds on the previous one (Borysenko, 1999; Harris, 1989).

Spiritual development for men has all the elements of the hero's journey. Regardless of the specific story, the hero's journey involves three stages: departure, initiation, and return (Campbell, 1968; Faiver, Ingersoll, O'Brien, & McNally, 2001; Vogler, 2007). Because something is amiss in his life or he faces a dilemma, the hero leaves home, to venture into an unknown land. Here, he faces tremendous challenges and as he meets them, he changes. It is "a journey from one way of being to the next; from despair to hope, weakness to strength, folly to wisdom" (Volger, 2007, p. 7). During the journey, he dies to his old self and finds meaning. And finally, bringing the "treasures," talents, and gifts discovered during his journey, the hero returns to his everyday life as a "whole (holy) person" (Faiver et al., 2001, p. 20). The male spiritual sojourner is brave and heroic (Borysenko, 1999).

FEMININE SPIRITUALITY

Each woman, like each man, develops in a unique, personal manner. However, certain patterns seem to emerge that are common to many women as they develop spiritually (Harris, 1989). Rather than a ladder or staircase, the circle or dance is a more apt metaphor for women's spiritual processes (Borysenko, 1999; Harris, 1989). Spiritual growth for women is not a logical progression, but is rhythmic, composed of a series of back and forth movements similar to the steps of a dance. Movement, therefore, is circular rather than vertical (Harris, 1989). The process is natural, intuitive, and unplanned. It leaves space for the unexpected, especially the possibility of Divine guidance (Borysenko, 1999). A woman grows spiritually at her own pace and in her own time. As she moves through each step of the dance, she circles back and begins the circle anew, deepening the process with each cycle. Unlike the heroic journeys of men, women are more likely to find and express their spirituality in the midst of their daily lives (Harris, 1989).

Men's spirituality is outer focused and transcendent. One needs to rise above the self to find the Divine (Kidd, 1996). For women, spiritual discovery is internally focused. The Divine is not transcendent, but immanent. The center of the circle is her heart, soul, and inner wisdom. Her journey involves quieting herself so she can access the Divine source of wisdom within (Borysenko, 1999; Kidd, 1996). Masculine spirituality emphasizes "movement over stillness," action, service to the world, speaking the truth, and social justice (Rohr & Martos, 2005, p. 10). A woman's spiritual journey is more natural than heroic, more relational than autonomous. Because we have previously focused on the metaphor of the labyrinth, we can see from the above description of the dance and the circle that the labyrinth is also a metaphor for women's spiritual development: She moves back and forth, at her own pace, to come ultimately to her center, to her heart, to the Divine.

For many women the Divine is found in the here and now, alive, and within (Divine immanence). Each moment is holy and important to embrace. Nurturing relationships are a natural part of her life and thus spirituality for women is relational rather than autonomous (Borysenko, 1999; Kidd, 1996). Her emphasis on relationships naturally leads to the awareness that all living things are interconnected (the web of life). Humans are not above other living creatures, but part of the whole. Each is not only responsible for herself but for others and the care of the planet (Kidd, 1996). Because spirituality takes place in the midst of a woman's daily life, it focuses on the themes of connection and brokenness, love and work, power and disenfranchisement, life and death (Harris, 1989). Through her spirituality she enters the Mystery and learns "to live the questions, love the questions, *dance* the questions" (italics in the original) (Harris, 1989, p. xi).

Awakening to the Spiritual

Awakening is the beginning of spiritual development (Harris, 1989). Clarissa Pinkola Estes (1992, p. 13), author of *Women Who Run with the Wolves*, says the female soul resides in the "guts." Thus, for women, awakening often begins internally, rather than in response to external events (Harris, 1989). She may find herself living in a spiritual wasteland (Bolen, 1994), with a sense of emptiness or a feeling that something is missing in her life (Harris, 1989). She remembers that there is a "different realm of existence with its own truth" (Carroll, 2008). She may become aware of limitations placed on her, feeling stifled and unheard (Kidd, 1996). Her soul stirs, calling her out of her slumber. It is a call to awaken from her spiritual lethargy and simultaneously an invitation to awaken "*to* and *toward* something" (italics in the original) (Harris, 1989, p. 3). It is a call to consciousness, a call to discover her inner self, her sacredness, and her relationship to the Divine (Harris, 1989). To find her true self, a woman needs "to remember and reclaim" the immanent Divine (Carroll, 2008). She is invited into the Mystery and called to live life more fully and deeply by embracing both its joys and sorrows (Harris, 1989).

Awakening may be a gradual, slow, private process. Or it may be sudden and dramatic, a flash of insight leaving her shaken to the core. Whether gradual or sudden, she begins to explore the depths of her inner landscape and begins the arduous task of birthing her feminine soul (Bolen, 1994; Kidd, 1996). The feminine soul is "a woman's inner repository of the Divine Feminine, her deep source, her natural instinct, guiding wisdom, and power" (Kidd, 1996, p. 20). To find herself and to grow spiritually, a woman must leave that which is secure to explore that which is more nourishing, more suitable. "Unknowing" replaces security (Anderson & Hopkins, 1991). Therefore, some anxiety is inevitable. She is not sure who she will become and is unclear of the response of others to her new-found feminine soul (Kidd, 1996).

Awakening may be accompanied by an increasing awareness of the role of women in patriarchal religious traditions or other experiences of oppression within her own society or other parts of the world. She may become increasingly aware of her "feminine wound," which Kidd (1996) describes as the internalization of all the societal and religious messages that see women as "less than" men (p. 30). Fearing they may lose everything (their belief system, their relationships), women may try to deny the growing awareness that their former spirituality no longer fits. She may be anxious that others will disapprove, ridicule, or even rebuke her (Kidd, 1996). Unlike Sleeping Beauty, she does not awaken from sleep with a kiss from Prince Charming to live happily ever after. More likely, her growing awareness and acknowledgment of patriarchal oppression will cause her to step on some toes, especially ecclesiastic ones.

Women may try to hush this growing awareness, but they will do so at a price: the price of their authenticity, the price of stifling silence, and the price of relinquishing their power. The call to feminine consciousness can be exciting or frightening. Some eagerly run forward to embrace with open arms their growing spiritual awareness; some respond cautiously, hesitantly moving forward and backward; and still others try to ignore the call altogether. Awakening is essentially the act of a woman remembering herself, remembering her power, remembering the deep well within, and connecting to the Divine Feminine source (Carroll, 2008; Kidd, 1996).

Recovering Her Feminine Soul

As her growing awareness becomes more urgent, a woman begins to peel away the layers of who she is. As she engages in this process, she temporarily resides in the space between who she was and who she will become (Harris, 1989). She must remember and reconnect to lost or forgotten aspects of herself. She brings them to consciousness and integrates them into her life, thus reclaiming her power and opening to the Divine in a fuller way (Anderson & Hopkins, 1991; Harris, 1989). She no longer accepts the myth that only men are powerful and women are not. She gracefully embraces her strength and recognizes that for women, spirituality must include heart as well as intellect, connection rather than autonomy (Geertsma & Cummings, 2004; Harris, 1989).

Looking Inward

Dwelling is the heart of the spiritual journey for women (Harris, 1989). She finds the Divine by coming to know her authentic self (Larkin, as cited in Fischer, 1988, p. 114). Thus, she needs a place of solitude and the ability to still herself internally. Within this quiet, inner space she is able to retreat, rest, and find spiritual succor. Many women may feel guilty of their need for time alone because they fear it is selfish. However, if a woman is to access her internal wisdom, she must shut out daily distractions, have a quiet time and space (Harris, 1989). It is within the silence that she is able to listen to the "guidance of the Spirit within," which can help her become inner directed rather than overly reliant on others (Fischer, 1988, p. 121). Like time spent in the center of the labyrinth, solitude allows her to connect to herself and the Divine, and to return refreshed to her daily life.

Therapy is the perfect place for women to do inner work. This, however, raises important questions about the types of therapy we offer. How do we make therapy a place where a woman can think, a place of gentle quietness where she can hear her own intuitive voice? Standardized treatment approaches that do not allow for individuality, flexibility, and moments of empathic silence do not meet this need. Some women may anxiously fill the quiet space with words. They need the support of their therapists to help them slow down, become still, and learn to trust their own wisdom.

Stilled Not Silenced

Solitude provides an opportunity to shut out daily distractions and quiet any internal noise. Silence allows one to "drop into stillness" (Siegel, 2007, p. 72), into the Source of Wisdom (Harris, 1989; Kidd, 1996), which, as a vehicle to explore her internal space, provides a fertile ground for spiritual growth. Too often for women, silence is used as a stifling tool of subjugation. Her voice may be drowned out by the dominant spiritual discourse. Along with the loss of her voice, she loses her identity, and her power. And when she is silenced, an entire community or culture suffers the loss of her perspective. Other women who share similar experiences may not have the courage to speak up, and are effectively silenced as well. It is tempting to think that women have freedom of speech, that their voices are heard. But are they really? Women who are attracted to the Divine Feminine may fear speaking up, afraid they will be ridiculed or ostracized. Because women are still the minority in religious leadership positions, how are women's voices heard? Historically, there have been far more male theologians than female. Within ultraconservative and fundamentalist denominations, women are expected to be submissive to their husbands and other male authorities. And internationally, many women are oppressed and subjugated by men. In the role of the "Silent Woman," a woman denies her truth (Kidd, 1996, p. 57). She keeps herself quiet, remains spiritually hidden to maintain the status quo within her spiritual community, to feel secure, or to remain safe. She may be discouraged from sharing her perspective or opinions, not speaking unless she agrees with the male authorities; she thus serves as "a mouthpiece for the party line" (Kidd, 1996, p. 57).

The need for silence and the need for voice are common themes for women. Their conversations are often marked by expressions such as "speaking up," "speaking out," "being silenced," and "not being heard" (Harris, 1989, p. 182). Harris (1989) refers to a quote by a prisoner under the Marcos regime, "If you really want to hear what we are saying, listen to what we are not allowed to say" (p. 182).

Being silenced is oppressive. When women are silenced, they are not allowed to have their own experiences, their own voices. Silence, stillness, solitude, and quiet, however, allow her to explore her inner space, discover her own experiences, and ultimately voice them. The need to speak her truth comes from deep within a woman. There is an "urgency to name what is seen, to tell what had been lived through, to put into words . . . what would otherwise remain mute" (Anderson & Hopkins, 1992, p. 112). This process sensitizes her to all the "the unheard voices" (Harris, 1989, p. 182). She connects with the oppressed, regardless of whether they are oppressed by patriarchy, racism, homophobia, poverty, or any of a host of societal structures that create barriers for others.

> ## Diversity in Practice
>
> ***Practice Behavior Example:*** *Recognize and communicate their understanding of the importance of differences in shaping life experiences.*
>
> **Critical Thinking Question:** Discuss the role of gender in shaping one's spiritual development. Address some potential differences between feminist and masculine spirituality.

WOMEN AND RELIGION

Reportedly, women are interested in spirituality (Rayburn & Comas-Diaz, 2008) and more religious than men (Bryant, 2007; Spilka, Hood, Hunsberger, & Gorsuch, 2003, p. 153). They often attend worship more frequently, pray more often, and express more agreement with traditional religious views (Donelson, 1999, as cited in Spilka et al., 2003, p. 114; Francis & Wilcox, 1998, as cited in Spilka et al., 2003, p. 121). Some argue that these findings reflect the socialization of women, but most likely socialization alone cannot account for all these factors. Women are less likely than men to leave their faith; however, when they do they are less likely to return (Spilka et al., 2003).

In the United States, most women who are affiliated with a religion are members of conventional Christian or Jewish denominations, which were developed and shaped by men. Many of these women are satisfied with these affiliations (Corbett, 1997, as cited in Canda & Furman, 2010, p. 130). However, some Jewish and Christian women attending spiritual retreats indicated that they did not feel spiritually nourished through traditional religion, and many were angry at the patriarchal and androcentric nature of it (Borysenko, 1999). Closer examination reveals that despite some advancement of women within traditional religion bias against them persists (Splika et al., 2003, p. 183). Women are excluded from formal leadership in some religious traditions. For example, although some strides have been made in increasing leadership roles for women in Judaism and among some Christian denominations, women are barred from leadership within the Catholic religion, and theological reasons have been used to justify exclusion (Hoge, 2005). Because God is perceived as male (see divine images), males hold the spiritual power. Women cannot be ordained; only men can, because Jesus is male. The idea that God is sexist is appalling (Chittister, 1998) and "religiously unconscionable" (Johnson, 1992, p. 15).

Women's concerns about institutionalized religion go beyond the issue of ordination. The sacred texts were written and interpreted by men who provide the authoritative view on them. The language of scripture, hymns, and other sacred rituals are frequently not inclusive (Chittister, 1998; Hoge, 2005, p. 38; Johnson, 1992; Kidd, 1996). In the early days of Christianity, the church fathers debated if women even had souls or if they could be saved. Thus, it is important to consider both the liberating and oppressive aspects of traditional religion in the lives of women (Canda & Furman, 1999, 2010).

PATRIARCHY

Patriarchy refers to social structures that privilege men (Johnson, 2007). However, not everything that is male or masculine is patriarchal (Chittister, 1998; Woodman & Dickson, 1996). As we will see below, patriarchy disadvantages men as well as women. And when a woman approaches others in a patriarchal manner, she is as destructive and domineering as patriarchal men (Woodman & Dickson, 1996).

Patriarchy is "a mindset, a way of looking at life, a worldview based on superiority, domination, effectiveness, and conformity" (Chittister, 1998, p. 24). Power is owned, controlled, and dominated by men; and women are pushed to the margins of society (Johnson, 2007). The power inherent in patriarchy is a "power over" model of domination, rather than a "power with" model of interdependence and cooperation (Chittister, 1998; Christ, 2003, p. 93). Patriarchy is androcentric. And being male centered, male thinking and development are viewed as normative, and variations in women's thinking or development are viewed as aberrant or inferior (Johnson, 2007).

The foundation of patriarchy is built on four interlocking concepts: dualism, hierarchy, domination, and essential inequality. From this perspective things are ranked and ordered, with some being powerful (and valuable) and others being powerless and expendable or utilitarian (Chittister, 1998). Being dualistic, patriarchy values rational thinking over emotions, material possessions over spiritual matters, empiricism over intuition, and men over women (Fox, 2008). The powerful build the world on the backs of the powerless (Chittister, 1998, p. 27).

Patriarchy purports that God is male, implying that maleness is more divine than femaleness. If this is so, "then what men want, what men think, what men value, God wants, thinks, values" (Chittister, 1998, p. 29). Thus, it minimizes women, fails to take into account their needs, and makes them unimportant and invisible (Chittister, 1998; Kidd, 1996; Rayburn & Comas-Diaz, 2008). Although patriarchy sometimes reveres women, it does so in a way that limits them. They are praised for knowing their place and honored for being docile, submissive, and obedient (Chittister, 1998, p. 27).

MEN AND PATRIARCHY

Although patriarchy privileges men, it ultimately destroys them (Chittister, 1998). Men believe "the false promises of the system" and although they appear to be the oppressor, they too are oppressed (Rohr, 2005, p. 12). Patriarchy stifles not only the spiritual lives of women but also those of men (Chittister, 1998; Kidd, 1996). Men often hide their spirituality, become disconnected from their feelings, and fail to connect with and develop their inner lives (Fox, 2008; Rohr, 2005). Men have given up a great deal emotionally and spiritually for the privileges patriarchy affords them (Chittister, 1998). In patriarchal structures men expect to have status and power. They expect others will listen to them and do as they bid. But they relinquish the right to be wrong, to not know, to not be in charge. They are denied the expression of feelings, especially gentler feelings, which cripples their relationships (Chittister, 1998, Wexler, 2009). They are allowed to have "buddies" but not true intimate friendships (Chittister, 1998). Denied the ability to be in touch with their own feelings, men "work till they drop, and they drop from their work" (Chittister, 1998, p. 28). When they fail to develop their inner lives they "build, explain, use, fix, manipulate, legislate, order and play" but never touch the essence of anything (Rohr, 2005, p. 9). By cutting themselves off from women, they lose the wisdom and grace she has to offer them. In a patriarchal structure, men become focused on independence and their spirituality becomes driven by dogma rather than feelings (Chittister, 1998, p. 28).

The path to the Sacred differs for women and men because they notice and take note of different things (Rohr, 2005). The struggle of women in their pursuit of the Sacred Feminine has stirred a yearning in men for an authentic expression of masculinity (Rohr, 2005). In the absence of the Sacred Masculine, men are left with pseudomasculinity and bravado (Fox, 2008; Rohr, 2005). In the past few decades, psychologists have been challenging traditional male paradigms that emphasize competition, achievement, and the lack of emotional connection (Levant & Pollack, 1995, p. 1). For men to heal spiritually, they need to become in touch with the Sacred Masculine (Fox, 2008; Rohr, 2005) and contact and embrace their authentic inner life rather than emphasize religious obligation, outward expressions of the spiritual life, and overreliance on external authority (Rohr, 2005).

> ### Diversity in Practice
>
> ***Practice Behavior Example:*** *Recognize the extent to which a culture's structures and values may oppress, marginalize, alienate, or create or enhance privilege and power.*
>
> **Critical Thinking Question:** Discuss the role of patriarchy in shaping spiritual life for both women and men.

FEMINIST SPIRITUALITY

A critique of patriarchy is needed to pave the way for forms of spirituality that address women's needs more adequately (Plaskow & Christ, 1989). Women can express their spirituality through traditional paths, but it is a "spirituality lacking an understanding and exploration of their femaleness" (Ochs, 1997, p. 27). To successfully meet the spiritual needs of women, religious structures must be transformed (Johnson, 2007). The integration of women into spiritual structures that continue the problems inherent in patriarchy and androcentrism is insufficient. For a vital spirituality women need more than "second-hand suits passed down from a male patriarchy to women on whom these garments may be quite ill fitting" (Rayburn & Comas-Diaz, 2008, p. xiv). An "add women and stir" approach continues a system that ignores women's spiritual needs and perpetuates their attempts to fit into a male-defined spiritual system (Johnson, 2007, p. 95).

Feminism, like patriarchy, is a worldview. But, unlike patriarchy, it is based on equality and inclusion (Chittister, 1998; Fischer, 1988). It takes into account those who have been overlooked, marginalized, and oppressed by patriarchal structures. A feminist approach to spirituality values diversity and questions (Chittister, 1998): Who holds power?

Who is entitled to hold power? How did they get it? Who said so? It is based on a "power with" model, one in which men and women equally share power and cooperate rather than compete (Chittister, 1998; Christ, 2003; Kidd, 1996). Thus, feminist spirituality is built on the principles of respect for others, interdependence and mutuality, nurturance and relationships (Chittister, 1998; Kidd, 1996), and the belief that equality extends to all sexes, races, and classes (Johnson, 2007). It emphasizes "inclusion rather than exclusion, connectedness rather that separateness, and mutuality in relationships rather than dominance and submission" (Fischer, 1988, p. 2). The goal of feminist spirituality is not to exclude men, but to invite them into women's struggle, to make them part of women's spiritual journeys (Kidd, 1996). The feminist perspective is based on the belief that community is essential to human development, but community must be "structured in justice," which requires societal change (Fischer, 1988, p. 2).

In developing an understanding about the differences between masculine and feminine spirituality it is important to avoid the development of new stereotypes that force men or women into boxes. Although the boxes may be different, they are nonetheless oppressive. To avoid this it is important to recognize that many men are drawn to aspects of the Sacred Feminine, whereas some women are more comfortable with traditional spiritual paths based on the Sacred Masculine. Images and symbols used with the Sacred Feminine are not superior to those used with the Sacred Masculine, but often are more relevant to women's experience.

Feminism and Diversity

Just as it is incorrect to assume that all women eagerly embrace the Sacred Feminine, it is naïve to believe that all women seek the same path to transform patriarchy and overcome oppression. Issues may differ based on background. For example, within the United States, feminists have often been white women of privilege or middle-class status. Womanist, Spirita, and mujerista theologies criticize feminists for failing to include issues of race and class along with the obstacles created by gender (Comas-Diaz, 2008; Grey, 2007; Johnson, 2007). (See chapter 11.)

Feminist spirituality needs to create a space to hear the voices of women who are marginalized or oppressed due to race or class. Patriarchy is criticized for neglecting the stories of women. Repeating the mistake constricts understanding of women's spirituality to some women, especially those from industrialized nations. To develop an inclusive spirituality, the stories of women from around the world, from all races, and from all socioeconomic classes, especially those who are oppressed, need to be invited to join the spiritual dialogue. Womanists and mujeristas remind us that at present we have only a partial picture of the role of oppression in women's spirituality.

IMAGES OF THE DIVINE

There is an old joke about a woman who makes a visit to a Catholic church one autumn afternoon. Feeling a close, personal relationship with Mary, the Mother of God, she often prayed aloud. And so, on this day she began, "Holy Mother of God, please hear my prayer." Two workmen, who were out of sight, decide to have some fun at her expense. One of them answered her. "This is Jesus Christ, how can I help you?" Again she intoned,

"Holy Mother of God, I beseech you." Again the workman answered, "This is Jesus, I am waiting to hear your plea." The woman tries to petition Mary again, and the workman responds once more. Exacerbated, the woman raises her fist to the heavens and shouts, "Quiet you, I'm trying to talk to your Mother."

This anecdote captures the need for women to find the Sacred Feminine, to connect to their "feminine soul" (Kidd, 1996). In Buddhism, Hinduism, and Taoism, there are positive feminine or androgynous images of the Divine. These religions are polytheistic or nontheistic (Canda & Furman, 2010). In monotheistic religions, such as Judaism, Islam, and Christianity, patriarchy has obscured the feminine aspects of the Divine (Canda & Furman, 2010; Chittister, 1998). Historically, men have named God and proclaimed the images developed as universal (Kidd, 1996). The images handed down through generations have been exclusively masculine (Chittister, 1997; Kidd, 1996). Simone de Beauvoir points out that traditional Western religion has gifted men with a God who is like them, male (Kidd, 1996, p. 50).

Symbols and Images

Symbols and images are used to point to a reality that lies beyond, something to help us glean some understanding of that which is not fathomable (Tillich, as cited in Johnson, 2007, p. 20). Process philosopher Charles Hartshorne (Christ, 2003, p. 227) states that we cannot approach spirituality and a relationship with the Divine through intellect alone. Reflection molds understanding, but symbols allow for the connection between insights and feelings and enables humans to share their experiences within a community. Symbols are the language of the soul and they are never neutral (Kidd, 1996). Johnson (1992) states that the language used by a faith community to define the Divine reflects that which they consider the "highest good, the profoundest truth" (p. 4). Images and symbols both shape and are shaped by the culture (Johnson, 1992; Kidd, 1996).

Traditional Images

In popular culture, the Divine is depicted, not only as male but also as white. The God of Michelangelo's painting on the ceiling of the Sistine Chapel permeates the imagination of many (Christ, 2003; Johnson, 2007). Without alternative images and symbols, the popular view of the Divine as old, white, and male is likely to persist (Christ, 2003). Masculine images are imbued with masculine traits. Thus, God is powerful, active, reasonable, concerned with justice, and headship. God is seen as lord, king, or a patriarchal father. Women may have difficulty relating to these images (Christ, 2003; Johnson, 2007), and they can create a spirituality that focuses on fear of "displeasing a male father-God" (Chittister, 1998, p. 29). The masculine conceptualization of the Divine poses a challenge to women in seeing themselves made in the image of God and embracing their own power (Christ, 2003). Women need symbols that reflect their experiences and spiritual needs, ones that resonant with what is important to them (Kidd, 1996).

Sacred Feminine

The Divine is spirit, neither male nor female (McFague, as cited in Kidd, 1996, p. 136). It is the "Eternal Thou" (Martin Buber, as cited in Christ, 2003, p. 31), an "incomprehensible mystery" that cannot be contained by words or concepts (Johnson, 1992, p. 7). If the Divine is neither male nor female, why is there such opposition to the use of feminine pronouns in the process of naming? References to the Divine as "She" or use of female images often cause discomfort or evoke ridicule.

"Without a vocabulary, the idea of feminine divinity is even hard to imagine" (Bolen, 2001, p. 37). Because of the history of androcentric theology, Johnson (1992, p. 42) states that the use of the term *God* is problematic. Despite attempts to imbue the Divine with feminine qualities, use of the term *God* will most likely suggest a male divinity, at least in Western worldviews (Christ, 2003, p. 17). Feminist theologians challenge the androcentric thinking and naming of the Divine (Christ, 2003). Rosemary Radford Ruether (as cited in Johnson, 1992, p. 42) suggests the term *Goddess*. Carol Christ (2003, p. 17) uses the term *Goddess/God* to capture a more complete picture of the divine, one that is not exclusively male. The very word *goddess* creates a great deal of discomfort for many. It is, however, merely a word, an archetype, another symbol to help women and men to connect to the feminine energy of the Divine.

Female images and symbols are necessary to embrace the whole of the Divine (Johnson, 1992, p. 49). These images are "not the expression of the feminine dimension of the divine, but the expression of the fullness of divine power and care shown in a female image" (Johnson, 1992, p. 56). In this section, we explore some images as alternatives to the traditional image of the Divine as male and white. It is important to note that although these images focus on the feminine, not all women are drawn to them and, as important, some men are.

We are therapists, not theologians. This section on alternative Divine images is included so we might recognize that some clients may present with negative images of the Divine, for example, a wrathful father. They may not give much thought to alternative images such as the "feminine face of God" (Anderson & Hopkins, 1992; Fincher, 2006), which may be more healing for them. Other clients may feel drawn to the Sacred Feminine and perceive the Divine using female images. For those who do not believe in the Divine or have traditional views, this section points out the importance of attending to potential countertransference reactions.

Goddess Archetype

The Goddess archetype is the archetype of the Great Mother who resides within each person and is realized as the capacity to nurture or create (Fincher, 2006). For women, the archetype speaks to her ability to find the Divine within, to relate to a Divine with a feminine face. This helps her to understand the Sacred Feminine not only intellectually but also in her soul (Kidd, 1996). The Sacred Feminine balances the masculine aspects of our culture and provides a greater sense of wholeness (Fincher, 2006).

Johnson (1992, 2007) cautions against substituting one literal interpretation of the Divine for another. Both the words *God* and *Goddess* are symbols to help women and men relate to the Divine mystery. The masculine and feminine are meant to complement each other, to be synthesized to create a whole (Christ, 2003). Female images that reflect similar underlying problems found in male images do not provide the needed counterbalance to the existing male images. For example, addressing female images of the Divine as "Lady" or "Queen" are no more healing than images of "Lord" and "King" (Christ, 2003).

Divine Mother

There are numerous images of the feminine in the Judeo-Christian Bible that evoke the image of God as Mother (Johnson, 2007). Process philosopher Hartshorne states that "the idea of a mother, influencing, but sympathetic to and hence influenced by her child and delighting in its growing creativity and freedom" contrasts with the traditional patriarchal God who is often portrayed as a "tyrant" (Hartshorne, as cited in Christ, 2003, p. 16). Some women, who are mothers themselves, are drawn to this image because it affirms the sacredness of their current life role (Fischer, 1988). Images of the Divine Mother are healing and comforting to many women and men. Johnson (2007), however, cautions that patriarchal conceptualizations of motherhood are oppressive and need to be avoided. However, images of the Divine Mother are often associated with comfort, nurturance, nourishment, and protection. It evokes images of being held and loved (Johnson, 2007).

Sophia/Wisdom

Sophia, derived from the Greek for wisdom, is the archetype of feminine spiritual wisdom. She represents "soul knowledge" (Bolen, 2001, p. 26), not knowledge that comes from an external authority, but the "wisdom that dwells in us" (Bolen, 2001, p. 27). Sophia (Wisdom) is a female image of the Divine introduced in the Old Testament and running "like a golden thread through the whole Christian tradition" (Johnson, 2007, p. 104). In the early Christian era, she was an important figure among the Gnostic Christians, but because the Gnostic literature was not included in the canonical scriptures, Sophia became a forgotten figure within monotheistic, patriarchal religion. She became "wisdom" with a lower case "w" (Bolen, 2001). Women biblical scholars argue that Sophia is not merely a feminine aspect of the Divine but is "the unfathomable mystery of the living God in female imagery," which goes beyond images of the Divine as mother to include a female deity who governs, teaches, exercises justice, and gives life" (Johnson, 2007, p. 105).

Marian Devotion

Within traditional spiritual paths, some find the Sacred Feminine through devotion to Mary, the Mother of God. This provides a vehicle to imbue feminine symbols with sacred significance (Kidd, 1996). In several places throughout the world, including France, Spain, and Switzerland, Mary is represented as the Black Madonna. These images are different from the usual portrayal of a fair-skinned Madonna. The Black Madonna reclaims the earthy qualities associated with the feminine suppressed by Western cultures and are especially important as they are more inclusive than the patriarchal images of God as white (Christ, 2003; Fincher, 2006).

Critics of Marian devotion state that the image of Mary reflects patriarchal gender stereotypes of submissiveness, docility, and obedience (Canda & Furman, 1999, 2010). They also contend that the belief that she conceived her son without the benefit of intercourse further implies that virtuous women will suppress their sexuality (Kidd, 1996; Walker, 2000).

Diversity in Practice

Practice Behavior Example: *Gain sufficient self-awareness to eliminate the influence of personal biases and values in working with diverse groups.*

Critical Thinking Question: Discuss the importance of feminine symbols in the spiritual lives of women. How would you address this in your work with women clients who are addressing spiritual concerns in treatment? What obstacles may arise?

RECONCILIATION AND INTEGRATION

Those who seek the Sacred Feminine within patriarchal structures may resolve their struggle in a variety of ways. Despite some oppressive characteristics, many women and men are able to find spiritual nourishment within their traditional religions (Corbett, 1997, as cited in Canda & Furman, 2010, p. 130). Some women may decide to augment patriarchal rituals by joining a women's spirituality group or attending feminist spiritual rituals (Chittister, 1998, p. 32). Some stay within traditional religions out of fear of censor or ridicule, whereas some leave their religions for a while, perhaps seeking alternative paths, but later return. Some others leave the oppressive dust of patriarchy behind, never to return (Chittister, 1998, p. 32); the absence of these dissenting voices leaves a void for all, a deafening silence. These voices are needed to help transform spiritual structures, making them more responsive to the spiritual needs of both women and men.

ALTERNATIVE PATHS

In the search for the Sacred Feminine some have sought women-centered spiritual paths, finding patriarchal traditions not viable. "All across the country, all around the world, women are picking up the discarded threads of patriarchal religions and reweaving new myths, rituals, and traditions for themselves" (Peay, 2002, p. 2).

There are a small number of women and men who belong to spiritual groups that are earth- or nature-centered and honor both the feminine and masculine aspects of the Divine. These movements include Wicca and Paganism or Neo-Paganism. Some members of such groups, fearing ridicule, may be reluctant to share their beliefs and practices with their therapists (Yardley, 2008). Careful attention to our biases and countertransference is called for when we work with clients who find spiritual fulfillment via these paths.

TREATMENT

We began this chapter by focusing on the lack of women's sacred stories. We also noted that not all men's spiritual experiences fit the dominant discourse. Therefore, our major focus of treatment when working with clients with spiritual issues should be on facilitating their ability to access and tell the story of their spiritual journey. Story telling, when authentic, is healing and transformative (Happel, as cited in Simpkinson & Simpkinson, 1993, p. 2). It is essential that clients' spiritual experience be respected (Fischer, 1988), even though it may not fit within a traditional path.

Narrative therapy is a postmodern approach to treatment and is applicable to helping women and men tell their sacred stories. An assumption of narrative theory is that individuals *story* their lives, and that often these stories are "saturated" with problems. Together, the therapist and client *deconstruct* the problem-saturated story and reconstruct a new one that is healing (Cooper & Lesser, 2011). Women and men may need to revise or reconstruct the parts of their sacred story that marginalize or harm them, replacing them with more affirming and growth-enhancing elements (Simpkinson & Simpkinson, 1993).

Stories told to a receptive listener bring self-acceptance, resolution, and an ability to transcend painful and constraining internal storylines (Maguire, 1998). Thus, the greatest gift of therapy is to listen to and listen for the unvoiced sacred story, especially those stories that have been silenced by oppression. We may need to gently help clients find their voice to bring these stories to light so they may weave them into their history and deconstruct those that limit them. Peay (2002), in her book *Soul Sisters: The Five Sacred Qualities of a Woman's Soul*, quotes an Arabian proverb that sums up well the focus of treatment for all, but which is especially important for therapeutic work focused on women's and men's unvoiced spiritual stories:

> [A therapist] is one to whom one may pour out all the contents of one's heart, chaff and grain together, knowing that the gentlest of hands will take and sift it, keep what is worth keeping and with a breath of kindness blow the rest away (p. 199).

Treatment techniques to assist clients in connecting with and voicing their experience are particularly suitable. For example, journaling, guided imagery, or creative art techniques provide a vehicle for them to connect with and express their sacred story (see chapter 5 for further details on interventions). Providing a sacred space and attentive listening is critical to this process (see chapter 3).

CONCLUSION

In this chapter we focused on the importance and the neglect of women's sacred stories. In particular, patriarchal religious structures have ignored or silenced the spiritual experiences of women. We also recognized that the dominant spiritual discourse does not include the experiences of all men, thereby silencing their stories as well. As an alternative to the patriarchal worldview, we explored a feminist approach to spirituality, including the search for the Sacred Feminine. We compared the variations of women's and men's spiritual development and included a section on the Divine images, and addressed traditional and alternative images and symbols to help individuals access the Sacred Feminine.

The purpose of feminist spirituality is not to demean men, but to affirm women. It is not to castrate men, but to empower women. It is not to exclude men, but to warmly invite them to join with women in creating a spirituality that honors both women and men. Without the other, either approach alone lacks wholeness, and thus cannot be holy. Rohr (2005) states that the Divine Feminine and the Sacred Masculine must join for a spirituality to be healthy.

It is important to note that much of the literature focuses on the oppressive effects of patriarchy on women and to some extent on men. Less is written about the internal spiritual experiences and development over the life span of women and men, especially those who do not fit the traditional paradigms. Furthermore, the primary focus of this chapter has been on women and men from the Judeo-Christian tradition and on those who have no religious affiliation. As mentioned previously, some of the Eastern religions have positive images of feminine deities. Among the indigenous spiritual traditions, women often hold prominent leadership positions (Canda & Furman, 1999). Although there is some literature on the subjugation of Muslim women, there is a paucity of literature about their inner experiences and what Islam means to them. How does she find spiritual nourishment? Is she drawn to the Sacred Feminine? If we attempt to provide therapy for such groups without answering these questions, we would be at risk of making assumptions based on non-Islamic values. For example, to criticize a woman's right to wear Islamic dress when she chooses to is as oppressive as those forms of religion or government that insist she wear it when she does not wish to or does not find meaning in doing so. Likewise, we do not know if some Muslim men feel pressure when their spiritual story does not fit with the dominant story for men in their tradition.

And finally, it is important to not romanticize feminist spirituality or to create new stereotypes. Not all women are drawn to the Sacred Feminine, just as some men are. My purpose is to provide alternatives so that women and men may find a healthy form of spirituality that fits their needs. Many women and men are able to take the fragments of different spiritual paths and stitch them together to create a spiritual patchwork quilt that fits their needs. A Catholic priest once raged that religion is not like a supermarket. One cannot pick and choose what one wishes. This comment reflects the worst of patriarchy; one is expected to follow a prescribed path, allowing the clergy to hold all the power and have control over all. The ability to create a spiritual path that encourages growth, connection, compassion, and concern for others reflects a mature and vital spirituality.

PRACTICE TEST

PRACTICE TEST The following questions will test your knowledge of the content found within this chapter and help you prepare for the licensing exam by applying chapter content to practice. For more questions styled like the licensing exam, visit **MySocialWorkLab.com**

1. Pamela told her social worker that she was not feeling spiritually nourished by her spiritual community. She believes her community views women as "second-class citizens." Her social worker should

   a. suggest she leave the community because it is oppressive.

   b. recommend she speak up in the community so all women congregants will benefit.

   c. point out other nurturing aspects of her community.

   d. ask if she is open to learning about feminist spirituality.

2. Melissa is very interested in the Sacred Feminine. Tonya, a religiously conservative social worker, is uncomfortable with the information Melissa is sharing. Tonya should

   a. try to avert discussion of the topic.

   b. sit in silence as Melissa discusses this topic.

   c. seek supervision to discuss her feelings and how to work effectively with Melissa.

   d. suggest Melissa discuss these issues within her spiritual community.

3. Henry, a 45-year-old, has been seeking a spirituality that sustains him. Although raised Catholic, religion was not important to him. The social worker should

   a. encourage him to explore many spiritual paths.

   b. use a narrative approach to help him voice his spiritual journey.

   c. encourage him to read about many traditions.

   d. share his or her own spiritual journey if Henry wants to hear it.

4. Veronica tells her social worker that she is attracted to the feminine aspect of the Divine. The social worker should

   a. explain that the Divine is neither male nor female.

   b. avoid using any pronouns in reference to the Divine.

   c. explore Veronica's attraction.

   d. tell Veronica that most people still think of the Divine as "He."

1. Some clients find spiritual nourishment in communities that may be categorized as patriarchal. Others experience difficulties in these communities. What are some issues that might arise when working with those who have difficulties? How should social workers handle ethical dilemmas, for example, if they believe the community is oppressive or harmful to their client?

2. Discuss why a narrative approach is helpful to understanding the spiritual stories of men and women.

SUCCEED WITH

PEARSON
mysocialworklab

Visit **MySocialWorkLab** for more licensing exam test questions, and to access case studies, videos, and much more.

Rachael was raised as a devout Roman Catholic. She attended Catholic school, went to Mass every Sunday, and followed all the rules and obligations of the Church. As far as Rachael knew, the world was Catholic and everyone practiced his or her religion. She socialized with her friends from school, and her parents socialized with family and the parents of Rachael's school friends. She remembers her parents talking about how excited they were when President Kennedy was elected. Although devout, her family was very liberal. They were actively involved in parish activities; discussions about religion and the Catholic Church's view on social issues were frequent, with lively conversations during dinner.

After graduating from Catholic High School, Rachael decided to attend a non-Catholic university. Although her parents would have preferred that she attend a Catholic college, they understood her need to expand beyond the parochial environment within which she had been raised thus far. Rachael had always been a good student and was excited about being away from home, the intellectual stimulation of the college world, and meeting new people. Her first year roommate, Lydia, was a nonpracticing Methodist. When Rachael attended Mass the first Sunday she was away, Lydia commented that she was surprised that Rachael would continue to practice her religion now that she was away from her parents. Rachael was surprised that Lydia did not attend church or seem to feel any sense of connection to her spiritual path. Despite the surprise each other felt about their religious or lack of religious practice, the two young women got along well and shared many interests. Although their religious backgrounds differed they enjoyed long conversations about the meaning of life and other existential concerns. Rachael was particularly surprised to hear that Lydia was not sure there was a God. When Rachael asked her, Lydia indicated that she could not see how there could be because there was so much suffering in the world. Because Rachael had been raised to be open to others' beliefs and opinions she tried to understand Lydia's point of view. She found it made her sad that Lydia did not believe in God or engage in any spiritual practices.

In sophomore year, Lydia met a young man whom she was convinced she was in love with; she was also convinced that he loved her. Rachael rarely saw her as Lydia frequently spent time with her boyfriend, often spending the night in his nearby apartment. One day, Rachael returned from classes to find Lydia in tears. She told Rachael she was pregnant and Danny (her boyfriend) had ended their relationship. Rachael tried to be as supportive as possible, but felt uncomfortable when Lydia decided to have an abortion. This incident stirred a great deal of confusion for Rachael. She started to become aware that for the past several months, she had been questioning her beliefs and this latest incident added to her confusion. She sought support through the campus ministry program. Rachael was surprised to encounter a woman spiritual director, but felt a strong connection to her. She was delighted to learn that the woman was also Catholic. In her conversations with the campus minister, Rachael began to clarify some of her own thoughts and beliefs. She realized that she was opposed to abortion, and struggled to understand Lydia's decision. Rachael decided to continue with the campus minister, raising other concerns that had recently troubled her. One issue that emerged was the institutional structure of her religion and the role of women. Rachael was taking a course on women's studies, and it raised her consciousness about the marginalization of women in her church. One day the campus minister used the word *She* in reference to God. Rachael questioned her and the minister talked about how God is beyond male or female. Rachael felt a sense of yearning to learn more about this. The campus minister gave her literature and invited her to a women's spiritual discussion group. After several weeks Rachael commented to the campus minister that she had always felt Catholicism was the right spiritual path for her. Even after being introduced to different religions and belief systems, she remained drawn to Catholicism but, even though she had not been previously aware of it, she felt like a second-class citizen. She had contemplated theology as her major, but questioned what she could do with it, because "she's not a man." The idea of the Sacred Feminine stirred her soul and she wanted to actively seek ways to integrate her Catholic beliefs and her newfound understanding of feminist spirituality. Rachael told her parents and friends, "I feel as though I've come home spiritually."

1. How do you think Rachael's spiritual development would have progressed without her discovery of the Sacred Feminine?

2. What elements of Rachael's spiritual journey indicated that she might be open to the Sacred Feminine when she discovered it?

3. How important do you think the gender of the spiritual director was to Rachael's discovery of feminist spirituality?

11

Leaving the Labyrinth: Gifting the World

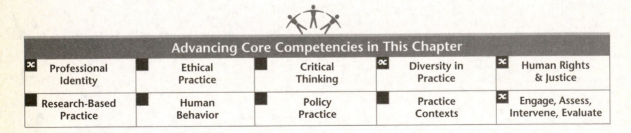

When we begin, we often do not think about the end. Both the labyrinth walk and therapy inevitably come to an end. If the experience is reflected on and processed well, the ending becomes a new beginning. Both require a move away from the sacred time and space, toward daily life, enriched, energized, and prepared to implement into our everyday activities the wisdom learned during the process.

In this chapter, continuing with our metaphor of the labyrinth, we explore the ending phase of therapy. This critical stage of treatment requires that we help clients reflect on the treatment process, the gains made, possible disappointments, the meaning of the therapeutic relationship, and plans to implement new skills and insights. As discussed in chapter 1, therapy, like the labyrinth walk, requires a decision to enter the process, moving through unknown territory, encountering challenges, gaining skills and insights, and a time of moving away from the process to implement the gifts from the journey. Some clients and therapists may relate to the metaphor of the labyrinth walk. This process is circular and the center of the labyrinth, like the sacred space in therapy, provides a place of respite from one's burdens, a time of stillness so one may encounter her feelings, gain insight, and make decisions. Others may prefer the metaphor of the epic spiritual journey, introduced in chapter 10, which is a more linear process. The hero or heroine heeds the call to leave the familiar, enter unknown territory, face a period of testing, and, enlightened and transformed, returns to his or her community to share the gifts (or boon) of the journey. Regardless of the metaphor, return from the sacred space to the ordinary world is a reality, and the ability to implement the gains made within the sacred space is the litmus test of success. In the epic journey, personal transformation and the implementation of the gifts justify the time away from the ordinary world (Volger, 1998). Implementation of the therapeutic gifts in the client's life validates the hard work the client did in treatment as well as her investment of time. Because she has resolved her issues, she is now more whole, and the benefits ripple out to those around her.

Although the gains made in therapy are beneficial to the individual and often to those in his immediate world, we discuss in this chapter expanding the implementation of therapeutic benefits to include the larger community. Thus, we discuss the relationship between the gifts of therapy and social justice. You might wonder why social justice is included in a chapter on ending therapy. As one develops spiritually, there is an increasing focus on altruism and the unit of transformation moves from the individual level to the community level. The compassion developed during therapy motivates the client to open her heart to the suffering of others and to become willing to "*take action*" to relieve it (italics in the original) (Thich Nhat Hanh, as cited in Bien, 2008, p. 84). Therefore, it seems logical that the benefits of spiritually focused therapy would emphasize not only implementing the gifts from the journey within one's immediate sphere but also expanding it for the greater good. Not all clients will bring the benefits of therapy beyond their immediate circle, but those who are motivated may find it helpful to integrate this into their developing spirituality.

TERMINOLOGY

Before we proceed further, I would like to address the commonly used terminology for the ending process: *termination* (Mahoney, 2003; Sperry, Carlson, & Kjos, 2003; Woods & Hollis, 2000). In a profession that seeks to create a holding environment (sacred space), to develop and maintain an empathic connection to clients (a sacred relationship), and to provide an emotionally corrective experience, why would we want to "terminate" clients when their therapy has been completed? I believe the word is cold, creates distance, and reflects our own feelings of loss or sadness when clients finish treatment. They have accomplished their goals, resolved their dilemmas, gained insight, and learned new skills. They are ready to move on, no longer needing our assistance or our support. Of course, we are thrilled that they have reached a resolution, we genuinely wish them well, and we have a sense of pride that they are able to complete treatment and have developed the skills to successfully negotiate the hills and valleys of life without us. But we are either mistaken or have failed to allow the client to mean something to us (Yalom, 2002) if we do not have some feelings of sadness, some sense that we will miss them. Therefore, I use the term *endings* to discuss the final phase of treatment. You may prefer the terms *closure*, *transitions*, or *new beginnings*.

THE ENDING PROCESS

The ending process is a transition from one form of support and problem solving (therapy) to a more natural, informal one (such as family, friends, or self-help groups) (Murphy & Dillon, 2003, p. 274). Mahoney (2003) believes the ending phase is the most important aspect of treatment. It provides the opportunity for clients to consolidate gains, celebrate accomplishments, process the ending of a valued relationship, and begin plans for life beyond therapy (Fortune, as cited in Murphy & Dillon, 2003, pp. 283–284). The therapist is pivotal to successful endings, which require more skill, sensitivity, and aplomb than any other phase of treatment (Walsh, 2007; Woods & Hollis, 2000). If not negotiated successfully, the benefits of therapy are not maximized; in fact, they may be reversed, and the expectation that clients will continue to grow beyond therapy will not be realized (Woods & Hollis, 2000). To end effectively, therapists must recognize the importance of the process and help clients work through their feelings about ending.

THE TRANSITION FROM THERAPY

Regardless of its gifts, after completion of therapy, as with the labyrinth walk, clients need to discover their "ordinary feet again" (Sands, 2001, p. 74). Along the winding path, the client has slipped into a rhythm, attending to her walking, her breathing, and opening to insights. Daily distractions vanish for a time, and she experiences a heightened sense of attention and attunement. She feels spiritually grounded, with a sense of peace and well-being, and a reluctance to leave the labyrinth and return to the stressors of everyday life (Curry, 2000). During therapy, the client also slips into a rhythm. She explores her feelings, is empathically supported by the therapist, and becomes accustomed to the therapist's warmth, concern, and attentive presence. She may be reluctant to leave this sacred space to face the challenges of life without therapeutic support. She may be uncertain about her ability to use her newly developed skills, and she may question the reliability of the nontherapeutic support system she now has to rely on. Even those who feel confident in their new abilities and certain of their support systems may be reluctant to leave the therapeutic relationship.

Pablo had been reluctant to enter therapy when he and his spouse were having serious relationship problems. Because the therapist was a woman, he expected her to take his partner's side as so many of his female coworkers had done. However, after several sessions, Pablo began to realize that the therapist was accepting of his perspective and respectful of his feelings. Rather than point out who was right or wrong, she gently explored both his and his spouse's feelings, thoughts and behaviors, helping them understand what had led them to act as they did. Pablo began to slip into the rhythm of expecting support rather than criticism. When it became time to end treatment he was anxious that he would be unable to continue to understand his marital relationship and make changes without compromising his integrity. With humor, Pablo remarked that he wanted to end therapy even less that he wanted to begin it.

ENDING TASKS

The process of ending involves several important tasks (Murphy & Dillon, 2003; Walsh, 2007; Woods & Hollis, 2000). The therapist must help the client reflect on the process of treatment, evaluate the work done, consolidate the gains made, address disappointments, point out remaining work, and plan the implementation of therapeutic gains in the client's life. In addition, the therapist and client need to discuss the ending of the therapeutic relationship, along with the accompanying feelings.

Reflection

The journey from the center of the labyrinth is a time of reflection. As one turns and leaves the labyrinth, he thinks about what has occurred on his walk, what insights he discovered, and he begins to plan how he can implement them into his everyday life (Curry, 2000). In an analogous process, the client ending therapy needs to reflect on the work done while in treatment, the goals accomplished, the remaining work, and the meaning of the therapeutic relationship. Reflection allows her to remember what issues brought her to treatment. She is able to compare her current situation to the one she originally presented with and realizes the progress she has made (Murphy & Dillon, 2003). She can reflect on what she expects from life without therapy and anticipate challenges and make plans to successfully meet them. Reflection helps the transition from learning within the process to implementation in the client's life (Curry, 2000). When therapists help clients to process the therapeutic relationship, clients are often able to internalize the relationship as a future resource. It can become a prototype of a healthy relationship and thus be used as a yardstick to measure future relationships (Murphy & Dillon, 2003; Woods & Hollis, 2000). In this fashion, reflection helps clients to implement therapeutic gains beyond therapy.

The ending phase is a time of reflection for the therapist as well. He evaluates the work done by the client, as well as the impact the client has had on him. He reflects on the gains or lack of gains made by the client and how this dovetails with his practice expertise. Has he been helpful to the client? Has he impeded her growth in any way? Has the client accomplished her goals with his help or in spite of him? How has this client helped him grow as a therapist, as a person? Regardless of the therapeutic outcome, all clients teach us something and the ending process is a time to reflect on and acknowledge our gratitude to them.

Recognizing Potential Growth in Endings

In a society that focuses on goals, the processing of endings is often overlooked. Curry (2000) remarks that within the labyrinth, energy is often expended in getting to the center, but after arriving there, one may tune out and miss the opportunity to continue to gain insight from reflecting on the return path. This reflection is needed to help implement the insights and wisdom gleaned from the walk. Likewise, in the therapeutic process, clients often do not recognize the benefit of processing the ending stage. If therapists are unaware or lack the necessary skills to help clients with this phase, the opportunity to evaluate the time together and the work done is likely to be missed. It is understandable that clients are focused on solving the problems that brought them to treatment and are eager to leave once they are resolved. But the ending phase provides a richness that cannot be recognized in the early phases of treatment (Walsh, 2003). Therefore, it is imperative that therapists help clients end well.

Theresa was a clinical social worker newly hired by a preventive service agency. Her client, Mrs. DeMarco, achieved her goals and her two children were returned to her care. Theresa discussed ending services with the client in her weekly supervision. She indicated that the client had not wanted to come for services, and now that she had her children back, Theresa thought she should begin closing the case at the next session. With supervision, Theresa began to reflect and realize that ending services might not be appropriate at this juncture. Even though the goals had been met, the client was experiencing a transition with her children's return home. More important, Theresa explored what treatment may have meant to Mrs. DeMarco and how she might feel ending services. Theresa reflected on her own feelings about working with this client, whom she initially did not like and blamed for losing custody of her children. She was surprised to realize that she had come to respect Mrs. DeMarco and validated the hard work she did. She developed more compassion for her in the course of treatment and was able to empathize with the struggles that had led to her to lose custody of her children. Without reflection, Theresa would have acted on the erroneous assumption that because Mrs. DeMarco did not initially want services, that she did not come to value them. Theresa was now more prepared to eventually help Mrs. DeMarco with the ending phase when it was appropriate.

Evaluating the Work

Within the twists and turns of the labyrinth, one finds resources she had previously not known she had (Curry, 2000, p. 8). Likewise, during therapy clients not only solve presenting problems and learn new skills but also discover strengths and abilities of which they had been unaware. To realize the strengths discovered and to consolidate the gains made by the client, it is critical that the therapist evaluate the client's work in the ending process. Furthermore, it prepares the client for ongoing growth (Woods & Hollis, 2000). As the therapist and client review the work and acknowledge the client's accomplishments, the therapist affirms the client's strengths, points out the work remaining, and encourages the client to implement the benefits of therapy in his everyday life (Murphy & Dillon, 2003; Woods & Hollis, 2000). During the evaluation, clients often benefit from comparing their life situation at the start of therapy to their current situation as they prepare to end therapy (Murphy & Dillon, 2003). Clients sometimes forget the extent of their suffering when they initiated treatment. The purpose is not to remind them of how distressed they felt, but to help them realize the progress they have made. This is particularly important as clients sometimes feel as if they have regressed in the ending phase (Walsh, 2003). Reminding them of how far they have come helps them acknowledge their growth and tells them that they are now well equipped to face future challenges (Murphy & Dillon, 2003). Explicit reflection on therapeutic gains in the final stage enhances the likelihood that gains will endure over time (Woods & Hollis, 2000). At times insights from the process are not recognized until later. This highlights the need to consolidate client learning and point out remaining work before saying good-bye (Hogan, 2003; Mahoney, 2003; Yalom, 1995).

In processing the ending phase of treatment, therapists need to elicit feedback on possible disappointments regarding the therapeutic process or the therapist (Murphy & Dillon, 2003; Woods & Hollis, 2000). The goals achieved may differ from the client's original expectations. As an individual enters the labyrinth, she may be looking for specific guidance on an issue but may receive something different from what she expected (Curry, 2000). When therapists open this topic for discussion, clients are able to voice disappointments or reveal that what they received surpassed what they had hoped for when they began. Evaluation allows us to learn what has been helpful to the client and what has not (Murphy & Dillon, 2003; Woods & Hollis, 2000).

Lorraine, a caring spouse and mother, was devoted to her family and friends. She focused on other's needs and tirelessly tried to help anyone she could. She was less aware of her own needs, and when she was aware, she minimized them, preferring to focus on others. Recently, she began to develop some health problems from her lack of self-care. When her therapy was ending, the therapist asked Lorraine what had been most helpful to her. After reflecting, she stated that although it had been difficult for her at the time, the therapist's gentle refocusing on her needs was the most beneficial. After a period of time she was able to balance her desire to care for others with her own needs for self-care.

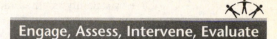

Engage, Assess, Intervene, Evaluate

Practice Behavior Example: *Critically analyze, monitor, and evaluate interventions.*

Critical Thinking Question: Discuss the importance of evaluation of the work when ending therapy with clients. What methods would you use to evaluate how effective treatment was?

Feelings and the Ending Phase

To help clients express their feelings about the ending process, therapists need to be aware of their own feelings about ending with the client. Does the therapist feel that the client is ready to end therapy? Was the ending planned? Is she satisfied with the therapy outcomes or filled with regret about how treatment proceeded? How does the therapist feel about saying good-bye to the client?

Clients often have a variety of feelings about ending therapy (Murphy & Dillon, 2003; Walsh, 2007; Woods & Hollis, 2000). Some are ready to end and eager to implement the skills learned in treatment. They may leave with little sadness or regret. Some are ambivalent, excited about their accomplishments, but perhaps sad to leave the therapist. Others are reluctant to end therapy. They may fear that the gains made will not endure, they may question their ability to implement them without the therapist's support, or feelings of loss and sadness may overshadow the gains made in treatment. Woods and Hollis (2000) state that clients may not have strong feelings about ending. This is assumed to be especially true when treatment is brief and does not focus on the therapeutic relationship. Regardless of whether clients entered treatment readily or reluctantly, endings stir up emotional reactions and for many feelings of sadness about saying good-bye. Within the sacred space of therapy clients experience compassion, genuine caring, insight, and recognition of their own strengths, abilities, and inner wisdom. The therapist serves as a role model for healthy relationships in which the client can have her needs met without sacrificing her integrity, her freedom, or her sense of self.

Treatment focused solely on behavioral outcomes may view the therapeutic relationship as utilitarian, rather than as a sacred relationship that enables an individual to transform the difficulties of his life and become more whole. In our current therapeutic climate, with its emphasis on brief treatment models, the power of the relationship and the importance of the ending process may be overlooked or minimized. The length of treatment is mistakenly assumed to predict the importance of the therapy and the therapist to the client. Clients can and often do develop strong attachments to the therapist in a relatively short period of time. This is especially true when clients are dealing with crises. When the importance of the therapeutic relationship is minimized, the client's attachment to the therapist can be seen as client pathology or mismanagement of treatment by the therapist. I have read student papers in which warm, engaging interns apologize or berate themselves because their clients formed a close relationship with them. They have mistakenly assumed that the natural sadness the client feels about ending indicates that they have "allowed" the client to become "dependent" on them. They believe they have done something wrong, rather than acknowledge that allowing the client to form a close relationship with them and rely on them has enabled him to do the work. Such dependence is temporary and is not pathology, but reflects a healthy attachment to the therapist. Therapeutic effectiveness is often contingent on the client's ability to form this attachment with the therapist. Certainly, therapists should not encourage dependency to meet their own needs (e.g., a desire to be needed by others). This is a misuse of the therapeutic relationship. However, the therapist who is open to the client's reliance on her until he is strong enough to negotiate life more independently provides good treatment and demonstrates a measure of courage. Such a therapist is willing to allow a connection and sense of intimacy, knowing that when the treatment ends, she will feel sadness. The therapist allows the connection because it is beneficial to the client, not because she wishes or needs it.

Feelings of sadness on the part of both the therapist and the client are expected during the ending phase. As therapists we anticipate that each client will react to endings in her own unique way, most often with a mixture of excitement, sadness, and uncertainty (Woods & Hollis, 2000). If we see common emotional reactions as pathology, we will not be in a position to help clients negotiate this important phase of treatment. Clearly, clients who have experienced traumatic separations or have abandonment issues will likely process the completion of therapy differently than those who have had more secure attachment over their life span. Such clients may need more help in negotiating the feelings this stage evokes and may need additional encouragement that they are ready to encounter life without therapeutic support. Even clients who do not appear to be connected to you may have strong feelings of which you were not aware until you begin the ending process. This may be especially true if it is not the client's decision to end.

Margarita, a 15-year-old high school student, had been reluctant to engage in the therapeutic process. She did not want to come to therapy and adamantly asserted that she did not need treatment. After several weeks of sessions, the social worker told Margarita that she would be leaving the agency in one month for another position. Margarita initially expressed anger but later admitted that she felt sad the therapist was leaving. Although she had opposed coming to treatment, she found the therapist's warmth and patience with her reluctance a different experience. She stated that "if she had to be in therapy," she wanted to stay with her current therapist. The therapist was surprised that the client felt so strongly about her leaving.

SAYING GOOD-BYE

After resting and reflecting at the center, it is time to retrace the path out of the labyrinth and return to the outside world. The hero or heroine on the epic journey needs to leave the special world and return to the ordinary world. And clients who have been in treatment need to transition back to a world that does not include the therapist or the therapeutic process. The ending, however, is the beginning (Curry, 2000). Curry (2000, p. 89) states, to honor her labyrinth walk as a sacred experience, she utters a "prayer of gratitude" as she turns from the center. When we process the ending stage and take time to say good-bye to our clients, we honor the time we have spent with them as a sacred experience. Although feelings of sadness often occur in the ending phase, the final good-bye is often more celebratory. The therapist's encouragement of the client's ability to continue without therapy helps the client to view the ending as a "launching" or as a new beginning. The goal is to help the client "remember" the therapist "as someone who is permanently in their corner, who believes in them, and who is rooting for them" (Murphy & Dillon, 2003).

IMPLEMENTING THE THERAPEUTIC GIFTS

During the ending phase, therapists help clients anticipate challenges and plan strategies to successfully implement their new skills and insights (Murphy & Dillon, 2003). They help them generalize the skills learned in the specific issues dealt with in therapy to anticipated challenges ahead (Gambrill, 2006). The time in therapy may provide support and respite, the labyrinth walk respite from the daily distractions of life, and the epic journey a great adventure, but without application of what was learned, the benefits of therapy are greatly limited (Curry, 2000).

The gains of the labyrinth walk are meant to be implemented in the walker's life (Curry, 2000). The sacred relationship with the therapist is meant to be a springboard to healthier relationships in the client's everyday world. And, therapy is meant to be more than respite from the burdens and difficulties clients bring to treatment. It is a "dress rehearsal" for life, not a substitution for it (Yalom, 2002, p. 182). Even if clients work hard in sessions, but do not integrate their insights into their daily lives, they will remain unchanged (Yalom, 2002). For therapy to be successful, clients must be able to implement the changes made in treatment in their daily lives. The gifts may include self-awareness, improved relationships, newly found self-esteem, openness to life, especially to his feelings, and a sense of personal agency (Mahoney, 2003, p. 187).

SPIRITUALITY AND SOCIAL JUSTICE

The challenge of the labyrinth is "to leave the center-point and return outward to perform deep, loving service to the world, carrying the gifts and knowings of this visit to the heart of things" (Curry, 2000, p. xi). Like the therapeutic benefits or the labyrinth gifts, spiritual benefits may initially refer to the relationship to self. Ultimately, however, spirituality requires that we recognize the interconnectedness of all beings (Kornfield, 1993). It is not uncommon to imagine spiritual life as a life lived by the cloistered nun, monk, or hermit, who shelters himself or herself from the practical world of everyday life, engaging in a solitary relationship with the Divine. And although there are some women and men who follow this path, most humans need to be spiritual beings in a secular world of human relationships and work. Modern spiritual life demands that, rather than retreat from it, one embrace the world and put his spirituality in action (Vladimiroff, 2007). "In today's world, the test of any authentic faith is action" (Wallis, 2002, p. xxiii). Spirituality needs to be a force for community, global, and planetary transformation as well as individual transformation (Wallis, 2002).

As one develops a more mature spirituality, self-transformation "spirals" outward and includes care and concern for others and has a "ripple effect of renewing the face of the earth" (Harris, 1989, p. 181). We embrace the knowledge that "spirituality is what we *do* because of what we say we believe, rather than the pursuit of belief itself" (italics in the original) (Chittister, 1998, p. 15). Spirituality is not something we have, but something we practice (Wallis, 2002). Thus, one moves from implementing the gifts from therapy in her personal life to a broader context and becomes interested in transforming the world to create a more harmonious planet and address issues of oppression and social injustices. We move from solitude toward hospitality (Nouwen, 1975) and engage in the process of opening our hearts and widening the circle of compassion. We go beyond being generous to our loved ones to embrace "royal giving," the act of spontaneously being generous to strangers (Kornfield, 1993).

From this perspective, spirituality demands that we confront oppression and social injustices, both in its blatant and subtle forms. As our heart awakens (Welwood, 2000), we become more compassionate and hear the voices of the downtrodden, the cries of those who suffer, and the pleas of those who are marginalized. We recognize a myriad of social ills, which we may read about in the newspaper, see on television, or experience firsthand. Some forms of oppression and injustice occur in far away places whose names we may not know how to pronounce or in countries we cannot locate on a map. Others happen in our own neighborhoods and communities. We recognize the spiritual and moral foundation of social problems (Wallis, 2002). Chittister (1998) challenges those who see racism, profiteering, and militarism as social problems, rather than spiritual problems. She states that many injustices are ignored "in the name of patriotism, capitalism, or even religion" (Chittister, 1998, p. 13).

For spirituality to be transformative, we must listen to and care about those who have been forgotten, silenced, or marginalized (Harris, 1989). We are called to question existing social conditions, especially those that foster oppression. The voices we hear and the questions that are raised "call for a sea of change" (Harris, 1989, p.187). These questions emanate from compassion and "beckon us to a deeper place and a more honest life; they are a call to conscience and ultimately, an invitation to transformation" (Wallis, 2002, p. 4). Personal devotion alone is insufficient in a world filled with injustices and oppression (Chittister, 1998; Wallis, 2002).

World Injustices

Throughout the world there are great discrepancies in the allocation of resources, including land and technological and scientific advances (Balasuriya, 2007). The pernicious effects of overwhelming poverty include the lack of basic necessities such as food, clothing, shelter, clean water, health care, suitable employment, and fair wages for work delivered (Johnson, 2007). The power systems of the world are unbalanced. Those who are disadvantaged are the victims of those who dominate and those who dominate are addicted to success and materialism (Duchrow, 2007). Those who live in poverty are "marginalized from the corridors of power where decisions are made that affect the conditions" under which they live (Johnson, 2007, p. 71). The status quo, which benefits the wealthy and powerful at the expense of the oppressed, is maintained because the oppressed are denied political and social power (Duchrow, 2007; Johnson, 2007). "The ship of concentrated poverty, built by systems that plunder the many to feed the wealth of the few and kept afloat by the denial of basic human rights, is laden with a cargo of grinding misery and cruel death" (Johnson, 2007, p. 72).

Social Justice

Social justice goes beyond what is fair for a specific individual to a concern for all (Capeheart & Milovanovic, 2007). Remedial efforts may focus on the allocation and distribution of life's necessities (distributive justice) or responses to harm done (retributive justice) (Capeheart & Milovanovic, 2007). Restorative justice attempts to involve those offended in the resolution of the conflict (Eglash, 1977, as cited in Capeheart & Milovanovic, 2007, p. 55).

The need for social justice is implied in many religious traditions. For example, in the Jewish tradition, justice is necessary for forgiveness (Schimmel, 2002). In fact, compassion demands justice (Faiver, Ingersoll, O'Brien, & McNally, 2001, p. 31). In the Old Testament, prophet Amos remarks poetically, "Let justice roll down like waters, and righteousness like an ever-flowing stream" (Johnson, 2007, p. 75). The New Testament is filled with passages urging good deeds toward those who suffer, including those in poverty. The Buddhists value "royal giving" or spontaneous generosity toward strangers (Kornfield, 1993). One of the Five Pillars of Islam is the giving of alms to those in need (Canda & Furman, 1999, 2010). And the importance of helping others is inherent among Hindus (Canda & Furman, 1999, 2010).

Human Rights and Justice

Practice Behavior Example: *Understand the forms and mechanisms of oppression and discrimination.*

Critical Thinking Question: In this section we address the importance of implementing the benefits of treatment into one's life and broaden this idea to include social justice. Discuss the role of spirituality in working toward social justice. Do you agree that the benefits of spiritually focused therapy should go beyond the individual's daily life?

Liberation Theology

Boff (2007) states that every crisis in the world poses an opportunity for transformation, along with the threat of devastating failure. One movement to address the injustices of the world is liberation theology. Drawing on the Judeo-Christian tradition, liberation theology focuses on the need to address issues of overwhelming poverty and massive injustices (Canda & Furman, 1999; Johnson, 2007). It is a grassroots movement, which emerged initially in Latin America and later in Africa, Asia, and among some populations within the United States as a response to the oppression of and injustice toward the collective poor (Boff & Boff, 1996; Gutierrez, 2007; Johnson, 2007). The movement aims to go beyond the provision of necessities and reforms, to challenge the maintenance of the status quo, and inspire the oppressed to "grasp their identity as active subjects who could shape their own history" (Johnson, 2007, p. 73; Boff, 1996).

Liberation theology does not consider distributive and retributive social justice to be sufficient. Aid, although well meaning, fails to recognize the oppression inherent in poverty. It is not the lack of necessities alone that keep people in poverty, but social structures that deny access to resources. Aid only provides immediate relief, not long-lasting solutions. Likewise, reforms are designed to improve conditions but not change the basic social structures and relationships that create and maintain poverty in the first place. For true liberation, the only appropriate strategies are those designed to increase consciousness (conscientization) among those affected by poverty and allow them to understand their rights, to organize themselves, and to challenge and transform the existing status quo (Boff, 1996).

Other Liberation Movements

Although several liberation movements aim to transform society and better the lives of those who are oppressed, there are nuances in the goals and foci of each. As stated in Chapter 10, *womanist*, *Spirita*, and *mujerista* theologies criticize traditional feminists for failing to include issues of race and class along with the obstacles created by gender (Comas-Diaz, 2008; Grey, 2007; Johnson, 2007). Gebara (1999) criticizes traditional liberation theology for ignoring the oppression of women and the earth.

Both Black and Latin American liberation theologies focus on social reform (Eppig, 2008). However, because traditional Christian and Catholic religion historically has been a tool of oppression for African Americans, questions arise in associating with the God of the oppressor. Black liberation theology conceptualizes a God, imaged as black, whose "action is liberating" (Johnson, 2007, p. 124). The movement is a serious reflection on the issue of racial justice (Althaua-Reid, Petrella, & Susin, 2007; Antonio, 2007). Black theology emerges from the need to affirm the black religious experience in the context of hostility and racism (Antonio, 2007, p. 81) and empowers the black community "to work to break the humiliating chains that hold them down, whether political, economic, legal, or cultural" (Johnson, 2007, p. 123). African American women, however, may distinguish themselves from black liberation theology developed by men and embrace the *womanist* theology, which focuses on "liberation for all who are oppressed by reason of race, sex, and class" (Johnson, 2007, p. 94). If we are to effectively address oppression and social injustice, all voices must be heard and respected. Only in collaboration can we transform the devastating effects of subjugation, marginalization, and oppression. In working with communities, we need to enter our work with a sense of mystery, inviting those we hope to help to teach us about themselves and their experience. Only in collaboration with them can we shape social and political movements that reflect the experiences of those who are affected by them, rather than recreating an oppressive form of helping.

Human Rights and Justice

Practice Behavior Example: *Engage in practices that advance social and economic justice.*

Critical Thinking Question: Discuss the role of liberation theology in addressing world injustices. Address the importance of diversity in liberation movements.

Eco-Liberation

Boff (2007) comments that not only do those living in poverty and oppression seek liberation but also the planet is in need of transformation. "It is not only the poor who cry out. The waters cry out, forests cry out, animals cry out, ecosystems cry out, the Earth cries out" (p. 4). He believes that the rationale that creates social injustices, leading to impoverishment, also leads to the exploitation of the world's resources. The position and attitude of "power over" and domination allow the planet to be exploited to benefit humankind, especially the privileged. Johnson (2007) states that each year 20 percent of the earth's population living in affluent nations use 75 percent of the world's resources and create 80 percent of the waste. Those living in poverty suffer disproportionately from the misuse of our planet. In some parts of the world, women in poverty struggle to birth their young in environments compromised by toxic waste, lack of clean water, healthy food, and fuel to keep them warm (Johnson,

2007). Our rivers and streams are filled with toxic waste, our forests stripped of trees, and our air filled with deadly carcinogens. Our assumption of superiority over other living things is used to justify the lack of respect for the earth and its abundance (Gebara, 1999).

Spirituality and liberation allow us to honor the sacredness of the earth, rather than see it as our handmaiden. Modern spirituality requires that we develop a different relationship with the planet. Technology untamed not only mars the earth but also negatively impacts on the human family (Boff, 2007). Ecofeminism, a form of feminist theology, equates the oppression of women and the domination of the earth. Arguing that patriarchal systems devalue both, ecofeminists strive to improve circumstances for each (Epigg, 2008). Ecofeminism aims to develop a new relationship with the planet and others. It is based on the understanding of the interconnectedness of all beings. "It is a stance, an attitude, a search for wisdom, a conviction that unfolds in close association with the community of all living beings" (Gebara, 1999, p. 23).

Implementing Spirituality and Social Justice in Everyday Life

As we reach beyond our self and our immediate circle of family, friends, and acquaintances, we begin to view the world and all those in it as our "temple" (Kornfield, 1993, p. 293). Our spiritual values may shape our work and our relationship to others and the planet; it demands an increasing concern for those who are oppressed. The relationship between spirituality and social justice may be modest, rather than dramatic. We may avoid goods manufactured by companies that exploit workers or engage in discriminatory or racist practices. Our recognition of the need for social justice and world peace molds our politics, our voting choices, and our position on domestic and international economic policies (Kornfield, 1993).

Spirituality and Politics

Lerner (2006) believes that the desire for social change and spiritual aspirations can be combined to form a powerful vision for the United States, a vision that counteracts one of intolerance and militaristic politics. We can forge a world in which "kindness, generosity, nonviolence, humility, inner and outer peace, love, and wonder at the grandeur of creation stand at the center of our political economic systems and become the major realities of our daily life experience" (Lerner, 2006, p. 24).

Although Wallis (1995, 2002) argues for separation of church and state, he remarks that spiritual values, ethics, and morals need to undergird our political system. Moral issues addressed in the political arena are often narrowly defined and used to exclude rather than being based on compassion and justice (Wallis, 1995). The spiritual life of the modern person needs to be bound up in concern for others (Wallis, 2002). We yearn for politicians who will bring diverse groups together to engage in finding solutions to persistent and pervasive social problems rather than "endless ideological posturing and partisan attack" (Wallis, 1995).

CONCLUSION

To achieve a new vision for ourselves, our communities, our world, and our planet, we need a spirituality for our time, one that weaves our relationship to the Divine with our relationship to others, including our planet. It needs to be inclusive, rather than exclusive of others, healing, and empowering so that all may be affirmed and flourish (Mananzan, 2007).

In this chapter we discussed the therapeutic process of ending therapy using the metaphor of the labyrinth. We focused on the tasks necessary to facilitate this important aspect of treatment, including supporting the client in implementing therapeutic gains in her everyday life. We also envisioned the rippling effects of these benefits to the local community, the world population, and our planet. Modern spirituality needs to address the pernicious effects of oppression. Therefore, we included in this chapter a section on the relationship between spirituality, social injustice, and misuse of the planet and our natural resources. Curry (2000, p. 8) states that the twists and turns of the labyrinth walk allow a person to "walk in meditation to that place within us where the rational merges with the intuitive and the spiritual is reborn. Quite simply, labyrinths are a way to discover the sacred in everyday life." Likewise, spiritually focused therapies are vehicles to develop the insight and skills needed for self-respect, to treat others as sacred beings, and to honor and protect the earth.

PRACTICE TEST

PRACTICE TEST The following questions will test your knowledge of the content found within this chapter and help you prepare for the licensing exam by applying chapter content to practice. For more questions styled like the licensing exam, visit **MySocialWorkLab.com**

1. Ursula has made a commitment to integrate her spirituality and her social work practice. She works in a large faith-based hospital and recently became aware that the hospital's hiring practices discriminate against gays and lesbians. Which of the following should she do if she wishes to integrate her beliefs and her work?

   a. Use her spiritual beliefs to sustain her in her distress about the hospital's hiring practices

   b. Keep silent so she can continue to provide care to her clients

   c. Using her spiritual beliefs would be proselytizing and inappropriate

   d. Use her spiritual beliefs as motivation to bring awareness to her employers about the issue

2. Krystal is ending treatment with an adolescent who had been mandated for treatment. As they process the ending phase, Krystal should

   a. remind the client how resistant he was in the beginning.

   b. focus on the positives of treatment because the client was negative.

   c. explore any disappointments the client had in either the therapist or the treatment process and validate his feelings.

   d. show the client how being negative creates problems for him.

3. Andrea is supporting a political candidate who is running for a local office. The candidate's platform is consistent with her spiritual beliefs. Andrea

   a. can tell her clients about the candidate, but cannot tell them how to vote.

   b. should not discuss the candidate because it would be inappropriate.

   c. cannot discuss the candidate, but can leave flyers outside her office door.

   d. cannot discuss the candidate, but can hang a political poster on the wall.

4. Thomas is committed to his own spiritual growth and in a recent session with his social worker expressed a desire to implement this in a broader context. His social worker should

   a. recommend a community group committed to social justice.

   b. explore what types of projects fit his interests.

   c. suggest he seek ideas within his spiritual community.

   d. focus on his presenting problem, but support his interest in social action.

1. Discuss the relationship between social action and spirituality. Richard is committed to social justice. What issue might arise if he is employed by a faith-based agency? How can he resolve these issues?

2. Discuss the role of spirituality in eco-liberation or other movements designed to preserve the earth's natural resources.

SUCCEED WITH

Visit **MySocialWorkLab** for more licensing exam test questions, and to access case studies, videos, and much more.

This case illustration describes the ending process of a therapy group composed of six women who met for approximately 15 months to work on issues related to sexual assault and early childhood sexual molestation. As the group ends the women decide to engage in a piece of social action to make young women aware of date rape by speaking at local high schools. Collectively they engage in a Take Back the Night event.* Below is a description of the members and the process that led to their decision to "do something to help other women."

Below are the profiles of the women when they began group therapy.

Angela, a 35-year-old white woman, was raped by a "friend" of the family when she was 15. Too afraid to tell anyone, she began to withdraw from friends and broke off her relationship with her boyfriend. Her grades dropped and she became depressed and moody. Her father pressed her to tell him what was wrong. When she eventually told him, he was outraged that this man known to their family should assault her. He confronted the man and ended their relationship. They never reported the incident to the police, nor did they seek counseling for her. Her parents felt as a family they "could help her better than strangers" through her ordeal. Despite their support, Angela remained depressed and after high school decided to work in a local insurance agency rather than go away to college as she had always dreamed. In her late 20s she met a man she trusted enough to develop a relationship with and ultimately married him. He is aware of her past assault and although he is supportive of her, he becomes frustrated when at times she becomes frightened and pushes him away. She occasionally has flashbacks of her rape. Angela began therapy to work on these issues. After six months of individual work, her therapist suggested a therapy group conducted by his colleague. Angela is grateful to her husband for his support and wants to be a "whole person" not only for herself but also "for him." Angela relies a great deal on her spirituality to help her cope. She describes it as "one of the most important things in my life."

Annie, a 31-year-old African American teacher, was raped by her boyfriend during her first year away at college. Initially, she was so traumatized she dropped out of school and cut off contact with her friends. She worked at a local bar and rarely dated or socialized. At the encouragement of a cousin, she eventually sought therapy, returned to school, completed her degree, and became a science teacher at a private high school. Annie loves her work, but at times becomes frightened when she is passed in the hallway by large groups of boys. Although she "truly believes she is safe" in this environment, the "raucousness" of high school boys reminds her of events leading to her assault. She learned of the therapy group through a community health center where she does volunteer work. Annie believes that her faith has helped her cope with her rape. She is dedicated in her "service to others" and hopes that reducing her fear will allow her to "serve more graciously and fully."

Colleen, a 28-year-old unemployed woman, was gang raped following a rock concert three years ago. She was acquainted with several of the boys in the group. She vacillates between anger at them for "ruining her life" and excusing them because they were "high and didn't know what they were doing to her." She also feels guilty that she was drink-

*For more information on Take Back the Night visit http://www.takebackthenight.org/history.html

ing that night and although she was not intoxicated, she "wonders if she had no alcohol, might have made a better choice and gone home." Colleen lives with her sister and stays home most of the time. She refuses to open the door of her apartment unless she is expecting someone. Even then, she insists they call her on the phone before she will open the door. She recognizes that this is "extreme caution" and joined the group so she could "lighten up a bit" but also learn how to "properly protect herself." Colleen had been a practicing Lutheran, but after the rape she has trouble "believing anything."

Marabella is a 35-year-old Mexican American married mother of three small children. When her abusive husband is intoxicated and she refuses to have sexual intercourse with him, he rapes her. A survivor of childhood incest, Marbella was unaware for a long time that her husband's behavior was not only inappropriate but also criminal. She is separated from him at the present time, but consistently contemplates returning to him. She worries about raising her children alone and feels he is trying to change his behavior and she should give him another chance. As a practicing Catholic, Marabella is opposed to divorce.

Denise, a 39-year-old administrative assistant, has struggled with anxiety and depression throughout her adult life. She has had a number of failed relationships. Denise, a survivor of father–daughter incest, trusts neither men nor women. She believes that "men will hurt you; women will let you down." She is angry at her father for the abuse and even angrier at her mother who did not protect her or believe her when she told her she was being abused. It was difficult for her to engage in therapy, but she has been committed and works hard to "believe she can trust her therapist." At the therapist's suggestion, Denise joined the group. She has been anxious about "talking to other woman about painful experiences." She is frightened they will "betray her like her mother." Denise describes herself as "anti-religious." Her parents were "real churchgoers," and she says, "Look what was happening at home." She believes those who are religious are "just a bunch of hypocrites like my parents."

April, a 25-year-old graduate student, was raped six months ago on her way home from work. April is struggling to stay in school and finish her degree in Special Education. She had been working at a fast food restaurant to earn spending money. Although she usually walked home with a friend after work, on the night of the rape, her friend had called in ill so he was not available to escort her home. Three blocks from her apartment, a man wearing a ski mask jumped from behind a bush, pushed her to the ground, and raped her. Since the attack, April has been anxious, has difficulty sleeping, and is afraid to be alone. She worries that her attacker will return and rape her again. April has not "thought too much about spirituality," although several months ago she attended many lectures on Buddhist philosophy and "felt a connection to their beliefs." Since the rape she has not "given it much thought."

Group-Ending Process

Over the course of the group meetings the women shared the details of their sexual abuse, but primarily focused on the impact the abuse has had on their current lives. Thus, they discussed relationship difficulties, the challenges of trusting others and allowing others to know them (intimacy), and fears about their safety, especially with men in close relationships. As they became more open with and trusting of each other their perceptions began to change. They voiced their changing attitude that "some women can be trusted" and expressed optimism that "some men can be as well."

When the group marked its first anniversary, the therapist introduced the idea of ending in a few months. Quite naturally the women were at first opposed. The conversations were marked by phrases such as, "Who can we talk to about this stuff?" "We aren't ready to move on," "We are just becoming really comfortable." Although they were angry about the idea of the group ending, they knew the therapist really cared about them. The therapist shared how she believed they were ready to end the group. She pointed out the progress each of them made individually and as a group. Each of the members acknowledged her own and each other's progress. They "remembered" how mistrustful they were of each other when the group began and now the other members are the "ones we trust most." Despite their recognition of the gains they have made, the members were still hesitant to end. "What if we go back to being scared all the time?"

Over the course of the ending process, Angela, who had previously shared with the group members that she meditated on a regular basis, told the women that recently during her meditation sessions she was feeling the need to "do something about the fear we all feel." As they began to talk about this several ideas emerged. Annie talked about how "service to others and God" has always been an important part of her spirituality. The rape survivors in the group wanted to help "protect" other young woman. As the discussion evolved, the members became enthusiastic about "not keeping our stories to ourselves" and committed to the idea that "they could take charge of their fear."

Annie mentioned her concern about the young women in her high school. She shared with the other women that as a result of hearing each of their stories she had begun to wonder if any of these young women were already in abusive relationships. She worried that some of them were vulnerable to date rape and perhaps some "are even being abused at home." She wanted to do "something" so they would "not get hurt" like her and the other members of the group. Colleen suggested she "tell them her story." The idea evolved that each of them had something to share that might help other young women. As the discussion progressed Annie arranged for April to come and talk at a student assembly. Other members contacted local schools, libraries, a community college, and two community centers. It took a few weeks, but each was able to "arrange a speaking engagement" to share her story. The women were nervous, but excited about their opportunity to help others. After their speaking engagements, each of the women shared that she felt inspired by the responses of young women to her story. Despite their sense of fulfillment and satisfaction with their "social action" the group members were concerned when April told them that she still becomes frightened that she will be attacked again. She and Colleen talked about how angry they are about being frightened and "feeling like they can't go anywhere alone at night."

The therapist told the group about an organization called Take Back The Night, which often holds marches, candlelight vigils, and other events to protest violence against women. She shared with the members that motivated by her work with women like themselves, she participated in a march organized to protest the gang rape of a young woman the previous year. She talked about her feeling of solidarity with the other women who marched alongside her and how it was empowering to stand up for those who have been brutally violated and those who were "robbed of their freedom to walk alone at night."

After a brief discussion the group members decided to participate in an upcoming candlelight vigil. Take Back the Night was sponsoring the vigil to protest a series of recent rapes on a local university campus. The women unanimously agreed that their participation was a "fitting" ending ceremony for their group. Marabella said she thought it was an indication of how far they had come as a group of women, "ready to stand together to take back the night not only for themselves, but for all women and men who are victims of violence everywhere."

1. Although all the women in this group agreed to participate in the same activity, do you think they may have been motivated by different reasons? Are all those reasons spiritual? How important is the role of spirituality in choosing to engage in social action for these women?

2. What are your feelings about the group members' decision to engage in social action as part of their own healing process?

3. Do you think it was appropriate for the group therapist to share with the group her experience of and participation in the Take Back the Night event?

12

The Therapist and Spirituality

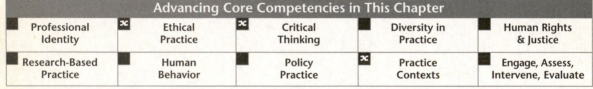

Advancing Core Competencies in This Chapter				
■ Professional Identity	✖ Ethical Practice	✖ Critical Thinking	■ Diversity in Practice	■ Human Rights & Justice
■ Research-Based Practice	■ Human Behavior	■ Policy Practice	✖ Practice Contexts	■ Engage, Assess, Intervene, Evaluate

Anna, aged 33, was overcome by grief. As she sat in her therapist's office she sobbed uncontrollably. In anguish she cried out, "I have lost everything that matters to me." "I see no reason to go on." "My life is meaningless." "Everything I believed in has fallen apart." "Why did this happen?" "Why did it happen to me?" "Where is God?"

As therapists we encounter the pain and suffering of clients like Anna throughout our professional careers. In the midst of their suffering, their previously held belief system fails to sustain them. In chapter 7, we explored the relationship between suffering and our clients' spirituality. For some, tragedy shatters their belief system, while for others, it strengthens and matures it. In this chapter, we will explore the therapist's experience of working with clients in the midst of a dark night of the soul. We will discuss therapists' relationship with spirituality and how it is affected by both the suffering of their clients and their clients' spiritual doubts in the midst of adversity. Are therapists' beliefs shattered, strengthened, or unaffected when they encounter their clients' suffering and crises of faith?

Although there is a growing focus on how clients and their stories change us, in this chapter, we focus more narrowly on the soul of the therapist. Thus, we pose the question, "Can therapists be affected by clients' spiritual anguish, their spiritual doubts, or the shattering of their spiritual beliefs?" Over time, does the cumulative exposure to either our

170

clients' suffering or their potential accompanying crises of faith touch our own souls? Is that impact positive or negative?

We are also interested in the experiences of therapists working with clients whose spiritual beliefs are vastly different from their own. What potential countertransference reactions exist? Are therapists' beliefs vulnerable to being shaped by clients' beliefs? If so, can the influence be positive as well as negative? And finally, in this chapter, we will discuss the use of spirituality to enhance our clinical work as well as a potential resource for therapist self-care.

THE THERAPIST'S EXPERIENCE

Quite naturally the clinical literature focuses primarily on how clients are able to heal within the context of the therapeutic encounter; several therapist characteristics are highlighted as necessary to the process. (See chapter 3 for a discussion of the therapeutic relationship.) Less attention is paid to the experience of the therapist during this encounter. When we overlook the effects of clinical work on therapists we do a disservice to them and their clients. Potentially adverse effects may not only be personally painful to therapists but may also negatively affect their professional work. Little research has been done on the effect of clinical work on the therapist's spiritual worldview. Therefore, the content of this chapter is conceptual and anecdotal, rather than empirical. In the course of our discussion, we will raise many questions, but we are limited in our ability to answer them. I hope that the questions will be thought provoking, stimulate further discussion, and ultimately generate both qualitative and quantitative research to further illuminate our understanding of therapists' experiences working with spiritual issues.

The Therapeutic Interaction

We have long recognized that therapists affect clients. More recently, we have become aware that clinical work, along with the personality of clients and the issues they present in treatment, affects therapists as well (Guy, 1987; Kottler, 1993; Mahoney, 2003; McCann & Pearlman, 1990; Pearlman & Saakvitne, 1995a). The therapeutic relationship, like other relationships, is an interaction. Each party affects and is affected by the other (Strean, 1998). Freud recommended that therapists take a neutral stance. The client is able to use this "blank screen" to project unconscious needs and conflicts onto the therapist and ultimately resolve them. Later analytic developments, especially object relations theorists such as Winnicott, proposed that clients heal within the context of a genuine relationship with the therapist (Applegate and & Bonovitz, 1995). It is not the therapist's skill and insight alone that brings about resolution, but the ability of the therapist to connect in a genuine way to the client, to care about him, and to provide an emotionally corrective experience. Thus, it is the genuine presence of the therapist that heals (Kottler, 1993). We create a space for clients to share their story and bear witness to their pain, communicating that they are worth listening to (Bien, 2008).

Genuine Presence

Although our genuine presence is healing for the client, it takes a toll on us. When we form an empathic connection to our clients, we open ourselves up to their stories and their influence (Figley, 1995; Pearlman & Saakvitne, 1995a). They may affect us positively and spur us to further growth, or we may develop adverse reactions. When we allow the client to awaken our heart (Welwood, 2000), we allow ourselves to feel their suffering, to be moved and touched by their experiences. We may feel their sadness, their anguish, or their anxiety. We may react to the horror of their tragedies. In our clinical work, we witness souls "in torment" (Kottler, 1993, p. 4), and it is not possible for us to remain "immune to the influence of prolonged exposure to human despair, conflict, and suffering" (p. xii). Our encounters with clients affect us profoundly; in fact they change us (Kottler, 1993; Mahoney, 2003). Mahoney (2003) states that although the renowned Milton Erickson captured the continued influence of the therapist on the client in his well-known phrase "My voice will go with you," he failed to capture the simultaneous truth that "our clients" voices also go with us" (Mahoney, 2003, p. 195). Clients' stories, their anguish, and the imagery they share with us fill our days and may haunt our dreams at night (Kottler, 1993; Mahoney, 2003). In this chapter, we narrow our focus to how our clients' stories may challenge or change us spiritually. To understand the potential effect of the client on the therapist, we need to discuss the personal life of the therapist and several concepts developed to capture the therapist's experience in the therapeutic encounter. These concepts include countertransference, burnout, vicarious traumatization, the wounded healer, and the sad soul of the therapist.

THE THERAPIST'S PERSONAL LIFE

We bring our history, our values, our beliefs, and our personal experiences to our clinical work. The greatest asset in our armamentarium of therapeutic skills is our humanity. Without it, our ability to understand, to connect with, and to empathize with our clients is severely compromised. However, our humanity is simultaneously that which puts us at greatest risk for the potentially adverse effects of therapeutic work as well as countertransference reactions. To what extent does our personal history influence our clinical work? Several authors (Guy, 1987; Kottler, 1993; Mahoney, 2003; Sussman, 1992, 1995) address the personal life of the therapist. In this section, I present several concepts to capture the experience of the therapist in the therapeutic process. These include the concepts of countertransference, burnout, vicarious traumatization, the "wounded healer," and the "sad soul" of the therapist. Although none of these concepts fits perfectly, each contributes to our theoretical understanding of the effect of clinical work on the therapist's spirituality. Below we briefly discuss each concept and use each of them to understand a series of vignettes.

Countertransference

Simply put, *countertransference* is the unconscious reaction the therapist has toward a client that derives from the therapist's personal history, most often with significant others, especially those from his or her past (Gorkin, 1987; Murphy & Dillon, 2003; Sperry, Carlson, & Kjos, 2003; Woods & Hollis, 2000). Historically, Freud believed countertransference to be a negative in working with clients. Although he made reference to the term only twice in all his writings, he argued that if therapists were unable to resolve counter-transference feelings they should transfer the client to another therapist (Gorkin, 1987). Theorists associated with the British school of object relations, for example, Winnicott, expanded and broadened the concept. These theorists postulate that reactions can be accounted for by understanding not only the therapist's unresolved issues but also the personality of clients with whom she works. By broadening the concept, countertransference is transformed from a negative occurrence to one that is inevitable and informative. By exploring his countertransference reactions, the therapist can develop a deeper understanding of the internal world of the client and how others may experience her (Gorkin, 1987). Despite the expansion of the term, there continues to be an implication that countertransference reactions stem from the unresolved experience of the therapist.

Burnout

Burnout is a concept that emerged in the 1970s and has been used to describe the emotional exhaustion that accompanies therapeutic work. Some authors believe that burnout best describes the effects of the bureaucratic structures within which therapists do their work. So rather than being related to the clinical material presented in session, burnout refers to issues such as large caseloads, poor or no administrative support, low wages, long hours, isolation, excessive paperwork, and the constraints of managed care (Freudenberger & Robbins, 1979; Murphy & Dillon, 2003; Woods & Hollis, 2000). The concept of burnout, because of the emphasis on the bureaucratic strains associated with therapeutic work, does not adequately describe the emotional toll that the nature of client issues may take on the therapist (Munroe, 1990; Pearlman & Saakvitne, 1995a).

Vicarious Traumatization

Vicarious traumatization (McCann & Pearlman, 1990; Pearlman & Saakvitne, 1995a) is a concept developed to describe the experience of therapists working with traumatized clients. These authors propose that, although countertransference issues and burnout are possible reactions to trauma work, neither of these concepts alone describes the effect on therapists of the shocking imagery that accompanies trauma work. Unlike countertransference reactions, vicarious traumatization develops over time and changes the internal world of the therapist. In short it is a reaction to the cumulative effect of therapists' work with all their traumatized clients, rather than a reaction limited to a specific client (countertransference).

An important contribution of the concept of vicarious traumatization is its emphasis on the disruption of the therapist's worldview from trauma exposure. In the role of witness, the therapist hears the horrific details of the client's suffering. We are intimately aware of human cruelty, intentional harm inflicted on others, and the randomness of some acts of violence and natural disasters. According to the concept of vicarious traumatization, over time, this exposure will alter the assumptions, beliefs, and frame of reference through which therapists view the world. Therapists may experience disruptions in their belief system, which, although milder, are similar to the disruptions in their clients' worldview (McCann & Pearlman, 1990; Pearlman & Saakvitne, 1995a).

Because spirituality is part of an individual's worldview and thus potentially affected when therapists witness their clients' suffering (Pearlman & Saakvitne, 1995a), vicarious traumatization is of particular interest to us. Alterations or disruptions in the spiritual domain are among the most painful consequences of vicarious traumatization (Neuman & Pearlman, 1994, as cited in Brady, Guy, Poelstra, & Brokaw, 1999; Pearlman & Saakvitne, 1995b). Like our suffering clients, we too may question the meaning and purpose of life or feel a sense of hopelessness or despair (Pearlman & Saakvitne, 1995b). A growing body of empirical literature supports the idea that therapists working with traumatized clients are affected by their work (Cunningham, 2003; Follette, Polusny, & Milbeck, 1994; Pearlman & MacIan, 1995), although exploration of the spiritual domain has been limited.

Interestingly, in one of the few studies on trauma work and spirituality, Brady et al. (1999) looked at the relationship between vicarious traumatization and spirituality in a national sample of women therapists. In this study, a positive correlation was found between working with survivors of sexual abuse and a spiritually satisfying life. These researchers hypothesize that their confrontation with trauma forces therapists to grapple with their own spirituality by bringing issues of meaning to the forefront (Neuman & Pearlman, 1994, as cited in Brady et al., 1999). Thus, the need to examine one's beliefs leads to a stronger sense of spirituality. Brady et al. (1999) suggest that when therapists witness their clients' suffering, they are compelled to examine their own beliefs, which may lead to their own spiritual development. Alternatively, these authors propose that therapists' spirituality is not strengthened due to their exposure to clients' suffering but that those who are more spiritually grounded may be more willing to engage in trauma work.

The concept of vicarious traumatization is most applicable to therapists working with clients in the midst of a dark night of the soul. When clients question the meaning and purpose of their suffering, therapists may be most vulnerable to their own period of spiritual questioning. However, not all clients bring trauma issues to treatment. Yet, I propose in this chapter that therapeutic work may alter the therapist's spiritual worldview. Can the concept of vicarious traumatization illuminate our understanding of the potential change in a therapist's beliefs if intense suffering is not present? Can we build on the essential truth of vicarious traumatization, that therapists can be changed by clients' experiences, to develop a concept that highlights the effect of clients' beliefs on therapists' spirituality?

The Wounded Healer

When we bring our personal lives to our work, we bring our life experiences, both positive and negative. Do our own difficulties impede our work or allow us to connect more empathically to our suffering clients? Some studies (Elliott & Guy, 1993; Pope & Feldman-Summers, 1992) have been used to support the idea that mental health professionals are more likely to have been raised in dysfunctional families with higher-than-average rates of alcoholism, mental illness, or child abuse. Therefore, some scholars hypothesize that many mental health professionals choose to engage in this work because of their own unresolved issues (Bugental, 1964, as cited in Farber, Manevich, Metzger, & Saypol, 2005, p. 1012; Maeder, 1989, as cited in Farber et al., 2005, p. 1012). Alice Miller (1981), in her book *The Drama of the Gifted Child*, proposes that children of narcissistic parents learn early to tune into other's feelings and many grow up to become sensitive and empathic therapists. They are drawn to a profession that requires them to focus on other's needs and do so quite well.

The concept of the *wounded healer* has been used to refer to those in the mental health field who have encountered problems and suffering in their own lives and become helping professionals to resolve their own difficulties. Chessick (1978, p. 6) states that those "whose souls are already anguished enter the field . . . looking for healing of the sadness of the soul"

(Chessick, 1978, p. 6). Is this a negative, as the literature often implies? Can the therapist's own experiences with suffering and sadness create a deeper sense of compassion and empathy and thus prepare therapists for therapeutic work in a way those who have not suffered are not?

The concept of the wounded healer traces back to ancient times and is prevalent in the myths of many cultures. Hippocrates, the father of medicine, was inspired by a mythical figure with extraordinary healing powers, despite a personal wound, unhealed by time (Mahoney, 2003, p. 197). The work of Eliade recounts the journey of the ancient shaman from a period of intense distress or illness to that of healer. The healing gift is a result of the person's ability to transcend this period of trial and suffering (Sussman, 1992, pp. 30–31). Thus, the shaman's wisdom and willingness to heal the suffering of others comes from the endurance of his own personal suffering (Bien, 2008). Although the personal wound is often incurable, it is because she is wounded and suffers that she is able to heal others (Meier, 1967, as cited in Sussman, 1992, p. 21).

The concept of wounded varies. For example, it can mean the healer has accumulated a great deal of life experience, which is now "a sacred source of wisdom" (Mahoney, 2003, p. 197). In some spiritual traditions *wound* refers to an openness to life. However, in industrialized societies, woundedness is equated with vulnerability, and thus seen as a negative. The healer then is someone who can heal others, but not himself (Mahoney, 2003).

Does personal suffering and successful resolution make the therapist more skilled in working with suffering clients? Does it allow the therapist to not only know firsthand what the client may be experiencing but also point the way to effective strategies to overcome adversity? Does the personal experience of the therapist prepare her for the difficult work of therapy or does it lead to assumptions of what the client is experiencing or how her dilemma should be resolved and thus impedes the work (Bien, 2008)? Although our own suffering can sensitize us to the suffering of others and allow us to be more effective therapists, it can create challenges in our countertransference reactions. We focus our discussion on whether wounded healers are more vulnerable to adverse affects when they witness their client's dark night of the soul. Does the client's suffering and anguish reopen the therapist's emotional wounds? Is he able to use his own pain to work more effectively with his client or does his pain interfere with his effectiveness?

The Sad Soul of the Therapist

Clinical work can be "among the most spiritually fulfilling" endeavors or one of the most "emotionally draining" (Kottler, 1993, p. xi). Over thirty years ago, Chessick (1978) wrote a short article entitled "The Sad Soul of the Psychiatrist." In this thought-provoking piece, he distinguishes the soul wound from "neurotic problems." The latter, like countertransference, results from the therapist's unresolved intrapsychic conflicts, whereas the "sad soul" develops as a result of the therapist's exposure to client problems. When therapists suffer from soul sadness they reverberate with the anguish and pain of their clients, and over time, it becomes a "gnawing theme in the back of their minds" (Chessick, 1978). The concept of the sad soul of the therapist contributed to the development of the concept of vicarious traumatization (McCann & Pearlman, 1990; Pearlman & Saakvitne, 1995a). Both the personal life of the therapist and the nature of the work converge to create the impact of therapeutic work on the therapist's soul (Pearlman & Saakvitne, 1995a). Kottler (1993) remarks that when we accompany our clients on their healing journey, our own wounds are reopened as we encounter our client's pain. In the midst of our "vicarious suffering" we struggle to wrestle "hope from hell" (Mahoney, 2003, p. 196). In the course of our work we are exposed to intentional cruelty, violation, manipulation, and random acts of tragedy. We witness the havoc wrought by natural disasters and one's human's inhumanity to another. The details and images of our clients' stories can erode our faith in human nature (Danieli, 1994; Mahony, 2003). We may be left grieving for a world we once knew (Cunningham, 1999), feel a sense of hopelessness, or question the existence or nature of a Supreme Being.

BEARING WITNESS

How is the therapist affected by, perhaps changed by, his or her encounter with clients? We are especially interested in how the therapist handles her confrontation with human suffering and tragedy in her role as witness for her clients. In this section I focus on the experience of the therapist in the face of suffering and tragedy. Do any of the above concepts used to describe the experience of the therapist in the clinical encounter illuminate our understanding of how the client's suffering can affect the therapist? Is anyone more appropriate, or does each contribute to our understanding?

From the literature on vicarious traumatization (McCann & Pearlman, 1990; Pearlman and Saakvitne, 1995a), we know that therapists may experience disruptions in their worldview as a result of their exposure to trauma material (Cunningham, 2003; Pearlman & MacIan, 1995). As stated before, I wish to build upon that theory and ponder how client's spiritual issues may affect the therapist.

When clients encounter and grapple with suffering, spiritual issues may emerge. When an individual's belief system fails to sustain him, he may experience a crisis as his spiritual worldview is shattered (Pearlman & Saakvitne, 1995a). I pose the question, "Are our spiritual beliefs challenged along with the client's when we witness their anguish and pain?" When we accompany them on their dark night of the soul, we are faced with hopelessness, doubt, and anguish. Does that experience shape us internally, permanently? Does our work with suffering clients raise existential questions for us as well? Do we ask why suffering exists? Do we question the existence or nature of an Ultimate Being when we witness our clients' unbearable tragedies? If our client's dark night of the soul affects us, is it always adversely? Many therapists are inspired by clients' ability to transcend sadness and suffering. Can our spirituality be strengthened as we witness clients overcome adversity? In short, I ask, "Is the soul of the therapist affected by clinical work when spiritual crises arise in the course of treatment?" Concern about the impact of spiritually focused work on therapists is often overlooked, but is an important focus. There may be adverse effects not only personally for the therapist but also in his professional work.

Martin had been providing social work services in a family service agency. His client George had been in treatment for mild depression related to the loss of his job. After several sessions, George called Martin distraught that his wife had died suddenly from an apparent heart attack. In the sessions following her death George poured out his grief and confusion surrounding the death of his wife. He shared with Martin that his wife Sophia had been considerably younger than he. She had always been in good health and did all the things we have come to believe as necessary to preserve health: nutritious diet, exercise, engaging in work she loved. Sophia had been very spiritual, and although she did not belong to a traditional religion she tended to her soul in many ways. She engaged in yoga, tai chi, and meditation practices. She loved nature and was altruistic toward those who needed her support. George commented that her spirituality "did her little good in the end." He questioned why God would take someone as good as her when the newspapers are filled with accounts of people who commit crimes and engage in horrendous deeds against others. George, a devout Presbyterian, was angry with God and shaken that his world could so abruptly change.

Martin too was shaken by the suddenness of Sophia's death. As he listened to George, he too questioned why Sophia should die. Why so suddenly, why so relatively young? And as the sessions continued, Martin found himself thinking, "What kind of God allows such tragic things to happen to such kind and caring people?" As these thoughts and feelings persisted, Martin felt guilty and frightened that he was having these doubts.

As a clinical social worker in a family service agency, Rene saw many abused children and worked with adults who had experienced both physical and sexual abuse as children. Initially, Rene was horrified that parents who were entrusted to care for and protect their children would abuse them. Over time, her thinking changed. She began to question the "type of God who would stand by and watch innocent children being mistreated." She began to fluctuate between anger with God and growing doubts about the existence of any sort of Ultimate Being. As the demands of her job increased and Rene faced more challenging cases with increasing severity of abuse, her existential questions became more prominent and more relevant. She began to think seriously about finding other work to protect herself from her growing doubts and anxiety.

Individuals respond spiritually in different ways to suffering. When Mabel was diagnosed with late stage breast cancer, she sought therapy at a community hospital for support and to explore her feelings throughout the ending stages of her life. Deirdre, who had lost her own mother to illness several years ago, was assigned the case. Mabel had a strong traditional faith and dealt with her diagnosis and impending death with a sense of resignation and grace. She frequently stated that God must have a plan for her and she was willing to surrender to it. Deirdre tried unsuccessfully to probe for feelings of anger, depression, fear, and anxiety. When Mabel maintained her equanimity, Deirdre found herself becoming angry with Mabel. Her attitude gradually shifted from one of admiration for her to seeing her as "naïve, duped, and in denial."

In understanding the reactions of these therapists we use the concepts described above. The sad soul of the therapist, described by Chessick (1978) (or by a spiritual variation of vicarious traumatization), may explain the reactions of both Martin and Rene. Martin was negatively affected by George's existential confusion, feeling of betrayal, and loss of faith. In the face of George's dark night, Martin found himself questioning his own beliefs. Thus, Martin's spiritual worldview was challenged both by his witnessing George's suffering, anguish, and his spiritual doubts raised by the tragic loss of his wife. Martin's inner experience reverberated with George's; George's spiritual doubts were "contagious" (Chessick, 1978).

The concepts of vicarious traumatization and burnout best describe Rene's reactions. It was the cumulative exposure, which over time, led to her crisis of belief. Although she initially blamed parents for the abuse and neglect, she ultimately came to blame God for abandoning these innocent children in their time of need. The pain she witnessed caused a disruption in the spiritual realm of her worldview. Simultaneously, bureaucratic issues affected her. Her already large caseload was increased and the complexity and severity of the cases made the work more difficult, leading to burnout. Therefore, it was the combination of vicarious traumatization and burnout that motivated her to seriously consider leaving her job.

Professional Identity

Practice Behavior Example: *Use supervision and consultation.*

Critical Thinking Question: Working with traumaitzed clients often creates emotional stress for therapists. Describe the reasons for this stress and how therapists should address it to assure continued quality of care for their clients.

Deidre's reactions to her client are best accounted for with the concept of countertransference. Upon exploration, Deidre realized that the anger she felt toward her client stemmed from her unresolved feelings about her own mother's death. Her mother, like her client, accepted her diagnosis and spent her remaining time at home with close family and friends. Deidre had wanted her to try extraordinary and alternative treatments to battle the cancer. But her mother chose to die peaceful without extreme medical intervention. Unlike her client, Deidre's mother was not religious, nor was she spiritual. But her client's resignation and acceptance, similar to her mother's, triggered a countertransference reaction in Deidre.

DIVERGENT SPIRITUAL WORLDVIEWS

Along with the impact on therapists of clients suffering and their subsequent dark night of the soul, we discuss the experience of therapists working with clients with very different spiritual beliefs. There are many combinations of divergent spiritual worldviews that may pose difficulties. These include, but are not limited to, therapeutic encounters between atheists and religiously conservative individuals. Likewise, difficulties can occur when one party is committed to an alternative spiritual path and the other is atheistic, agnostic, or traditionally religious. Countertransference reactions are one concern. But these differences may also affect the therapist in a more personal manner.

Historically, religion and spirituality were taboo topics within the therapeutic encounter. Following in the tradition of Freud, religion was viewed negatively as a delusion, or as a search for the omnipotent parent. Studies (Shafranske, 2001, as cited in Pargament, 2007, p. 9; Worthington, Kurusu, McCullough, & Sandage, 1996, as cited in Smith & Orlinsky, 2004, p. 144) indicate that therapists are often not followers of traditional spiritual paths, yet polls indicate that the overwhelming majority of Americans believe in an Ultimate Being, who many call "God" (Pargament, 2007). Others conclude that although the profession is not spiritual, many of the therapists who practice within it are either religious or spiritual (Bergin & Jensen, 1990; Smith & Orlinsky, 2004). However, it is still likely that a therapist–client dyad may be made up of a nonbelieving therapist and a believing client (Pargament, 2007). This poses significant concerns about possible countertransference reactions. Does the therapist dismiss or disapprove of the client's beliefs and spiritual practices? Does she see the client's beliefs as a form of wishful thinking or believe him to be naïve or foolish?

Or there may be incidents of atheistic or agnostic clients who seek help from spiritually committed therapists. What if these therapists are religiously conservative? Does the therapist think that there is a flaw in the client who is unable to believe? Does it make a difference if the lack of belief is viewed as temporary or is a permanent characteristic of the client? Ideally, therapists should recognize the validity of the client's belief system, even if they do not share it. In chapter 2, we discussed ethical concerns about therapists and clients who have divergent spiritual belief systems. I mentioned, for example, that therapists who either overtly or covertly impose their beliefs (or lack of) on vulnerable clients violate ethical principles.

Although countertransference and ethical violations are important considerations, in this chapter, we also discuss the emotional experience of therapists who work with clients with very different spiritual beliefs. Can those beliefs influence the personal life of the therapist in any way? Do therapists ever find themselves wishing that they could have a strong spiritual belief system like their clients? We are particularly interested in the cumulative effect of different spiritual beliefs on the therapist. Can clients' lack of belief chip away at the therapist's beliefs? Can clients' faith and trust influence the therapist?

Thomas sought therapy to deal with a mild, but unrelenting, depression. His therapist, Crystal, was raised as an Episcopalian, but as an adult embraced a more generic sense of the spiritual. In the course of treatment, Thomas related many periods of difficulty throughout his life. During each period of crisis, Thomas had prolonged periods of spiritual questioning. He was adamant that anyone who believed there was an Ultimate Being or any source of spiritual guidance was a fool. During unrelenting questioning, Crystal began to feel uncomfortable working with Thomas. As she explored this in supervision, she realized that Thomas was causing her to question her own beliefs, and she feared she would, like him, be left with unrelenting doubts.

As mentioned above, divergent spiritual beliefs can occur when both client and therapist do not adhere to traditional belief systems. Atheists, agnostics, or traditionally religious individuals may have difficulties with those who have strong spiritual beliefs that fit the description of New Age spirituality.

Sara was raised as a conservative Christian and was firmly committed to her faith. Although she was open to other traditional faith systems, she became troubled while working with a woman who was a Wiccan. Wicca is an alternative earth-bound spiritual path that emphasizes harmony with all living creatures and pays special attention to the feminine. Although Wicca is referred to as "witchcraft," it does not include satanic worship or involve the casting of evil spells (Canda & Furman, 1999, 2010). Sara, however, equated witchcraft with satanic worship. She felt frightened when her client described her spiritual beliefs and practices. Images of devil worship haunted Sara, and she began to have nightmares. As a devout Christian, Sara felt offended by her client's spirituality. Sara's supervisor recommended that she learn about Wicca and understand the distinction between its practices and those of satanic worship. Sara felt this would upset her further and asked to have her client transferred to another therapist.

Marilyn, an agnostic, began treatment with James, a 30-year-old who professed belief in many New Age practices. Prior to treatment, James had consulted with psychic readers and engaged mediums to help him make contact with his deceased girlfriend. James was passionate in his belief in the gifts of these healers. As treatment progressed, James shared more of his beliefs with Marilyn. He believed in karmic forces and angels and said that he could sense one's energy. Marilyn struggled to avoid judging James for his beliefs. She believed that anything that could not be tested by scientific principles was suspect and had a great deal of difficulty accepting his beliefs, which she believed were "too different, too weird." His beliefs reinforced for her that "spirituality was based on wishful thinking."

We also raise the following question in this chapter: Can therapists' beliefs be positively affected by their clients' spiritual beliefs?

Henrietta had never given much thought to her spirituality. She was raised by agnostics and never had any positive thoughts about religion or spirituality. She began work with a 50-year-old woman who described herself as a spiritual seeker. In the course of her treatment, the client talked about her upbringing within the Jewish tradition. Although her family was not devout, they observed the major holy days. When she was 40, she began an exploration of different spiritual paths, including Jewish mysticism, Buddhism, and several New Age practices. As she talked about what had drawn her to each and her experiences with different faith groups, Henrietta began to feel a longing for her own sense of the spiritual. She began querying friends about their spiritual lives, which led to an active search for spirituality that would sustain her and connect her to something beyond herself. She remarked that she does not know if she would have ever begun this journey without her exposure to her client's search.

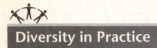

Diversity in Practice

Practice Behavior Example: *Gain sufficient self-awareness to eliminate the influence of personal biases and values in working with diverse groups.*

Critical Thinking Question: What clinical or ethical dilemmas may arise for therapists working with clients whose spiritual beliefs are very different from their own? How should they address these concerns to en sure quality services to their clients?

SPIRITUALITY AND OUR WORK

It is truly a privilege to accompany clients on their therapeutic journey. However, clinical work is uncertain. Despite being well versed in theories and having a repertoire of skills, we never really know what we will encounter in our sessions with clients or how treatment will turn out (Johanson & Kurtz, 1991). Uncertainty can frighten and challenge us. In chapter 3 we discussed several spiritual practices to enhance the effectiveness of our work. These include being mindfully present to the client, awakening our hearts to clients' experience, and surrendering to not knowing. Here we summarize how spiritual practice can enhance our work and then explore the role of spirituality in our own self-care.

Spiritual Practices to Enhance Our Work

Our genuine presence and mindful attention are the most healing gifts we bring to our therapeutic work. To be truly present to the client we must be grounded in our own experience, being aware of and embracing whatever feelings arise in the course of our work. Rather than close our feelings off, we use them as a springboard for personal and professional understanding (Cunningham, 2004; Welwood, 2000). Our compassion arises from our ability to awaken our hearts, allowing the client's story to touch us and despite the pain remain open to it (Welwood, 2000). We resist being swept away by our client's experience by surrendering the need to know and the need to control. We release our expectations and attachments to specific outcomes (Bien, 2008; Welwood, 2000). We enter into the mystery of the person seated before us with a beginner's mind and a respectful sense of "not knowing" (Bien, 2008; Johanson & Kurtz, 1991). We invite clients to tell us who they are and in partnership, we discover together what will be most healing for them. Thus, we bear witness to what is, rather than what we wish was, and offer what Welwood (2000) calls the "greatest gift" when we invite and allow a client to have "his or her experience just as it is" (p. 144).

Therapeutic Work and the Therapist's Soul

Therapeutic work takes courage. Our clients need courage to enter into the unknown process, but we also need courage to enter the unknown with them. It takes courage to wait and to trust that the client will lead us. It takes wisdom to recognize what they need and skill to provide it for them. It takes courage to be grounded in our own experience, while simultaneously allowing the client's experience to awaken our heart. We allow ourselves to feel their pain and not shun from it. Therapeutic work is a dance, moving back and forth between grounding ourselves and allowing our hearts to be awakened by the client's story. The challenge is staying with the painful feelings that emerge, both theirs and those that are stirred within us. Pema Chodron (2001) says that true spiritual awakening comes when we are able to remain present to shakiness, a broken heart, or feelings of hopelessness. In the remainder of this chapter, I focus on how therapists can sustain themselves while awakening their hearts to their client's pain.

Spiritual Nourishment for the Therapist's Soul

In the course of our therapeutic lives we witness both the ordinary trials and tribulations of human life as well as those more profound experiences of sorrow and suffering. If we are to awaken our hearts and stay present to our clients in the midst of their pain, we need something to help us endure the hardships of life and work. What helps you endure your personal and professional challenges? What nourishes your spirit and sustains your soul? What protects you from the scarring thumbprint of human tragedy? How do you renew yourself daily so you come to your work refreshed and invigorated, ready to take on the privilege of accompanying clients on their therapeutic journey toward wholeness?

From a spiritual perspective, we recognize that there is a source of wisdom at our core. For some, this is the immanent Divine, our soul, or our true and authentic self. When we are aligned with this divine source, we are resourceful, we are open to new options, and we are able to make wise decisions and choices (Hogan, 2003, p. 41). Wittine (1995) calls this inner source that lies deep within us a "sacred well" (p. 289). And when we access this spiritual well, we can sustain ourselves through the fundamental existential realities we face in our daily encounters with clients. Our spiritual center provides a source of strength when we bear witness to suffering, anguish, and despair. It keeps us grounded and centered (Wittine, 1995).

To access this sacred well within we need to embrace silence and create an inner stillness. Given the demands of our daily lives, this is not always easy. However, Silf (1999) reminds us that in the midst of tumultuous sea storms, it is calm 10 feet below the crest of the highest waves. Stillness allows us to connect with "the deeper currents of our heart" and enables us to know what we are really feeling (Silf, 1999, p. 11). Spiritual practices (Hermes, 2001; Kabat-Zinn, 1994; Teasdale, 1999) such as mindfulness, meditation, contemplative or centering prayer are designed to help us access that place of stillness and calm within the storms of our personal and professional lives. Silence allows us to hear our soul's voice, to be in touch with our internal wisdom, allowing insights to emerge (Hogan, 2003). It grants us the gift of solitude, necessary for inner exploration and a staple of spiritual practice. When we withdraw our attention from the external world, we are able to focus on our internal landscape. In the midst of solitude we are able to sort out the essential and the trivial (Teasdale, 1999). And within this place of silence and solitude, we find space to connect to our essence and thus our internal sense of wisdom. For some, this is the place where they connect with the Divine.

The goal of meditation practice is personal transformation. Because it prepares one for the inevitable ups and downs of life (Gunaratana, 1991), it is a resource for therapists in dealing with the vicissitudes of therapeutic work. When we are mindful, we are fully awake and aware of the present moment. We are freed from past and future entanglements, judgments, and the process of rejecting our experiences. Being free, we experience more joy, energy, and clarity and are open to insights (Germer, 2005). Through meditation, the mind becomes still and calm (Gunaratana, 1991). And because contemplation contrasts with action (Teasdale, 1999), it provides the perfect antidote for social workers, who expend tremendous energy in actions aimed at bringing about change and transformation. The goal is not to privilege reflection over action, but to recognize that both are necessary and complementary to each other.

Chessick (1978) reminds us that to counteract the sad soul we need to be reminded of those things in life that are good and beautiful. These reminders ignite a flicker of hope and nourish our souls. For him, the beauty of art and music help to transcend the ordinary as well as the suffering we encounter as therapists. You may find your flicker of hope in nature or some other meaningful way. It may be walking on the beach, watching a sunset, listening to a piece of music that stirs your soul, or viewing a piece of artwork so beautiful you are moved to tears. Regardless of the form this reminder takes, we need to remember that although we encounter suffering daily in our role as witnesses for our clients, there are incredible moments of joy and beauty in this life and we need to embrace them to feed our own souls.

Our Own Sacred Space

In chapter 3 we discussed the need to create a sacred space so our clients can engage in the difficult work of therapy. We too need a sacred space to replenish our souls so that we can continue to be available to our clients.

Sacred space is space set apart from ordinary space (Eliade, 1957). A chosen sacred space may vary. For some it may be a place in nature. You may cherish a walk in the meadow or sitting by the seashore. You might bike through the mountains or walk an actual labyrinth. It may be a place designated as a sacred site, such as a Buddhist temple, a synagogue, a church, or a mosque. You may have created a sacred space within your home, such as a corner of a room, which you fill with objects that are meaningful to you. Sue Monk Kidd (1996), author of *The Dance of the Dissident Daughter*, created an altar on which she displayed objects that represented her journey toward the Sacred Feminine. Pargament (2007, p. 47) talks about a hospital chaplain who worked with seriously ill children. She created a small garden in her yard, which she called her "sacred garden." Her family members knew that when she was there, she was not to be disturbed. Regardless of where this place is, it is a space that helps you find inner stillness and allows you to connect with your inner self. Thus, the sacred space needs to be internal as well as external.

Sacred or Sabbath Time

We are all challenged to find the needed time for reflection and self-care. We may resist it, fearing it to be selfish (Thorne, 2002). However, self-love or self-compassion and therefore self-care is rooted in many spiritual traditions. Essential to self-care is creating a sacred time to restore our souls. To embrace the fullness of life one needs to pause and appreciate the sacred moment, which provides a "stopping place, a listening post" (Lynn, 1999, as cited in Pargament, 2007, p. 48).

Sabbath time is a sacred practice rooted in several spiritual traditions. During the Sabbath, the individual refrains from his or her usual work activities. It is a period of rest, relaxation, and reflection. Within religious traditions, there may be guidelines about sacred rituals, meals, and prohibitions against or mandates for certain activities. For our purposes, we can look at the concept more broadly. What is the essence of Sabbath time and how can it enhance our need for self-care?

For many, a day off from work is filled with necessary chores, doing the laundry, catching up on bills, running to do errands. We may take a day to attend a professional conference. Although chores are necessary and conferences an important professional activity, these are not Sabbath time. Sabbath time goes beyond time off. It is a time set aside for contemplation, genuine rest (both body and spirit), and relaxation. We may spend part of the day in silence or solitude. We use the time to reflect and contemplate the meaning of our lives, our purpose. When the time is used to contemplate our work, it has a qualitative difference. Rather than focusing on our usual work concerns Sabbath time is devoted to stepping back and thinking about our work from a different perspective. What draws you to this work? How is it meaningful to you? Are you passionate about what you do? Are you fully engaged with clients? Are you satisfied that you are making some difference in your clients' lives? Are you emotionally exhausted? Do you need an extended break from your work? So rather than thinking about what needs to be done at work, the focus is on your relationship to your work and how it affects you physically, spiritually, and emotionally.

Rabbi Heschel (1986, as cited in Pargament, 2007, p. 48), says, "Six days a week we live under the tyranny of things of space; on the Sabbath we try to become attuned to holiness in time." In the Jewish tradition it is believed that "a blessing of wholeness descends upon all those who observe the Sabbath" (Frankel, 2003, p. 218). Yet observance of the Sabbath is a waning tradition, perhaps limited to some Orthodox and conservative religious groups. Loss of Sabbath time is a sacred loss. I do not suggest that we reinstate rigid adherence to a set of behaviors or prohibitions but that we carve out time that provides the spiritual sustenance of the Sabbath. Although setting aside a day a week is traditional and perhaps ideal, it may not be possible given the realities of your life. Be creative and design something that works for you. Perhaps one day a month is more practical or a few days each season of the year. It is the essence of Sabbath time that is important. Our work is important, but difficult. It may take a toll on us physically, emotionally, and spiritually. If we do not find meaningful ways to nourish our souls it is unlikely we will endure over time and provide quality services to those vulnerable souls who seek our help. Adequate self-care, including attention to our spirits, is imperative.

Professional Identity

Practice Behavior Example: *Demonstrate professional demeanor in behavior, appearance, and communications.*

Critical Thinking Question: Discuss the importance of self-care in your professional development and its importance in assuring quality services to clients.

CONCLUSION

Throughout this book, we have focused on the use of spirituality in our clinical practice with clients. In this chapter we discussed our own spirituality and how it may be affected by our work with clients, especially those who are suffering and experience a dark night of the soul. We have chosen several concepts that describe the experience of the therapist in the therapeutic encounter and proposed that the soul of the therapist may be affected by clients' beliefs. In addition, we discussed spirituality as a resource in our own self-care.

To be effective therapists we need to be able to sustain our resiliency over time. Being grounded in our own experience and authentically present to ourselves are important tools in our own self-care. To access our internal wisdom, we need solitude and the ability to achieve inner stillness. Mindfulness practice allows us to still our minds and encounter inner silence so we can tap the wellspring of our internal wisdom. Therefore, it both enables us to practice effectively in the moment with clients and provides an excellent resource for our own self-care. This will also enable us to continue our work over the long haul. Along with spiritual practices such as meditation or mindfulness, we proposed that therapists need both a sacred space and sacred time to nourish their souls.

The material presented in this chapter is primarily theoretical and anecdotal because therapists' spirituality has not been the focus of empirical literature. Although we posed many questions, we are limited in our ability to answer them. One area that may be interesting to explore is the evolution of the therapist's spiritual journey juxtaposed with her professional development. Are there periods where he may be more vulnerable to disruptions in his own spiritual beliefs? Are there periods when she may be more immune to adverse effects from her client's dark night of the soul? I hope that this chapter points out the need for both qualitative and quantitative research to illuminate the experience of the therapist working with client's spiritual issues.

And so our journey together comes to an end. We have conceptualized spirituality and clinical practice as a labyrinth walk throughout this text. We have now come full circle and it is time to step back over the threshold. Take whatever benefits you may have gained from your reading and implement them into your practice. Take care of yourself as you bear witness to your clients' suffering. I wish you well as you continue your journey. Namaste!

PRACTICE TEST

PRACTICE TEST The following questions will test your knowledge of the content found within this chapter and help you prepare for the licensing exam by applying chapter content to practice. For more questions styled like the licensing exam, visit **MySocialWorkLab.com**

1. Rory, an experienced social worker, joined a group for professionals to deal with the stress of working with traumatized clients. The group leader should provide understanding of

    a. spirituality as a coping resource.

    b. vicarious traumatization so that group members understand professional reactions.

    c. posttraumatic growth theory to expand group members' personal growth.

    d. countertransference issues to help group members explore a possible personal history of trauma.

2. Jeanette requested therapy because she is having difficulties working with women who are in violent relationships. Jeanette grew up in a violent home and finds herself becoming frequently angry with her clients. Which of the following concepts best describes her reaction?

    a. countertransference

    b. burnout

    c. vicarious traumatization

    d. wounded healer syndrome

3. When social workers begin to question the meaningfulness of life as a result of their work with traumatized clients, which of the following concepts best describes their reaction?

    a. burnout

    b. vicarious traumatization

    c. countertransference

    d. wounded healer syndrome

4. When social workers feel a sense of disconnection because of large caseloads and little administrative support, which of the following concepts best describes their reactions?

    a. burnout

    b. vicarious traumatization

    c. countertransference

    d. wounded healer syndrome

1. Describe the spiritual concept of Sabbath time in dealing with the stresses related to clinical work. Include the distinction between this concept and time off from work. Include the ethical responsibility of the therapist's self-care in effective social work practice.

2. Arnold has 30 years experience in a mental health clinic. Due to budget cutbacks there has been limited supervision, increased caseloads, and no staff development. Although Arnold describes himself as spiritual, he has recently been feeling emotionally drained and having difficulty connecting to his clients. Describe whether countertransference, vicarious traumatization, or burnout best describes his reactions and why. What are some spiritual strategies for social workers like Arnold?

SUCCEED WITH

Visit **MySocialWorkLab** for more licensing exam test questions, and to access case studies, videos, and much more.

References

Albertsen, E. J., O'Conner, L. E., & Berry, J. W. (2006). Religion and interpersonal guilt: Variations across ethnicity and spirituality. *Mental Health, Religion & Culture, 9*(1), 67–84.

Altemeyer, B., & Hunsberger, B. (1992). Authoritarianism, religious fundamentalism, quest, and prejudice. *International Journal for the Psychology of Religion, 2*(2), 113–133.

Altemeyer, B., & Hunsberger, B. (2005). Fundamentalism and authoritarianism. In R. F. Paloutzian & C. L. Park (Eds.), *Handbook of the psychology of religion and spirituality* (pp. 378–393). New York: Guilford Press.

Althaua-Reid, M., Petrella, I., & Susin, L. C. (2007). *Reclaiming liberation theology: Another possible world*. London: SCM Press.

Anderson, S. R., & Hopkins, P. (1992). *The feminine face of God: The unfolding of the sacred in women*. New York: Bantam.

Antonio, E. (2007). Black theology. In C. Rowland (Ed.), *The Cambridge companion to liberation theology* (pp. 79–104). Cambridge, England: Cambridge University Press.

Applegate, J. S., & Bonovitz, J. M. (1995). *The facilitating partnership: A Winnicottian approach for social workers and other helping professionals*. Northvale, NJ: Jason Aronson.

Armstrong, K. (2001). *The battle for God: A history of fundamentalism*. New York: Random House.

Armstrong, K. (2002). Fundamentalism. In B. Reed (Ed.), *Nothing sacred: Women respond to religious fundamentalism and terror* (pp. 11–21). New York: Thunders' Mouth Press/Nation Book.

Arrien, A. (1995). Walking the mystical path with practical feet. In A. Simpkinson, C. Simpkinson, & R. Solari (Eds.), *Nourishing the soul: Discovering the sacred in everyday life* (pp. 103–110). San Francisco, CA: HarperCollins.

Artress, L. (1996). *Walking a sacred path: Rediscovering the labyrinth as a spiritual tool*. New York: Riverhead Books.

Attig, T. (2007). Relearning the world: Making and finding meanings. In R. A. Neimeyer (Ed.), *Meaning reconstruction & the experience of loss* (pp. 33–53). Washington, DC: American Psychological Association.

Baer, R. A., & Krietemeyer, J. (2006). Overview of mindfulness- and acceptance-based treatment approaches. In R. A. Baer (Ed.), *Mindfulness-based treatment approaches: Clinician's guide to evidence base and applications* (pp. 3–27). Burlington, MA: Academic Press.

Balasuriya, T. (2007). Religion for another possible world. In M. Althaus-Reid, I. Petrella, & L. C. Susin (Eds.), *Another possible world: Reclaiming liberation theology* (pp. 10–15). London: SCM Press.

Barbs, J. (1991). New age fundamentalism. In C. Zweig & J. Abrams (Eds.), *Meeting the shadow: The hidden power of the dark side of human nature* (pp. 160–161). New York: Jeremy P. Tarcher/Putnam.

Baumeister, R. F., Stillwell, A. M., & Heatherton, T. F. (1994). Guilt: An interpersonal approach. *Psychological Bulletin, 115*(2), 243–267.

Baumeister, R. F., & Vohs, K. D. (2004). Four roots of evil. In A. G. Miller (Ed.), *The social psychology of good and evil* (pp. 85–101). New York: Guilford Press.

Benner, D. G. (2005). Intensive soul care: Integrating psychotherapy and spiritual direction. In L. Sperry & E. P. Shafranske (Eds.), *Spiritually oriented psychotherapy* (pp. 287–306). Washington, DC: American Psychological Association.

Bergin, A. E., & Jensen, J. P. (1990). Religiosity of psychotherapists: A national survey. *Psychotherapy, 27*(1), 3–7.

Bien, A. W. (2008). *The zen of helping: Spiritual principles for mindful and open-hearted practice*. Hoboken, NJ: John Wiley & Sons.

Bloomfield, H., & Goldberg, P. (2003). *Making peace with God: A practical guide*. New York: Jeremy P. Tarcher/Putnam.

Boff, L. (2007). Two urgent utopias for the twenty-first century. In M. Althaus-Reid, I. Petrella, & L. C. Susin (Eds.), *Another possible world: Reclaiming liberation theology* (pp. 4–9). London: SCM Press.

Boff, L., & Boff, C. (1996). *Introducing liberation theology*. Maryknoll, NY: Orbis Books.

Bolen, J. S. (1994). *Crossing to Avalon: A woman's midlife pilgrimage*. San Francisco, CA: HarperCollins.

Bolen, J. S. (2001). *Goddesses in older women: Archetypes in women over fifty*. New York: HarperCollins.

Borysenko, J. (1995). Minding the body, mending the mind and soul. In A. Simpkinson, C. Simpkinson, & R. Solari (Eds.), *Nourishing the soul: Discovering the sacred in everyday life* (pp. 23–31). San Francisco, CA: HarperCollins.

Borysenko, J. (1999). *A woman's journey to God: Finding the feminine path*. New York: Riverhead Books/Penguin Putman.

Brach, T. (2003). *Radical acceptance: Embracing our life with the heart of a Buddha*. New York: Bantam Books.

Bradley, R., Schwartz, A. C., & Kaslow, N. J. (2005). Posttraumatic stress disorder symptoms among low-income, African-American women with a history of intimate partner violence and suicidal behaviors: Self-esteem, social support, and religious coping. *Journal of Traumatic Stress, 18*(6), 685–696.

Brady, J. L., Guy, J. D., Poelstra, P. L., & Brokaw, B. F. (1999). Vicarious traumatization, spirituality, and the treatment of sexual abuse: A national survey of women psychotherapists. *Professional Psychology: Research and Practice, 30*(4), 386–393.

Braun, K. L., & Zir, A. (2001). Roles for the church in improving end-of-life care: Perceptions of Christian clergy and laity. *Death Studies, 25*(8), 685–704.

Brewin, C. R., & Power, M. J. (1997). Meaning and psychological therapy: Overview and introduction. In M. Power & C. R. Brewin (Eds.), *The transformation of meaning in psychological therapies: Integrating theory and practice* (pp. 1–14). New York: John Wiley & Sons.

Bryant, A. (2007). Gender differences in spiritual development during the college years. *Sex Roles, 56,* 835–846.

Bullis, R. K. (1996). *Spirituality in social work practice.* Bristol, PA: Taylor & Francis.

Cameron, J. (1992). *The artist's way: A spiritual path to higher creativity.* New York: Tarcher/Putman.

Campbell, J. (1968). *The hero with a thousand faces.* Princeton, NJ: Princeton University Press.

Canda, E. R., & Furman, L. D. (1999). *Spiritual diversity in social work practice: The heart of helping.* New York: The Free Press.

Canda, E. R., & Furman, L. D. (2010). *Spiritual diversity in social work practice: The heart of helping.* New York: Oxford University Press.

Capeheart, L., & Milovanovic, D. (2007). *Social justice: Theories, issues and movements.* New Brunswick, NJ: Rutgers University Press.

Carey, M., Fox, R., & Penney, J. (2002). *The artful journal: A spiritual quest.* New York: Watson-Guptill Publications.

Carroll, L. (2008). *Remember who you are: Seven stages on a woman's journey of spirit.* San Francisco, CA: Conari Press.

Carroll, M. (2004). *Awake at work.* Boston, MA: Shambhala.

Castillo, R. J. (1997). *Culture and mental illness: A client-centered approach.* Pacific Grove, CA: Brooks/Cole.

de Chardin, P. T. (1955). *The phenomenon of man.* London: Perennial. Retrieved July 15, 2010, from www.en.wikiquote.org/wiki/Pierre_Teilhard_de_Chardin

Chessick, R. D. (1978). The sad soul of the psychiatrist. *Bulletin of the Menninger Clinic, 42*(1), 1–9.

Chittister, J. D. (1998). *Heart of flesh: A feminist spirituality for women and men.* Grand Rapids, MI: Wm. B. Eerdmans Publishing.

Chochinov, H. M., & Cann, B. J. (2005). Interventions to enhance the spiritual aspects of dying. *Journal of Palliative Medicine, 8*(Suppl. 1), S103–S110.

Chodron, P. (2001). Fear. In C. Willis (Ed.), *Why meditate? The essential book about how meditation can enrich your life* (pp. 201–230). New York: Marlowe.

Christ, C. P. (2003). *She who changes: Re-imaging the divine in the world.* New York: Palgrave.

Coffman, S. J., Dimidjian, S., & Baer, R. A. (2006). Mindfulness-based cognitive therapy for prevention of depressive relapse. In R. A. Baer (Ed.), *Mindfulness-based treatment approaches: Clinician's guide to evidence base and applications* (pp. 31–50). Burlington, MA: Academic Press.

Coholic, D., Nichols, A. W., & Cadell, S. (2008). Spirituality and social work practice: Introduction. *Journal of Religion and Spirituality, 27*(1–2), 41–46.

Comas-Diaz, L. (2008). 2007 Carolyn Sherif award address: *Spirita*: Reclaiming womanist sacredness into feminism. *Psychology of Women Quarterly, 32,* 13–21.

Congress, E. P. (1996). Gestalt theory and social work treatment. In F. J. Turner (Ed.), *Social work treatment: Interlocking theoretical approaches* (4th ed.), (pp. 341–361). New York: The Free Press.

Connor, K. M., Davidson, J. R. T., & Lee, L. (2003). Spirituality, resilience, and anger in survivors of violent trauma: A community survey. *Journal of Traumatic Stress, 16*(5), 487–494.

Connors, G. J., Toscova, R. T., & Tonigan, J. S. (1999). Serenity. In W. R. Miller (Ed.), *Integrating spirituality into treatment: Resources for practitioners* (pp. 235–250). Washington, DC: American Psychological Association.

Cooper, M. G., & Lesser, J. G. (2011). *Clinical social work practice: An integrated approach* (4th ed.). Boston, MA: Pearson.

Covey, S. R. (2004). *The 7 habits of highly effective people: Powerful lessons in personal change.* New York: Free Press.

Cullinan, A. (1993). Bereavement and the sacred art of spiritual care. In K. J. Doka & J. D. Morgan (Eds.), *Death and spirituality* (pp. 195–205). Amityville, NY: Baywood Publishing.

Cunningham, M. (1999). The impact of sexual abuse treatment on the social work clinician. *Child and Adolescent Social Work Journal, 16*(4), 277–290.

Cunningham, M. (2000). Spirituality, cultural diversity and crisis-intervention. *Crisis Intervention, 6*(1), 65–77.

Cunningham, M. (2003). Impact of trauma work on social work clinicians: Empirical findings. *Social Work, 48*(4), 451–459.

Cunningham, M. (2004). Avoiding vicarious traumatization: Support, spirituality, and self-care. In N. B. Webb (Ed.), *Mass trauma and violence: Helping families and children cope* (pp. 327–346). New York: Guilford Press.

Curry, H. (2000). *The way of the labyrinth: A powerful meditation for everyday life.* New York: Penguin Compass.

Danieli, Y. (1994). Countertransference, trauma and training. In J. P. Wilson & J. D. Lindy (Eds.), *Countertransference in the treatment of PTSD* (pp. 368–388). New York: Guilford Press.

Davenport, L. (2009). *Healing and transformation through self-guided imagery.* Berkeley, CA: Celestial Arts.

Derezotes, D. S. (2006). *Spiritually oriented social work practice.* Boston, MA: Pearson.

Djupe, P. A., & Sokhey, A. E. (2003). American rabbis in the 2000 elections. *Journal for the Scientific Study of Religion, 42*(4), 563–576.

Doka, K. (2002). How could God? In J. Kauffman (Ed.), *Loss of the assumptive world: A theory of traumatic loss* (pp. 49–54). New York: Brunner-Routledge.

Doka, K. J. (1993a). The spiritual needs of the dying. In K. J. Doka & J. D. Morgan (Eds.), *Death and spirituality* (pp. 143–150). Amityville, NY: Baywood Publishing.

Doka, K. J. (1993b). The spiritual crisis of bereavement. In K. J. Doka & J. D. Morgan (Eds.), *Death and spirituality* (pp. 185–193). Amityville, NY: Baywood Publishing.

Donahue, M. J., & Nielsen, M. E. (2005). Religion, attitudes, and social behavior. In R. F. Paloutzian & C. L. Park (Eds.), *Handbook of the psychology of religion and spirituality* (pp. 274–291). New York: Guilford Press.

Doucet, L. H. (2002). *A healing walk with St. Ignatius: Discovering God's presence in difficult times.* Chicago, IL: Loyola Press.

Duchrow, U. (2007). Difficulties and opportunities for theology in today's world. In M. Althaus-Reid, I. Petrella, & L. C. Susin (Eds.), *Another possible world: Reclaiming liberation theology* (pp. 16–22). London: SCM Press.

Duncan, B. L., Miller, S. D., & Sparks, J. A. (2004). *The heroic client: A revolutionary way to improve effectiveness through client-directed, outcome-informed therapy.* San Francisco, CA: Jossey-Bass/Wiley.

Dyslin, C. W., & Thomsen, C. J. (2005). Religiosity and risk of perpetrating child physical abuse: An empirical investigation. *Journal of Psychology and Theology, 33*(4), 291–298.

Eliade, M. (1957). *The sacred and the profane: The nature of religion.* Orlando, FL: Harvest Book/Harcourt, Inc.

Elkins, D. N. (1998). *Beyond religion: Eight alternative paths to the sacred.* Wheaton, IL: Quest Books.

Ellerbe, H. (1995). *The dark side of Christian history.* Windermere, FL: Morningstar & Lark.

Elliott, D. M., & Guy, J. D. (1993). Mental health professionals versus non-mental health professionals: Childhood trauma and adult functioning. *Professional Psychology: Research and Practice, 24,* 83–90.

Ellis, G. F. R. (2001). Exploring the unique role of forgiveness. In R. G. Helmick, S. J. & R. L. Petersen (Eds.), *Forgiveness and reconciliation: Religion, public policy and conflict transformation* (pp. 395–410). Philadelphia, PA: Templeton Foundation Press.

Emmons, R. A. (2005). Emotion and religion. In R. F. Paloutzian & C. L. Park (Eds.), *Handbook of the psychology of religion and spirituality* (pp. 235–252). New York: Guilford Press.

Enright, R. D. (2002). *Forgiveness is a choice: A step-by-step process for resolving anger and restoring hope.* Washington, DC: American Psychological Association.

Enright, R. D., & Fitzgibbons, R. P. (2000). *Helping clients forgive: An empirical guide for resolving anger and restoring hope.* Washington, DC: American Psychological Association.

Epigg, E. (2008). Worldviews and women's spirituality. In C. A. Rayburn & L. Comas-Diaz (Eds.), *Woman soul: The inner life of women's spirituality* (pp. 3–17). Westport, CT: Praeger.

Exline, J. J., & Baumeister, R. F. (2000). Expressing forgiveness and repentance: Benefits and barriers. In M. E. McCullough, K. I. Pargament, & C. E. Thoresen (Eds.), *Forgiveness: Theory, research, and practice* (pp. 133–155). New York: Guilford Press.

Exline, J. J., & Rose, E. (2005). Religious and spiritual struggles. In R. F. Paloutzian & C. L. Park (Eds.), *Handbook of the psychology of religion and spirituality* (pp. 315–330). New York: Guilford Press.

Faiver, C., Ingersoll, R. E., O'Brien, E., & McNally, C. (2001). *Explorations in counseling and spirituality: Philosophical, practical, and personal reflections.* Belmont, CA: Brookes/Cole.

Fall, K. A., Holden, J. M., & Marquis, A. (2004). *Theoretical models of counseling and psychotherapy.* New York: Brunner-Routledge.

Falsetti, S. A., Resick, P. A., & Davis, J. L. (2003). Changes in religious beliefs following trauma. *Journal of Traumatic Stress, 16*(4), 391–398.

Farber, B. A., Manevich, I., Metzger, J., & Saypol, E. (2005). Choosing psychotherapy as a career: Why did we cross that road? *Journal of Clinical Psychology/In Session, 61*(8), 1009–1031.

Farhi, D. (2003). *Bringing yoga to life: The everyday practice of enhanced living.* San Francisco, CA: HarperCollins.

Farrelly-Hansen, M. (2001). Introduction. In M. Farrelly-Hansen (Ed.), *Spirituality and art therapy* (pp. 17–28). London: Jessica Kingsley.

Feuerstein, G. (1991). The shadow of the enlightened guru. In C. Zweig & J. Abrams (Eds.), *Meeting the shadow: The hidden power of the dark side of human nature* (pp. 148–150). New York: Jeremy P. Tarcher/Putnam.

Figley, C. R. (Ed.). (1995). *Compassion fatigue: Coping with secondary traumatic stress disorder in those who treat the traumatized.* New York: Brunner/Mazel.

Fincher, S. F. (2006). *Coloring mandalas: Circles of sacred feminine.* Boston, MA: Shambhala.

Fischer, K. (1988). *Women at the well: Feminist perspectives on spiritual direction.* New York: Paulist Press.

Follette, V., Polusny, M., & Milbeck, K. (1994). Mental health and law enforcement professionals: Trauma history, psychological symptoms, and impact of providing services to child sexual abuse survivors. *Professional Psychology: Research and Practice, 25,* 275–282.

Fowler, J. W. (1981). *Stages of faith: The psychology of human development and the quest for meaning.* San Francisco, CA: Harper.

Fox, M. (2000). *One river, many wells: Wisdom springing from global faiths.* New York: Jeremy P. Tarcher/Putman.

Fox, M. (2008). *The hidden spirituality of men: Ten metaphors to awaken the sacred masculine.* Novato, CA: New World Library.

Fox, R. (2001). *Elements of the helping process: A guide for clinicians* (2nd ed.). New York: Haworth Press.

Frankel, E. (2003). *Sacred therapy: Jewish spiritual teachings on emotional healing and inner wholeness.* Boston, MA: Shambhala.

Frankl, V. E. (1984). *Man's search for meaning* (Rev. ed.). New York: Washington Square Press.

Frankl, V. E. (1986). *The doctor and the soul: From psychotherapy to logotherapy* (Rev. ed.). New York: Vintage Books/Random House.

Frankl, V. E. (1988). *The will to meaning: Foundations and applications of logotherapy.* New York: Meridian Books/Penguin.

Frankl, V. E. (2000). *Man's search for ultimate meaning.* New York: Basic Books.

Freudenberger, H., & Robbins, A. (1979). The hazards of being a psychotherapist. *The Psychoanalytic Review, 66*(3), 371–378.

Friedemann, M. L., Mouch, J., & Racey, T. (2002). Nursing the spirit: The framework of systemic organization. *Journal of Advanced Nursing, 39*(4), 325–332.

Galanter, M. (2005). Cults and charismatic group psychology. In E. P. Shafranske (Ed.), *Religion and the clinical practice of psychology* (pp. 269–296). Washington, DC: American Psychological Association.

Galek, K., Flannelly, K. J., Vane, A., & Galek, R. (2005). Assessing a patient's spiritual needs: A comprehensive instrument. *Holistic Nursing Practice, 19*(2), 62–69.

Gall, T. L. (2006). Spirituality and coping with life stress among adult survivors of childhood sexual abuse. *Child Abuse & Neglect, 30,* 829–844.

Gambrill, E. D. (2006). *Social work practice: A critical thinker's guide* (2nd ed.). New York: Oxford University Press.

Gebara, I. (1999). *Longing for running water: Ecofeminism and liberation*. Minneapolis, MN: Fortress Press.

Geertsma, E. J., & Cummings, A. L. (2004). Midlife transition and women's spirituality groups: A preliminary investigation. *Counseling and Values, 49*(1), 27–49.

Germer, C. K. (2005). Mindfulness, what is it? What does it matter? In C. K. Germer, R. D. Siegell, & P. R. Fulton (Eds.), *Mindfulness and psychotherapy* (pp. 5–27). New York: Guilford Press.

Geyer, A. L., & Baumeister, R. F. (2005). Religion, morality, and self-control: Values, virtues, and vices. In R. F. Paloutzian & C. L. Park (Eds.), *Handbook of the psychology of religion and spirituality* (pp. 412–432). New York: Guilford Press.

Glaser, A. (2001). *A call to compassion: Bringing Buddhist practices of the heart into the soul of psychotherapy*. Berwick, ME: Nicholas-Hays.

Goldstein, E. G. (1995). *Ego psychology and social work practice* (2nd ed.). New York: Free Press.

Gorkin, M. (1987). *The uses of countertransference*. Northvale, NJ: Jason Aronson.

Gorsuch, R. L., & Miller, W. R. (1999). Assessing spirituality. In W. M. Miller (Ed.), *Integrating spirituality into treatment: Resources for practitioners* (pp. 47–64). Washington, DC: American Psychological Association.

Gotterer, R. (2001). The spiritual dimension in clinical social work practice: A client perspective. *Families in Society: The Journal of Contemporary Human Services, 82*(2), 187–193.

Gray, M. (2008). Viewing spirituality in social work through the lens of contemporary social theory. *British Journal of Social Work, 38*, 175–196.

Grey, M. (2007). Feminist theology: A critical theology of liberation. In C. Rowland (Ed.), *The Cambridge companion to liberation theology* (2nd ed.), (pp. 105–122). New York: Cambridge University Press.

Griffith, J. L., & Griffith, M. E. (2002). *Encountering the sacred in psychotherapy: How to talk with people about their spiritual lives*. New York: Guilford Press.

Gunaratana, H. (1991). *Mindfulness in plain English*. Boston, MA: Wisdom Publications.

Guth, J. L., Beail, L., Crow, G., Gaddy, B., Montreal, S., Nelsen, B., Penning, J., & Walz, J. (2003). The political activity of evangelical clergy in the election of 2000: A case study of five denominations. *Journal for the Scientific Study of Religion, 42*(4), 501–514.

Gutierrez, G. (2007). The tasks and content of liberation theology. In C. Rowland (Ed.), *The Cambridge companion to liberation theology* (pp. 19–38) (J. Condor, Trans.). Cambridge, England: Cambridge University Press.

Guy, D. J. (1987). *The personal life of the psychotherapist: The impact of clinical practice on the therapist's intimate relationships and emotional well-being*. New York: John Wiley & Sons.

Hagberg, J. O. (1995). *Wrestling with your angels: A spiritual journey to great writing*. Holbrook, MA: Adams Publishing.

Hamman, J. (2000). The rod of discipline: Masochism, sadism, and the Judeo-Christian religion. *Journal of Religion and Health, 39*(4), 319–327.

Harris, M. (1989). *Dance of the spirit: The seven steps of women's spirituality*. New York: Bantam.

Hartz, G. W. (2005). *Spirituality and mental health: Clinical applications*. New York: Haworth Pastoral Press.

Helmick, R. G., S.J. (2001). Does religion fuel or heal in conflicts? In R. G. Helmick, S.J. & R. L. Petersen (Eds.), *Forgiveness and reconciliation: Religion, public policy, and conflict transformation* (pp. 81–95). West Conshohocken, PA: Templeton Foundation Press.

Hermes, K. J., FSP. (2001). *Beginning contemplative prayer: Out of chaos into quiet*. Ann Arbor, MI: Charis/Servant Publications.

Hogan, E. E. (2003). *Way of the winding path: A map for the labyrinth of life*. Ashland, Oregon: White Cloud Press.

Hoge, D. R. (2005). Religion in America: The demographics of belief and affiliation. In E. P. Shafranske (Ed.), *Religion and the clinical practice of psychology* (pp. 21–41). Washington, DC: American Psychological Association.

Hollis, J. (2007). *Why good people do bad things: Understanding our darker selves*. New York: Gotham Books.

Hunsberger, B., & Jackson, L. M. (2005). Religion, meaning, and prejudice. *Journal of Social Issues, 61*(4), 807–826.

Ibrahim, F. A., Roysircar-Sodowshy, G., & Ohnishi, H. (2001). Worldview: Recent developments and needed directions. In J. G. Ponterotto, J. M. Casas, L. A. Suzuki, & C. M. Alexander (Eds.), *Handbook of multicultural counseling* (2nd ed., pp. 425–456). Thousand Oaks, CA: Sage Publications.

Ingerman, S. (1995). The shamanic journey: A way to retrieve our souls. In A. Simpkinson, C. Simpkinson, & R. Solari (Eds.), *Nourishing the soul: Discovering the sacred in everyday life* (pp. 111–120). San Francisco, CA: Harper.

Irion, P. E. (1993). Spiritual issues in death and dying for those who do not have conventional religious belief. In K. J. Doka & J. D. Morgan (Eds.), *Death and spirituality* (pp. 93–112). Amityville, NY: Baywood Publishing.

Janoff-Bulman, R. (1992). *Shattered assumptions: Toward a new psychology of trauma*. New York: The Free Press.

Janoff-Bulman, R. (1999). Rebuilding shattered assumptions after traumatic life events: Coping processes and outcomes. In C. R. Snyder (Ed.), *Coping: The psychology of what works* (pp. 305–323). New York: Oxford University Press.

Janoff-Bulman, R. (2002). Introduction. In J. Kauffman (Ed.), *Loss of the assumptive world: A theory of traumatic loss* (pp. xi–xii). New York: Brunner-Routledge.

Janoff-Bulman, R., & Frantz, C. M. (1997). The impact of trauma on meaning: From meaningless world to meaningful life. In M. Power & C. R. Brewin (Eds.), *The transformation of meaning in psychological therapies: Integrating theory and practice* (pp. 91–123). New York: John Wiley & Sons.

Johanson, G., & Kurtz, R. (1991). *Grace unfolding: Psychotherapy in the spirit of the tao-te-ching*. NY: Random House.

Johnson, E. A. (1992). *She who is: The mystery of God in feminist theological discourse*. New York: Cross.

Johnson, E. A. (2007). *Quest for the living God: Mapping frontiers in the theology of God*. New York: The Continuum International Publishing Group.

Johnson, R. A. (1986). *Inner work: Using dreams and active imagination for personal growth*. San Francisco, CA: HarperCollins.

Kabat-Zinn, J. (1990). *Full catastrophic living: Using the wisdom of your body and mind to face stress, pain, and illness.* New York: Dell Publishing.

Kabat-Zinn, J. (1994). *Wherever you go, there you are: Mindfulness meditation in everyday life.* New York: Hyperion.

Kahle, P. A., & Robbins, J. M. (2004). *The power of spirituality in therapy: Integrating spiritual and religious beliefs in mental health practice.* New York: Haworth Press.

Kauffman, J. (1993). Spiritual perspectives on suffering the pain of death. In K. J. Doka & J. D. Morgan (Eds.), *Death and spirituality* (pp. 165–170). Amityville, NY: Baywood Publishing.

Keyes, C. L. M., & Lopez, S. J. (2005). Toward a science of mental health. In C. R. Snyder & S. J. Lopez (Eds.), *Handbook of positive psychology* (pp. 45–59). New York: Oxford.

Khalsa, S. K. (2002). *Yoga for women.* New York: DK Publishing.

Kidd, S. M. (1996). *Dance of the dissident daughter: A woman's journey from Christian traditions to the sacred feminine.* New York: HarperCollins.

Kimball, C. (2002). *When religion becomes evil.* San Francisco, CA: Harper/HarperCollins.

Kirkpatrick, L. A. (1999). Attachment and religious representations and behavior. In J. Cassidy & P. R. Shaver (Eds.), *Handbook of attachment: Theory, research, and clinical applications* (pp. 803–822). New York: Guilford Press.

Koenig, H. G. (2005). *Faith & mental health: Religious resources for healing.* West Conshohocken, PA: Templeton Foundation Press.

Koenig, H. G., Pargament, K. I., & Nielsen, J. (1998). Religious coping and health status in medically ill hospitalized older adults. *The Journal of Nervous and Mental Disease, 186*(9), 513–521.

Kornfield, J. (1993). *A path with heart: A guide through the perils and promises of spiritual life.* New York: Bantam Books.

Kornfield, J. (1995). Awakening a sacred presence. In A. Simpkinson, C. Simpkinson, & R. Solari (Eds.), *Nourishing the soul: Discovering the sacred in everyday life* (pp. 131–140). San Francisco, CA: HarperCollins.

Kornfield, J. (2002). *The art of forgiveness, lovingkindness, and peace.* New York: Bantam Books.

Kornfield, J. (2008). *The wise heart: A guide to the universal teachings of Buddhist psychology.* New York: Bantam Books.

Kottler, J. A. (1993). *On being a therapist* (Rev. ed.). San Francisco, CA: Jossey-Bass Publishers.

Kramer, K. (1988). *The sacred art of dying: How world religions understand death.* New York: Paulist Press.

Krieglstein, M. (2006). Spirituality and social work. *Dialogue and Universalism, 16*(5/6), 21–29.

Kristjanson, L. (2006). A palliative approach to spirituality in residential aged care. *Journal of Religion, Spirituality & Aging, 18*(4), 189–205.

Kubler-Ross, E. (1969). *On death and dying.* New York: Scribner.

Kurtz, E., & Ketcham, K. (1994). *The spirituality of imperfection: Storytelling and the journey to wholeness.* New York: Bantam Books.

Landsman, I. S. (2002). Crises of meaning in trauma and loss. In J. Kauffman (Ed.), *Loss of the assumptive world: A theory of traumatic loss* (pp. 13–30). New York: Brunner-Routledge.

Langer, E. J. (1989). *Mindfulness.* Cambridge, MA: Da Capo Press.

Lantz, J. (1996). Integration of problem-oriented and mystery-centered approaches in existential psychotherapy. *Journal of Contemporary Psychotherapy, 26*(3), 295–305.

LeFavi, R. G., & Wessels, M. H. (2003). Life review in pastoral counseling: Background and efficacy for use with the terminally ill. *The Journal of Pastoral Care & Counseling, 57*(3), 281–292.

Lerner, M. (2006). *The left hand of God: Healing America's political and spiritual crisis.* San Francisco, CA: Harper/HarperCollins.

Lerner, M. J. (1980). *The belief in a just world.* New York: Plenum.

Lesser, E. (1999). *The seeker's guide: Making your life a spiritual adventure.* New York: Villard.

Levant, R. F., & Pollack, W. S. (1995). Introduction. In R. F. Levant & W. S. Pollack (Eds.), *A new psychology of men* (pp. 1–8). New York: Basic Books.

Levin, J. (2002). Is depressed affect a function of one's relationship with God? Findings from a study of primary care patients. *International Journal Psychiatry in Medicine, 32*(4), 379–393.

Loewenthal, K. (2007). *Religion, culture, and mental health.* New York: Cambridge University Press.

Lovell, S. (2001). Loving body is embracing spirit: Coming home stories. In M. Farrelly-Hansen (Ed.), *Spirituality and art therapy: Living the connection* (pp. 182–203). London: Jessica Kingsley.

Lovinger, R. J. (2005). Considering the religious dimension in assessment and treatment. In E. P. Shafranske (Ed.), *Religion and the clinical practice of psychology* (pp. 327–363). Washington, DC: American Psychological Association.

Luyten, P., Corveleyn, J., & Fontaine, J. R. J. (1998). The relationship between religiosity and mental health: Distinguishing between shame and guilt. *Mental Health, Religion & Culture, 1*(2), 165–184.

Maguire, J. (1998). *The power of personal storytelling: Spinning tales to connect with others.* New York: Jeremy P. Tarcher/Putnam.

Mahoney, A., Pargament, K. I., Tarakeshwar, N., & Swank, A. (2001). Religion in the home in the 1980s and 1990s: A meta-analytic review and conceptual analysis of religion, marriage, and parenting. *Journal of Family Psychology, 15,* 559–596.

Mahoney, M. J. (2003). *Constructive psychotherapy: Theory and practice.* New York: Guilford Press.

Malchiodi, C. A. (2002). *The soul's palette: Drawing on art's transformative powers of health and well-being.* Boston, MA: Shambhala.

Mallon, B. (2008). *Dying, death and grief: Working with adult bereavement.* Los Angeles, CA: Sage.

Mananzan, M. J., OSB. (2007). Globalization and the perennial question of justice. In M. H. Snyder (Ed.), *Spiritual questions for the twenty-first century: Essays in honor of Joan D. Chittister* (pp. 153–161). Maryknoll, NY: Orbis Books.

Manetta, A. A., Bryant, D. F., Cavanaugh, T., & Gange, T. (2003). The church—Does it provide support for abused women? Differences in the perceptions of battered women and parishioners. *Journal of Religion and Abuse, 5*(1), 5–21.

Mann, R. L. (1998). *Sacred healing: Integrating spirituality with psychotherapy.* Nevada City, CA: Blue Dolphin Press.

Marlatt, G. A., & Kristeller, J. L. (1999). Mindfulness and meditation. In W. M. Miller (Ed.), *Integrating spirituality into treatment: Resources for practitioners* (pp. 67–84). Washington, DC: American Psychological Association.

Martin, J. P. (2005). The three monotheistic world religions and international human rights. *Journal of Social Issues, 61*(4), 827–845.

Maslow, A. H. (1962). *Toward a psychology of being.* Princeton, NJ: Van Nostrand Insight Books.

McCann, L., & Pearlman, L. A. (1990). Vicarious traumatization: A framework for understanding the psychological effects of working with victims. *Journal of Traumatic Stress, 3,* 131–149.

McCullough, D. W. (2004). *The unending mystery: A journey through labyrinths and mazes.* New York: Anchor Books/Random House.

McCullough, M. E., Bono, G., & Root, L. M. (2005). Religion and forgiveness. In R. F. Paloutzian & C. L. Park (Eds.), *Handbook of the psychology of religion and spirituality* (pp. 394–411). New York: Guilford Press.

McCullough, M. E., & Witvliet, C. V. (2005). The psychology of forgiveness. In C. R. Snyder & S. J. Lopez (Eds.), *Handbook of positive psychology* (pp. 446–458). New York: Oxford.

McGrath, P. (2003). Religiosity and the challenge of terminal illness. *Death Studies, 27,* 881–899.

McNiff, S. (2004). *Art heals: How creativity cures the soul.* Boston, MA: Shambhala.

Meyers, R. (2006). *Why the Christian right is wrong: A minister's manifesto for taking back your faith, your flag, your future.* San Francisco, CA: Jossey-Bass.

Miller, A. (1981). *The drama of the gifted child.* New York: Basic Books.

Miller, K. K., Chibnall, J. T., Videen, S. D., & Duckro, P. N. (2005). Supportive-affective group experience for persons with life-threatening illness: Reducing spiritual, psychological, and death-related distress in dying patients. *Journal of Palliative Medicine, 8*(2), 333–343.

Miller, W. R. (Ed.). (1999). *Integrating spirituality into treatment: Resources for practitioners.* Washington, DC: American Psychological Association.

Moon, J. (2001). *Stirring the waters: Writing to find your spirit.* Boston, MA: Journey Editions.

Moore, T. (1992). *Care of the soul: A guide for cultivating depth and sacredness in everyday life.* New York: HarperCollins.

Moore, T. (1995). The art and pleasure of caring for the soul. In A. Simpkinson, C. Simpkinson, & R. Solari (Eds.), *Nourishing the soul: Discovering the sacred in everyday life* (pp. 14–21). San Francisco, CA: HarperCollins.

Moore, T. (2004). *Dark nights of the soul: A guide to finding your way through life's ordeals.* New York: Gotham Books/Penguin.

Morgan, J. D. (1993). The existential quest for meaning. In K. J. Doka & J. D. Morgan (Eds.), *Death and spirituality* (pp. 3–9). Amityville, NY: Baywood Publishing.

Moss, E. L., & Dobson, K. S. (2006). Psychology, spirituality, and end-of-life care: An ethical integration. *Canadian Psychology, 47*(4), 284–299.

Moyers, B. (1993). *Healing and the mind.* New York: Doubleday.

Munroe, J. F. (1990). *Therapist traumatization from exposure to clients with combat-related post-traumatic stress disorder: Implications for administration and supervision.* Unpublished dissertation, Northwestern University, Evanston, IL.

Murphy, B. C., & Dillon, C. (2003). *Interviewing in action: Relationship, process, and change* (2nd ed.). Pacific Grove, CA: Brooks/Cole.

Murray, S. A., Kendall, M., Boyd, K., Worth, A., & Benton, T. F. (2004). Exploring the spiritual needs of people dying of lung cancer or heart failure: A prospective qualitative interview study of patients and their careers. *Palliative Medicine, 18,* 39–45.

Nakashima, M. (2007). Positive dying in later life: Spiritual resiliency among sixteen hospice patients. *Journal of Religion, Spirituality, & Aging, 19*(2), 43–66.

Naparstek, B. (2004). *Invisible heroes: Survivors of trauma and how they heal.* New York: Bantam Books.

Neimeyer, R. A. (2007). The language of loss: Grief therapy as a process of meaning reconstruction. In R. A. Neimeyer (Ed.), *Meaning reconstruction & the experience of loss* (pp. 261–292). Washington, DC: American Psychological Association.

Nouwen, H. J. (1975). *Reaching out: The three movements of the spiritual life.* New York: Image Books/Doubleday.

Ochs, C. (1997). *Women and spirituality* (2nd ed.). New York: Rowman & Littlefield.

O'Connor, L. E., Berry, J. W., & Weiss, J. (1999). Interpersonal guilt, shame, and psychological problems. *Journal of Social and Clinical Psychology, 18*(2), 181–203.

O'Connor, P. (1993). A clinical paradigm for exploring spiritual concerns. In K. J. Doka & J. D. Morgan (Eds.), *Death and spirituality* (pp. 133–141). Amityville, NY: Baywood Publishing.

Orsillo, S. M., Roemer, L., & Holowka, D. W. (2005). Acceptance-based behavioral therapies for anxiety: Using acceptance and mindfulness to enhance traditional cognitive-behavioral approaches. In S. M. Orsillo & L. Roemer (Eds.), *Acceptance and mindfulness-based approaches to anxiety: Conceptualization and treatment* (pp. 3–35). New York: Springer.

Palmer, M. (1997). *Freud and Jung on religion.* London: Routledge.

Paloutzian, R. F. (2005). Religious conversion and spiritual transformation: A meaning-system analysis. In R. F. Paloutzian & C. L. Park (Eds.), *Handbook of the psychology of religion and spirituality* (pp. 331–347). New York: Guilford Press.

Pargament, K. I. (1997). *The psychology of religion and coping: Theory, research, practice.* New York: Guilford Press.

Pargament, K. I. (2005). Religious methods of coping: Resources for the conservation and transformation of significance. In E. P. Shafranske (Ed.), *Religion and the clinical practice of psychology* (pp. 215–239). Washington, DC: American Psychological Association.

Pargament, K. I. (2007). *Spiritually integrated psychotherapy: Understanding and addressing the sacred.* New York: Guilford Press.

Pargament, K. I., Ano, G. G., & Wachholtz, A. B. (2005). The religious dimension of coping: Advances in theory, research, and practice. In R. F. Paloutzian & C. L. Park (Eds.), *Handbook of the psychology of religion and spirituality* (pp. 479–495). New York: Guilford Press.

Pargament, K. I., Magyar-Russell, G. M., & Murray-Swank, N. A. (2005). The sacred and the search for significance: Religion as a unique process. *Journal of Social Issues, 61*(4), 665–687.

Pargament, K. I., Murray-Swank, N. A., & Mahoney, A. (2008). Problem and solution: The spiritual dimension of clergy sexual abuse and its impact on survivors. *Journal of Child Sexual Abuse, 17*(3), 397–420.

Pargament, K. I., Smith, B. W., Koenig, H. G., & Perez, L. (1998). Patterns of positive and negative religious coping with major life stressors. *Journal of the Scientific Study of Religion, 37*(4), 710–724.

Park, C. L. (2005). Religion and meaning. In R. F. Paloutzian & C. L. Park (Eds.), *Handbook of the psychology of religion and spirituality* (pp. 295–314). New York: Guilford Press.

Parkes, C. M. (2002). Grief: Lessons from the past, visions for the future. *Death Studies, 26,* 367–385.

Pearlman, L. A., & MacIan, P. S. (1995). Vicarious traumatization: An empirical study of the effects of trauma work on trauma therapists. *Professional Psychology: Research and Practice, 26,* 558–565.

Pearlman, L. A., & Saakvitne, K. (1995a). *Trauma and the therapist: Countertransference and vicarious traumatization in psychotherapy with incest survivors.* New York: W.W. Norton.

Pearlman, L. A., & Saakvitne, K. (1995b). Treating therapist with vicarious traumatization and secondary traumatic stress disorders. In C. R. Figley (Ed.), *Compassion fatigue: Coping with secondary traumatic stress disorder in those who treat the traumatized* (pp. 150–177). New York: Brunner/Mazel.

Peay, P. (2002). *Soul sisters: The five sacred qualities of a woman's soul.* New York: Jeremy P. Tarcher/Putnam.

Peck, M. S. (1983). *People of the lie: The hope for healing human evil.* New York: Touchstone Book/Simon & Schuster.

Phillips, D. Z. (2005). *The problem of evil and the problem of good.* Minneapolis, MN: Fortress.

Pinkola Estes, C. (1992). *Women who run with the wolves: Myths and stories of the wild woman archetype.* New York: Ballantine Books.

Plante, T. G. (2009). *Spiritual practices in psychotherapy.* Washington, DC: American Psychological Association.

Plaskow, J., & Christ, C. P. (Eds.). (1989). *Weaving the visions: New patterns in feminist spirituality.* New York: HarperCollins.

Pollitt, K. (2002). Introduction. In B. Reed (Ed.), *Nothing sacred: Women respond to religious fundamentalism and terror* (pp. ix–xiv). New York: Thunders' Mouth Press/Nation Books.

Pope, K. S., & Feldman-Summers, S. (1992). National survey of psychologists' sexual and physical abuse history and their evaluation of training and competence in these areas. *Professional Psychology: Research and Practice, 23,* 353–361.

Price, J. R., III., & Simpkinson, C. H. (1993). Sacred stories and our relationship to the divine. In C. Simpkinson & A. Simpkinson (Eds.), *Sacred stories: A celebration of the power of stories to transform and heal* (pp. 11–26). San Francisco, CA: HarperSanFrancisco.

Puchalski, C. M. (2008). Spirituality and the care of patients at the end-of-life: An essential component of care. *Omega, 56*(1), 33–46.

Rayburn, C. A., & Comas-Diaz, L. (Eds.). (2008). *Womansoul: The inner life of women's spirituality.* Westport, CT: Praeger.

Richards, P. S., & Bergin, A. E. (2002). *A spiritual strategy for counseling and psychotherapy.* Washington, DC: American Psychological Association.

Rilke, R. M. (2004). *Letters to a young poet* (Rev. ed.) (M. D. Herter Norton, Trans.). New York: W. W. Norton.

Roemer, L., Salters-Pedneault, T., & Orsillo, S. M. (2006). Incorporating mindfulness- and acceptance-based strategies in the treatment of generalized anxiety disorder. In R. A. Baer (Ed.), *Mindfulness-based treatment approaches: Clinician's guide to evidence base and applications* (pp. 51–74). Burlington, MA: Academic Press.

Rogers, C. (1989). *On becoming a person: A therapist's view of psychotherapy.* Boston, MA: Houghton Mifflin.

Rohr, R., & Martos, J. (2005). *From wild man to wise man: Reflections on male spirituality.* Cincinnati, OH: St. Anthony Messenger Press.

Rose, E. M., Westefeld, J. S., & Ansley, T. N. (2001). Spiritual issues in counseling: Clients' beliefs and preferences. *Journal of Counseling Psychology, 48*(1), 61–71.

Rosen, S. J. (2008). Introduction. In S. J. Rosen (Ed.), *Ultimate journey: Death and dying in the world's major religions* (pp. vii–ix). Westport, CT: Praeger.

Rosenberg, M. B. (1999). *Nonviolent communication: A language of compassion.* Del Mar, CA: PuddleDancer Press.

Rossman, M. L. (2000). *Guided imagery for selfhealing: An essential resource for anyone seeking wholeness.* Tiburon, CA: H J Kramer Book.

Roth, R. (1999). *Prayer and the five stages of healing.* Carlsbad, CA: Hay House.

Ruether, R. R. (2002). The war on women. In B. Reed (Ed.), *Nothing sacred: Women respond to religious fundamentalism and terror* (pp. 3–9). New York: Thunders' Mouth Press/Nation Books.

Rupp, J. (2000). *Dear heart, come home: The path of midlife spirituality.* New York: Crossroad Publishing.

Rye, M. S., Pargament, K. I., Amir Ali, M., Beck, G. L., Dorff, E. N., Halisey, C., Narayanan, W., & Williams, J. G. (2000). Religious perspectives on forgiveness. In M. E. McCullough, K. I. Pargament, & C. E. Thoresen (Eds.), *Forgiveness: Theory, research, and practice* (pp. 17–40). New York: Guilford Press.

Saakvitne, K., & Pearlman, L. A. (1996). *Transforming the pain: A workbook on vicarious traumatization for helping professionals who work with traumatized clients.* New York: Norton.

Sahlein, J. (2002). When religion enters the dialogue: A guide for practitioners. *Clinical Social Work Journal, 30*(4), 381–401.

Sanderson, C., & Linehan, M. M. (1999). Acceptance and forgiveness. In W. R. Miller (Ed.), *Integrating spirituality into treatment: Resources for practitioners* (pp. 199–216). Washington, DC: American Psychological Association.

Sands, H. R. (2001). *The healing labyrinth: Finding your path to inner peace.* Hauppauge, New York: Barron's Educational Services.

Savary, L. M., Berne, P. H., & Williams, S. K. (1984). *Dreams and spiritual growth: A Judeo-Christian way of dreamwork.* Mahwah, NJ: Paulist Press.

Schimmel, S. (2002). *Wounds not healed by time: The power of repentance and forgiveness*. Oxford, UK: Oxford University Press.

Schwartz, R. M. (1997). *The curse of Cain: The violent legacy of monotheism*. Chicago, IL: Chicago, IL Chicago University Press.

Schwartzberg, S. S., & Janoff-Bulman, R. (1991). Grief and the search for meaning: Exploring the assumptive worlds of bereaved college students. *Journal of Social and Clinical Psychology, 10*(3), 270–288.

Segal, Z. V., Williams, J. M. G., & Teasdale, J. D. (2002). *Mindfulness-based cognitive therapy for depression: A new approach to preventing relapse*. New York: Guilford Press.

Shafir, R. Z. (2003). *The zen of listening: Mindful communication in the age of distraction*. Wheaton, IL: Quest Books.

Shafranske, E. P., & Sperry, L. (2005). Addressing the spiritual dimension in psychotherapy: Introduction and overview. In L. Sperry & E. P. Shafranske (Eds.), *Spiritually oriented psychotherapy* (pp. 11–29). Washington, DC: American Psychological Association.

Shea, S. (1998). *Psychiatric interviewing: The art of understanding* (2nd ed.). Philadelphia, PA: W.B. Saunders Company.

Siegel, D. J. (2007). *The mindful brain: Reflection and attunement in the cultivation of well-being*. New York: W. W. Norton and Company.

Silberman, I. (2005a). Religious violence, terrorism, and peace. In R. F. Paloutzian & C. L. Park (Eds.), *Handbook of the psychology of religion and spirituality* (pp. 529–549). New York: Guilford Press.

Silberman, I. (2005b). Religion as a meaning system [Special issue]. *Journal of Social Issues, 61*(4).

Silberman, I., Higgins, E. T., & Dweck, C. S. (2005). Religion and world change: Violence and terrorism versus peace. *Journal of Social Issues, 61*(4), 761–784.

Silf, M. (1999). *Close to the heart: A guide to personal prayer*. Chicago, IL: Loyola Press.

Simpkinson, C., & Simpkinson, A. (Eds.). (1993). *Sacred stories: A celebration of the power of stories to transform and heal*. San Francisco, CA: HarperSanFrancisco.

Smidt, C. (2003). Clergy in American politics: An introduction. *Journal for the Scientific Study of Religion, 42*(4), 495–499.

Smith, D. P., & Orlinsky, D. E. (2004). Religious and spiritual experience among psychotherapists. *Psychotherapy: Theory, Research, Practice, Training, 41*(2), 144–151.

Solari, R. (1995). Introduction. In A. Simpkinson, C. Simpkinson, & R. Solari (Eds.), *Nourishing the soul: Discovering the sacred in everyday life* (pp. 103–110). San Francisco, CA: Harper Press.

Sperry, L. (2001). *Spirituality in clinical practice: Incorporating the spiritual dimension in psychotherapy and counseling*. Philadelphia, PA: Brunner-Routledge.

Sperry, L., Carlson, J., & Kjos, D. (2003). *Becoming an effective therapist*. Boston, MA: Allyn & Bacon.

Sperry, L., & Giblin, P. (2005). Marital and family therapy with religious persons. In E. P. Shafranske (Ed.), *Religion and the clinical practice of psychology* (pp. 511–532). Washington, DC: American Psychological Association.

Sperry, L., & Shafranske, E. P. (Eds.). (2005). *Spiritually oriented psychotherapy*. Washington, DC: American Psychological Association.

Spilka, B., Hood, R. W., Hunsberger, B., & Gorsuch, R. (2003). *The psychology of religion: An empirical approach* (3rd ed.). New York: Guilford Press.

Staub, E., & Pearlman, L. A. (2001). Healing, reconciliation, and forgiving after genocide and other collective violence. In R. G. Helmick, S. J., & R. L. Petersen (Eds.), *Forgiveness and reconciliation: Religion, public policy and conflict transformation* (pp. 205–227). Philadelphia, PA: Templeton Foundation Press.

Steinhauser, K. E., Clipp, E. C., NcNeilly, M., Christakis, N. A., McIntyre, L. M., & Tulsky, J. A. (2000). In search of a good death: Observations of patients, families, and providers. *Annals of Internal Medicine, 132*(10), 825–832.

Stoebe, M. S., & Schut, H. (2007). Meaning making in the dual process model of coping with bereavement. In R. A. Neimeyer (Ed.), *Meaning reconstruction & the experience of loss* (pp. 55–73). Washington, DC: American Psychological Association.

Stone, R. (1996). *The healing art of storytelling: A sacred journey of personal discovery*. New York: Hyperion.

Storr, A. (1996). *Feet of clay: Saints, sinners, and madmen: A study of gurus*. New York: Free Press.

Strean, H. (1998). *When nothing else works: Innovative interventions with intractable individuals*. Northvale, NJ: Jason Aronson.

Suarez, Z. E., Newman, P. A., & Reed, B. G. (2008). Critical consciousness & cross-cultural/intersectional social work practice: A case analysis. *Families in Society, 89*(3), 407–417.

Surya Das, L. (1999). *Awakening to the sacred: Creating a spiritual life from scratch*. New York: Broadway Books.

Sussman, M. B. (1992). *A curious calling: Unconscious motivations for practicing psychotherapy*. NJ: Jason Aronson.

Sussman, M. B. (Ed.). (1995). *A perilous calling: The hazards of psychotherapy practice*. NY: John Wiley & Sons.

Suzuki, S. (2006). *Zen mind, beginner's mind*. Boston, MA: Shambhala.

Swinton, J. (2001). *Spirituality and mental health care: Rediscovering a 'forgotten' dimension*. London: Jessica Kingsley.

Swinton, J. (2007). *Raging with compassion: Pastoral responses to the problem of evil*. Grand Rapids, MI: William B. Eerdmans Publishing.

Take Back The Night Organization. (n.d.). *A history of take back the night*. Retrieved June 23, 2010, from http://www.takebackthenight.org/history.html

Tangney, J. P. (1990). Assessing individual differences in proneness to shame and guilt: Development of the self-conscious affect and attribution inventory. *Journal of Personality and Psychology, 59*(1), 102–111.

Tangney, J. P., & Stuewig, J. (2004). A moral-emotional perspective on evil persons and evil deeds. In A. G. Miller (Ed.), *The social psychology of good and evil* (pp. 327–328). New York: Guilford Press.

Tangney, J. P., Wagner, P., Flecher, C., & Gramzow, R. (1992). Shamed into anger? The relation of shame and guilt to anger and self-reported aggression. *Journal of Personality and Social Psychology, 62*(4), 669–675.

Taylor, J. (1983). *Dream work: Techniques for discovering the creative power in dreams*. New York/Mahwah, NJ: Paulist Press.

Taylor, J. (1992). *Where people fly and water runs uphill: Using dreams to tap the wisdom of the unconscious*. New York: Warner Books.

Teasdale, W. (1999). *The mystic heart: Discovering a universal spirituality in the world's religions*. Novato, CA: New World Library.

Teasdale, W. (2001). *The mystic heart: Discovering a universal spirituality in the world's religions.* Novato, CA: New World Library.

Tedeschi, R. G., Park, C. L., & Calhoun, L. G. (1998). Posttraumatic growth: Conceptual issues. In R. G. Tedeschi, C. L. Park, & L. G. Calhoun (Eds.), *Posttraumatic growth: Positive changes in the aftermath of crisis* (pp. 1–22). Mahwah, NJ: Lawrence Erlbaum Associates.

Thorne, B. (2002). *The mystical power of person-centered therapy: Hope beyond despair.* London: Whurr Publications.

Tix, A. P., & Frazier, P. A. (1998). The use of religious coping during stressful life events: Main effects, moderation, and mediation.*Journal of Consulting and Clinical Psychology, 66*(2), 411–422.

Tsang, J. A., McCullough, M. E., & Hoyt, W. T. (2005). Psychometric and rationalization accounts of the religion-forgiveness discrepancy. *Journal of Social Issues, 61*(4), 785–805.

Ulmer, A., Range, L. M., & Smith, P. C. (1991). Purpose of life: A moderator of recovery from bereavement. *Omega, 23*(4), 279–289.

Vladimiroff, C., OSB. (2007). God and rice bowls in a new age. In M. H. Snyder (Ed.), *Spiritual questions for the twenty-first century: Essays in honor of Joan D. Chittister* (pp. 57–61). Maryknoll, NY: Orbis Books.

Vogler, C. (2007). *The writer's journey: Mythic structure for writers* (3rd ed.). Studio City, CA: Michael Wiese Productions.

Wakefield, D. (1990). *The story of your life: Writing a spiritual autobiography.* Boston, MA: Beacon Press.

Walker, B. G. (2000). *Restoring the Goddess: Equal rites for modern women.* Amherst, NY: Prometheus Books.

Wallis, J. (1995). Restoring the soul of politics. In A. Simpkinson, C. Simpkinson, & R. Solari (Eds.), *Nourishing the soul: Discovering the sacred in everyday life* (pp. 251–259). San Francisco, CA: HarperSanFrancisco.

Wallis, J. (2002). *Faith works: Lessons on spirituality and social action.* London: Society for Promoting Christian Knowledge (SPCK).

Wallis, J. (2005). *God's politics: Why the right gets it wrong and the left doesn't get it.* San Francisco, CA: Harper/HarperCollins.

Walsh, F. (1999). Opening family therapy to spirituality. In F. Walsh (Ed.), *Spiritual resources in family therapy* (pp. 28–58). New York: Guilford Press.

Walsh, J. (2003). *Endings in clinical practice: Effective closure in diverse settings.* Chicago, IL: Lyceum Books.

Walsh, J. (2007). *Endings in clinical practice: Effective closure in diverse settings* (2nd ed.). Chicago, IL: Lyceum Books.

Welwood, J. (2000). *Toward a psychology of awakening: Buddhism, psychotherapy, and the path of personal and spiritual transformation.* Boston, MA: Shambhala.

West, M. G. (2000). *Exploring the labyrinth: A guide for healing and spiritual growth.* New York: Random House.

Wexler, D. B. (2009). *Men in therapy: New approaches for effective treatment.* New York: W. W. Norton.

Wiesenthal, S. (1997). *The sunflower: On the possibilities and limits of forgiveness.* New York: Schoken.

Williams, L. (2006). Spirituality and gestalt: A gestalt-transpersonal perspective. *Gestalt Review, 10*(1), 6–21.

Wittine, B. (1995). The spiritual self: Its relevance in the development and daily life of the psychotherapist. In M. B. Sussman (Ed.), *A perilous calling: The hazards of psychotherapy practice* (pp. 288–301). New York: John Wiley & Sons.

Woodman, M., & Dickson, E. (1996). *Dancing in the flames: The dark goddess in the transformation of consciousness.* Boston, MA: Shambhala.

Woods, M. E., & Hollis, F. (2000). *Casework: A psychosocial therapy* (5th ed.). Boston, MA: McGraw-Hill.

Worden, J. W. (2009). *Grief counseling and grief therapy: A handbook for the mental health practitioner* (4th ed.). New York: Springer.

Worthington, E. L., Mazzeo, S. E., & Canter, D. W. (2005). Forgiveness-promoting approach: Helping clients reach forgiveness through using a longer model that teaches reconciliation. In L. Sperry & E. P. Shafranske (Eds.), *Spiritually oriented psychotherapy* (pp. 235–257). Washington, DC: American Psychological Association.

Wortmann, J., & Park, C. L. (2008). Religion and spirituality in adjustment following bereavement: An integrative review. *Death Studies, 32,* 703–736.

Yalom, I. D. (1980). *Existential psychotherapy.* New York: Basic Books.

Yalom, I. D. (1995). *The theory and practice of group psychotherapy.* New York: Basic Books/HarperCollins.

Yalom, I. D. (1998). *The Yalom reader: Selections from the work of a master therapist and storyteller.* New York: Basic Books.

Yalom, I. D. (2002). *The gift of therapy: An open letter to a new generation of therapists and their patients.* New York: HarperCollins.

Yardley, M. (2008). Social work practice with Pagans, Witches, and Wiccans: Guidelines for practice with children and youths. *Social Work, 53*(4), 329–336.

Yeats, W. B. (2001). *A dialogue of self and soul.* Retrieved April 8, 2010, from www.poemhunter.com/poem/a-dialogue-of-self-and-soul

Zimbardo, P. (2004). A situationist perspective on the psychology of evil: Understanding how good people are transformed into perpetrators. In A. G. Miller (Ed.), *The social psychology of good and evil* (pp. 21–50). New York: Guilford Press.

Zimbardo, P. (2007). *The Lucifer effect: Understanding how good people turn evil.* New York: Random House.

Zinnbauer, B. J., & Pargament, K. I. (2005). Religiousness and spirituality. In R. F. Paloutzian & C. L. Park (Eds.), *Handbook of the psychology of religion and spirituality* (pp. 21–42). New York: Guilford Press.

Zweig, C., & Abrams, J. (1991). Introduction: The shadow side of everyday life. In C. Zweig & J. Abrams (Eds.), *Meeting the shadow: The hidden power of the dark side of human nature* (pp. xvi–xxv). New York: Jeremy P. Tarcher/Putman.

Index